ROUGH TACTICS

ROUGH TACTICS

Black Performance in Political Spectacles, 1877–1932

Mark A. Johnson

UNIVERSITY PRESS OF MISSISSIPPI / JACKSON

The University Press of Mississippi is the scholarly publishing agency of the Mississippi Institutions of Higher Learning: Alcorn State University, Delta State University, Jackson State University, Mississippi State University, Mississippi University for Women, Mississippi Valley State University, University of Mississippi, and University of Southern Mississippi.

www.upress.state.ms.us

The University Press of Mississippi is a member of the Association of University Presses.

An earlier version of Chapter 4 originally appeared in *Southern Cultures* 20 (Summer 2014). An earlier version of the Bridge originally appeared in *Louisiana History* 56 (Summer 2015).

Copyright © 2021 by University Press of Mississippi
All rights reserved

First printing 2021
∞

Library of Congress Control Number available

Hardback ISBN 978-1-4968-3282-5
Trade paperback ISBN 978-1-4968-3283-2
Epub single ISBN 978-1-4968-3284-9
Epub institutional ISBN 978-1-4968-3285-6
PDF single ISBN 978-1-4968-3286-3
PDF institutional ISBN 978-1-4968-3287-0

British Library Cataloging-in-Publication Data available

I dedicate this book to my parents, Neil and Sandy, who showed me unconditional support and taught me to work hard and love the past.

CONTENTS

ACKNOWLEDGMENTS · IX ·
INTRODUCTION · 3 ·

CHAPTER 1
"Out in Full Force":
Black Participation in Spectacular Politics before Disfranchisement,
1877–99
· 14 ·

CHAPTER 2
"A Contest in Music"
Election-Day Spectacles in the Central Georgia Temperance Campaigns,
1885–99
· 51 ·

BRIDGE
"A Strictly Social Function"
The Contest of Black Labor and Confederate Memory
at the 1903 UCV Reunion
· 87 ·

CHAPTER 3
"Furious Music"
African Americans, Political Spectacles, and Street Theater in the
Post-Disfranchisement South, 1909–32
· 127 ·

CHAPTER 4
"To Do Our Bit for Good Government"
W. C. Handy, E. H. Crump, and the 1909 Memphis Mayoral Election
· 158 ·

EPILOGUE
"I Didn't Really Know How to Show My Opposition"
Street Theater in the Twenty-first Century
- 188 -

NOTES - 191 -
BIBLIOGRAPHY - 219 -
INDEX - 230 -

ACKNOWLEDGMENTS

I AM GRATEFUL FOR THIS OPPORTUNITY TO THANK THE NUMEROUS PEOPLE who have helped me in several ways with this book. I am particularly appreciative for the financial support from the University of Alabama Department of History. I would like to thank the librarians at Louisiana State University, the Hogan Jazz Archive at Tulane University, the University of Georgia, the Memphis & Shelby County Room at Memphis Public Library, and Hoole Special Collections at the University of Alabama. Specifically, I would like to thank Brett Spencer, Bruce B. Raeburn, G. Wayne Dowdy, and Germain J. Bienvenu for sharing their expertise on archival collections.

I could not have started nor completed this project without the initial support and encouragement from faculty at Purdue University. I appreciate the efforts of Whitney Walton, Caroline E. Janney, John Larson, Frank Lambert, and Randy Roberts, who pushed me to start thinking like an historian early in my collegiate career.

At the University of Maryland, I stumbled upon the initial inspiration for this project, and I am indebted to the faculty who helped me cultivate it. Specifically, I would like to thank Ira Berlin for advising the original research project. I have used the material and ideas from that project throughout this book. I am also grateful to Rick Bell for sharing his insights on history and storytelling.

At the University of Alabama, I learned many lessons and gained many friends. I am particularly grateful for the guidance and expertise of Kari Frederickson. Throughout the process, she has been thoughtful and encouraging. I am also thankful for the help of W. Fitzhugh Brundage, Sharony Green, Andrew Huebner, George Rable, and Joshua Rothman. At various stages, they read chapter drafts and provided helpful suggestions.

I could not have completed this book without strong friendships, especially at work. I looked forward to going to work every day because of the camaraderie present at the University of Alabama, Georgia State University, and now the University of Tennessee at Chattanooga. Since the beginning, I have shared this journey with Megan L. Bever, who has been a dear friend but also a professional role model. I am indebted to Laura Mammina, Mike Thompson, and Susan Eckelmann Berghel, who read drafts of this book and mentored me through its production. I am thankful to the friends and teammates of local basketball and soccer teams, as well. I needed them more than they could ever know.

I could not have done this book without the people closest to me. To Kate, I want to thank you for your support and companionship as I wrote this book. To Aaron and Caleb, I want to thank you for being my best friends. To Mom and Dad, I want to thank you for nurturing my love of the past and teaching me how to do things the right way.

ROUGH TACTICS

INTRODUCTION

IN 1902, BLACK BANDLEADER WILLIAM CHRISTOPHER HANDY, WHO HAD NOT yet achieved fame as the Father of the Blues, settled in Clarksdale, Mississippi. Before he became a famous musician and music producer, he took whatever work he could find to make ends meet, which sometimes resulted in seemingly unlikely alliances with white supremacists. "We were frequently hired . . . to furnish music for political rallies," recalled Handy. At these rallies, Handy and his band of Black musicians had to "absorb a 'passel' of oratory of the brand served by some Southern politicians." At this time, Mississippi's race relations had grown especially violent as vigilante groups, like the Whitecaps, terrorized and murdered Black farmers. During Handy's brief stay in Mississippi, white terrorists lynched hundreds of African Americans, seventeen of them within a small radius around Clarksdale. In this climate, Mississippians propelled politician and notorious white supremacist James K. Vardaman to prominence and the governorship.[1]

Handy and his band played for Vardaman, who enchanted white audiences with his vitriol. Before the Black musicians took the stage, Vardaman gave a speech, in which he promised his audience that his government would not fund Black schools because he considered education unsuitable for African Americans. He praised the former Confederacy and explained that enslaved African Americans, who had little or no education, had protected "like so many faithful watch-dogs" the mothers, daughters, wives, and sweethearts of white southern soldiers during the Civil War. He had given, and would continue to give, similar speeches throughout the campaign, which condemned racial mixing and education for African Americans, and expressed nostalgia for the Old South.[2]

After Vardaman finished his hateful speech, Handy and his Black band played the southern anthem "Dixie" for the white audience. Southern Democrats often chose "Dixie" or other songs of the Confederacy for their campaign rallies because the unofficial Confederate anthem would have helped the audience reminisce on the mythical Old South, when and where white supremacy reigned supreme and masters and slaves, as the myth goes, loved one another. Handy and his band, as Black musicians, helped reinforce this image in the spectacle of the campaign rally.[3]

From Handy's perspective, Vardaman's comments recalled to his mind previous instances of racial abuse, but they had done their job and, assumedly, had been paid. When the event concluded and Handy and his band removed themselves from public gaze, they laughed off these comments. Handy explained, "We could laugh and we could make rhythm. What better armor could you ask?"[4]

Although Vardaman put Handy in a tough spot with his rhetoric, Handy enjoyed playing for the campaigns of some of the South's less menacing politicians because of the opportunity to showcase his and his band's talents. He admitted that it was "not always the bitter pill this particular candidate made it." On one occasion, he and his band played for Senator John Sharpe Williams of Mississippi, "a great favorite of the people." He enjoyed playing for Williams because it provided them an opportunity to demonstrate their appreciation for him and showcase their "good music and gay uniforms." At this time, Handy had not yet achieved fame and fortune, so he still had financial considerations, and these gigs helped enhance his profile around town.[5] By 1909 he still had not yet caught his big break and had moved to Memphis, where he composed a campaign song for mayoral candidate Edward Hull Crump. Handy's composition would help launch both of their famous careers.

From the end of Reconstruction in 1877 to the election of Franklin D. Roosevelt in 1932, Black southerners, like Handy, influenced local, state, and national politics and challenged white supremacy by performing at the political and cultural spectacles essential to the southern politics. These spectacles consisted of many different events, such as parades, rallies, orations, flag-raisings, and many forms of street theater. African Americans often held their own spectacles, but they also infiltrated seemingly white-only spaces, where they demanded recognition of their economic rights and their place in the political sphere. At these events, African Americans often participated as musicians, like Handy, but they also contributed in a variety of ways: as spectators, performers, street artists, actors, marchers, and more. In all these roles, they generated enthusiasm, demonstrated the strength of the party or movement, mobilized voters, legitimized electoral results, and expressed their viewpoints.

Before Reconstruction ended in 1877, African Americans voted and held office. In fact, African Americans reached levels of government that would, after Reconstruction ended, remain unattainable until the mid- to late twentieth century. In the Reconstruction South two Black men, Hiram Revels and

Blanche K Bruce, won election to the Senate. They were the only two Black senators for almost a century.

After the election of Franklin D. Roosevelt in 1932, African American political activity surged upwards. Roosevelt consulted with Black advisors from the Federal Council of Negro Affairs. Then World War II created an opportunity for African Americans, who viewed the war effort as a chance to improve their own situation. During World War II, membership in Black organizations, like the National Association for the Advancement of Colored People and new organizations like the Congress of Racial Equality, skyrocketed. They would play a fundamental role in the civil rights movement of the 1950s, 1960s, and beyond.

Between these two periods of Black political mobilization, African Americans suffered through a period characterized by historians as the nadir of race relations. African Americans faced segregation, disfranchisement, and lynching.

In the post-Reconstruction South, white southerners reinvigorated antebellum racial hierarchy by tailoring their methods of oppression to suit a modernizing, industrializing region.[6] By the 1890s, white southerners passed segregation and disfranchisement laws after receiving the blessing of the Supreme Court, which condoned segregation by redefining the Fourteenth Amendment and Fifteenth Amendments to allow these discriminatory practices.[7] In the South, white politicians justified segregation and disfranchisement by claiming that Black men, including even the well-mannered and prosperous, posed a threat to white women in public spaces and white men needed control of politics to protect white women. When poll taxes and literacy tests failed, white southerners used intimidation and violence, especially the spectacle of lynching to keep Black voters away from the polls, respond to rumors of sexual assault, and punish upwardly mobile Black entrepreneurs who competed with white businesses.[8] Whenever African Americans fought back, white southerners ratcheted up the violence.

African Americans recognized that a successful attack on Jim Crow required economic empowerment, legal expertise, and strong community foundations to gain political power.[9] African Americans hoped to gain status, and therefore political influence, by acquiring property and wealth. They trained in law and politics and used their talents to claim political and civil rights through the court system and other political processes. They built up their own communities by strengthening churches, schools, and civic organizations.[10]

Among these many forms of resistance, African Americans used their musical and theatrical talents to challenge white supremacy, attain economic opportunity, and transcend segregation. African Americans, especially performers, manipulated negatives stereotypes and segregation laws to their advantage. They performed for Black audiences in segregated clubs and juke joints, which provided safe spaces for Black expression because they could vocalize their hopes and frustrations with white society and their own condition beyond the eyes and ears of white employers and neighbors.[11]

In the early twentieth century, Black folk musicians took their music from the rural South to mainstream America, and their musical styles became popular with white and Black audiences. They played for audiences eager for a modern and urban aesthetic, such as jazz. Professional musicians migrated out of the South, taking their music with them to northern, urban locales, such as Chicago. They recorded their sound with emerging technology, and record companies distributed the music throughout the country. In this way, Black musicians relied on the social and cultural forces of modernity, such as urbanization, immigration, migration, and new technologies. They manipulated white America's anxieties about the modern world and their nostalgia, as well, and they popularized folk music and blues.[12]

African Americans broke down racial barriers in the entertainment industry because white audiences, who had been charmed by previous decades of blackface performances, wanted to see authentic products. For working-class white Americans, blackface minstrel shows mocked African Americans and justified their enslavement, so these shows temporarily eased economic anxieties concerning competition from Black workers. Although these performances insulted African Americans, the response of white Americans to these shows proved that Black culture existed and that it appealed to the masses. In this ironic way, blackface minstrelsy helped integrate Black music styles into the national mainstream.[13] African Americans took the stage to satisfy white desires to see the real thing. In the modern age, with its assembly lines and mechanical reproduction, people demanded authentic and unique products, especially in their art and music. By satisfying this demand, Black musicians popularized blues, jazz, ragtime, and social dancing.[14] In addition to using blackface minstrelsy as a form of economic and cultural uplift, African Americans also adopted the characteristics, in terms of body language, speech patterns, and fashion, of white Americans in order to mock their sense of supremacy and entitlement.[15]

In these blackface performances, Black musicians and thespians still adorned the role of the humble servant, but they critiqued white society and expressed their frustrations with segregation and racial violence. They escaped retribution for their opinions because their characters, which eased white anxieties, protected them. Likewise, musicians adapted typical musical themes, including unrequited love and vanished lovers, to address lynching. They also expressed a desire for personal freedom and enjoyment, such as sexual pleasure and financial wealth, during a period of circumscribed rights and privileges. With these characters and themes, Black performers spoke to their Black audiences without offending white spectators.[16]

Off the stage, Black performers distinguished themselves from the image of the humble plantation servant and cultivated an image of professionalism and civility that their plantation characters lacked. They assumed demeaning roles, no matter how much they hurt, to attain economic success and gain recognition of their status as professionals.[17] In search of economic opportunity, African Americans played for white supremacist organizations, political candidates, and reformers. In some cases, Black performers leveraged these economic opportunities into political influence by publicly expressing their political loyalties and expressing frustrations with the post-Reconstruction political and social order. In an entertainment and political culture that reached the masses through spectacles, African Americans participated as marchers, spectators, speakers, and more; Black musicians proved especially visible and, in many cases, desirable.

Spectacles consisted of different types of events, and African Americans participated in them in a variety of ways, which resulted in a spectrum of political expression. At political rallies and speeches, they often simply attended as guests, which nonetheless had political implications, especially after they had lost the right to vote. As part of the crowd, they reminded their white neighbors of their presence and, therefore, claimed membership in the citizenry and proved their allegiance to a political party or cause. They also forced the speaker to acknowledge their presence, which speakers did by either extending a welcoming word or condemning them. In a way, these spectators were performers because they attended the speeches and rallies not only to hear the candidates but also to make themselves publicly visible.

Beyond observing speeches, African Americans also participated in political spectacles as musicians and actors. They generated enthusiasm, attracted audiences, and helped spread a message about the candidate or cause. They got paid or earned other favors for their talents and gained access to larger audiences. They either played their role as scripted, or they took the opportunity to improvise by spreading a message other than the one intended by the candidate or the cause. They honored and humiliated public officials and candidates. In mobs, they exhibited potentially threatening behavior. They burned or hanged white people in effigy. They dressed in military-style uniforms and paraded the streets. In an era of lynching, they even confronted and harassed white women in public. With this behavior, African Americans adopted the European tradition of rough music, or chivaree, as their own. Like their predecessors, African Americans voiced their disapproval in their target's words or deeds through public shaming, which remained a tool available to them even as voting rights disappeared.[18]

African Americans employed a tactic known as rough music as an especially useful tool for expressing their politics in the Jim Crow South. Previously, Europeans had used rough music, known in France as *charivari* and Italy as *scampanate*, to enforce community boundaries and norms, and harass violators. In its earliest forms, Europeans used the practice to welcome newlywed couples to married life. Outside of the newlywed's quarters, a crowd clanged pots and pans and blew horns to endorse the marriage. Similarly, Europeans and Americans used clanging, rattling, discordant sounds to humiliate and intimidate violators of community standards. At the end of the seventeenth century, rough music became increasingly employed by English people and colonial Americans as a form of spectacular street theater designed to draw public attention to social offenders, such as spousal abusers and adulterers. The mobs carefully designed the performances to highlight the offender's behavior. Amid the noise, they might act out domestic squabbles to highlight spousal abuse. Similarly, they might mock a young bride's infertility or old man's impotence to criticize a marriage between partners of extremely different ages. For the most part, the community used these methods when it did not have any legal alternative, such as in cases of domestic violence long before its criminalization. As a tool of the otherwise powerless, African Americans claimed it as one of their own methods. In the Jim Crow South, they employed street theater or rough music to honor or humiliate candidates and officeholders as their voting rights increasingly disappeared.[19]

Spectacles have political implications because they influence the way that people understand and interact with the people and world around them and sensationalize society's norms, mores, and values. To win audiences and sell newspapers, politicians and newspaper editors used sensational images that resembled an extraordinary version of reality. For politicians, spectacles served to spread an ideology. When people viewed spectacles, they used past experiences and assumptions to give meaning to the images presented to them, so spectators had an active role in the spectacle, which means that the audience could make inferences different from one another and from the intended message. When people encounter these images, in other words, the sensationalized words and images take on a life of their own.[20]

For centuries Americans, including disfranchised Americans, have demonstrated their party and national loyalties with political spectacles. During the American Revolution and early national period, Americans frequently made use of public spectacle, which delineated new citizenship boundaries and differentiated between groups. As part of the revolt against British rule, Americans publicly harassed tax collectors and government officials. When elite representatives made decisions in the national capital, patriots and citizens endorsed these decisions with street demonstrations, such as parades and processions, which they infused with patriotism and partisanship and thereby claimed citizenship in the nation and membership in the party.[21]

During the antebellum period, Americans continued to participate in political spectacles regardless of age, ethnicity, class, and sex. The people reflected the democratic, freedom-loving spirit of the age with their actions at these spectacles by enjoying gluttonous amounts of food and drink. Women and African Americans, both free and enslaved, attended these events in segregated capacities and thereby enlarged the political sphere to include them when it otherwise excluded their formal participation.[22]

After the Civil War, Americans continued these practices and imbued the spectacles with militaristic elements. In the post-Reconstruction South, Black and white civilians raised flags and poles in their towns and cities to demonstrate their party's strength. Like their colonial and antebellum forebears, they believed that political decisions and electoral results did not have legitimacy until the people endorsed them in the streets. Led by lieutenants, political clubs marched through the streets with torches and banners in military-style uniforms. It was typical for Black musicians to dress in military-style uniforms, and Black voters in military garb marched in crowds to the polls to protect themselves from attack. To white audiences the sight of crowds of Black men in uniform would have been an aggressive statement, given the legacy of conflict and aggression directed by white southerners toward Black soldiers and Black veterans. After the Civil War, white southerners frequently and often violently objected to the sight of Black men in uniform. By putting on these uniforms, Black performers seemingly put themselves in danger.[23]

In the postwar period, women resumed their important role at these events and lent their support to political parties despite lacking the right to vote. They attended barbecues, spoke before large audiences, raised flags and poles, presented flowers, persuaded voters outside of polling booths, sang hymns, and marched in parades.[24] African Americans, who had their citizenship recognized with the Fifteenth Amendment, had a role at these events, too.

In the late nineteenth and early twentieth centuries, party leaders and reformers, especially in northern communities, lamented the persistence of political spectacles. By the 1880s, white northerners had accepted a new masculine ideal emphasizing composure and domesticity instead of passion and aggressiveness. As the war grew distant, northerners also wanted to distance themselves from militancy. In their politics, they preferred to act like refined intellectuals rather than soldiers. They wanted fewer parades and more debate. They condemned political spectacles, which they perceived as a ploy to attract illiterate and so-called gullible voters, especially African Americans and immigrants.[25]

In terms of voting numbers, the campaign against political spectacles in the North succeeded in eliminating a substantial portion of the electorate. By 1924, northerners only voted at a rate of 58 percent. As politics became less partisan and spectacular and more intellectual, most northerners lost interest, especially as entertaining cultural spectacles, such as baseball, boxing, and theme parks, took their attention away from consulting the newest political treatises.[26]

In the South, voters stayed away from the polls for entirely different reasons. Through disfranchisement measures, southerners kept poor Black and white citizens away from the polls. By 1924 southerners voted only at a rate of 20 percent.[27] Although voting numbers plummeted, Black and white southerners found ways to express themselves anyway.

In the post-Reconstruction South, white Americans used spectacle to disseminate their ideology of white supremacy. By lynching African Americans, white Americans dramatically demonstrated their continued mastery of Black bodies, because it punished real or perceived transgressions but also sent a message to the rest of society. Beyond its immediate effects on Black victims and white assailants, lynching became representational of white supremacy because souvenirs, images, and accounts of the violence and death reinforced its message across the nation. When Black and white people encountered the stories and images of lynching, they remained assured that white people continued to rule.

The lynching impetus resulted, in part, from white people's anxieties over living and working in closer to proximity to African Americans in increasingly urbanized and industrialized spaces. Lynching did not always have its intended effect on audiences, because images of hanged and burned bodies helped galvanize resistance to white supremacy.[28] Despite lynching, segregation, and disfranchisement, white supremacy never dominated as much as white southerners hoped.

Disfranchised southerners, including African Americans, used spectacles to publicize their politics, but in different ways.[29] In the late nineteenth and early twentieth centuries, southerners continued to use militaristic, aggressive displays for political purposes. Despite disfranchisement, African Americans participated in politics by taking to the streets to join their Black and white neighbors in popular demonstrations to support candidates, legitimize results, celebrate victories and defeats, and endorse political decisions. Unable to participate in official political activity on a large scale, these seemingly powerless men and women used what they had available to them, such as their artistic talents, to gain small concessions and achieve a measure of visibility from a system crafted to oppress, disfranchise, and lynch them.[30]

I have arranged the chapters of this book to explain how Black participation in political spectacles of all types changed from end of Reconstruction in 1877 to the election of Franklin D. Roosevelt in 1932. I have ordered the book into two parts. Part 1 covers from the end of Reconstruction to the end of the nineteenth century, when African Americans frequently appeared in public events of both major political parties, numerous reform movements, and the labor movement. Around the turn of the twentieth century, two developments threatened this behavior. First, white southerners passed laws and constitutional amendments to eliminate Black voting; by 1908 all the former Confederate states had disfranchised Black southerners, and the laws wiped out the voting rights for many poor white southerners, too. Second, many elitist politicians championed an intellectual style of politics that favored written and oral debate instead of public spectacle.[31] Part 2 covers from 1900 to 1932, when African Americans continued to participate in the spectacles in the South, where it remained a vital element of politics, perhaps because disfranchisement had eliminated the most direct tool of political expression. African Americans had to make different alliances and change some of their methods, but they remained quite active in the public sphere.

In chapter 1, I reveal the extent to which African Americans pervaded the spectacles of late nineteenth-century southern politics. They performed on behalf of the major political parties, third parties, and reform movements. African Americans attended rallies, paraded through the city, played campaign songs, and performed theater in the streets. They also voted, especially in the referenda on reform movements, such as prohibition, and for third parties, such as the Readjuster Party in Virginia and the People's Party. African Americans used the same methods generations of Americans had used to claim membership in a political party or as a member of a movement, and the body politic.

In chapter 2, I highlight an example of how African Americans used public spectacle and voting rights to express their politics on the prohibition issue in central Georgia. In 1885 and 1887, African Americans voted on the issue in Atlanta, but they also hit the streets and turned out for the election-day spectacle. By 1898, when Maconites decided the issue for themselves, white southerners had become increasingly hostile to Black voting rights, especially after the success of the People's Party, the Wilmington Insurrection, and military mobilization for the Spanish-American War. These events heightened racial tensions. In the 1898 campaign, a spectacle-based political culture thrived, and African Americans continued to vote and participate in the spectacle. They even confronted and harassed white female prohibitionists on the streets, which would have been dangerous in the racial climate of the moment.

Before moving on to Part 2, in a section I call the Bridge I share the story of the unionized Black musicians who fought for the right to perform at the 1903 United Confederate Veterans reunion in New Orleans. It serves as the most complete example, from all sides involved, of the strange alliances between white supremacists and opportunistic Black performers. In the debates over the rights of the Black musicians, the veterans and union leaders expressed their complicated thoughts on Black artistry, labor rights, and proper roles in politics and society. In this episode, white southerners publicly portrayed Black talent as an apolitical vestige of the Old South but nonetheless would not let them play at the reunion. Publicly, they explicitly separated political functions from social functions and argued that Black musicians should participate in social functions, like the reunion. They portrayed Black musical aptitude as natural, thus separating it from professional and intellectual achievement. They knew, however, that the reunion was not simply a social event and that it had political implications, so they privately organized to keep them away. To the veterans and supporters, as everyone knew, the sight of Black professional musicians with union rights would have threatened the romanticized image of the Old South that justified white supremacy. From the perspective of the Black musicians, the reunion offered economic opportunity, and they wanted their share and access to the massive audience of spectators, who flooded into New Orleans from all over the country.[32] By using this story as a bridge to the twentieth century with disfranchisement and segregation, I argue that similar dynamics continued to play out as white politicians and Black performers interacted with one another at political events.

In chapter 3, I document that spectacles remained an important part of the political process when disfranchisement limited formal expressions of political power. As performers at campaign rallies, parades, and other public events, African Americans manipulated stereotypes to enter seemingly off-limit spaces. After disfranchisement, African Americans had to get more creative with their political alliances if they wanted to maintain any power. The Republican Party struggled in the South because it did not have steady access to the Black votes upon which it depended. The region's Black voters, furthermore, had become a bit disenchanted with the Republican Party. In the solidly Democratic South, African Americans used their performances to humiliate Democratic candidates, but they also pitted Democrats against one another with their artistic and electoral support to gain concessions. They also confronted the Lost Cause, which white southerners used to justify their superiority over the region's Black population. On issues that split white voters, such as prohibition and other reforms, African Americans remained present in the public spectacles. They also continued to participate in the labor movement and, eventually, the Communist Party. They lent their support to many of the third-party alternatives to the Democratic Party that sprung up in the era of Jim Crow. During World War I, African Americans displayed their patriotism in militaristic fashion and lent their talents to the war effort. They also packed their bags and took their talents to northern cities, where they continued to use these methods to express political power.

In Chapter 4, I analyze the relationship between Memphis mayoral candidate Edward Hull Crump and Black bandleader W. C. Handy because they took advantage of spectacle to achieve power and fame. In post-disfranchisement Memphis, Crump's supporters employed Handy and his band to generate enthusiasm for the campaign and mobilize Black voters on Beale Street to register and cast ballots. Given this opportunity, Handy created a song that inspired Black and white voters to support Crump, but the song also made Handy famous and launched his successful career as a composer and publisher.[33]

African Americans remained surprisingly aggressive in the face of the law and the threat of lynching, which claimed thousands of victims and put fear into the hearts of Black southerners. Unlike Black lawyers and politicians, who challenged white supremacy in the courts and legislatures, Black performers like W. C. Handy and his band demonstrated that the seemingly smallest forms of resistance softened white supremacy's harshest elements. At some of these spectacles, African Americans could only expect to make their presence known, secure a couple extra dollars, gain some modest publicity, or have a laugh at someone else's expense. At times, however, their performances generated national attention, toppled politicians, and helped African Americans secure and exercise economic and political rights.

CHAPTER 1

"OUT IN FULL FORCE"

Black Participation in Spectacular Politics before Disfranchisement, 1877–99

ON NOVEMBER 16, 1892, DEMOCRATS IN CLINTON, NORTH CAROLINA, BURIED an effigy of twenty-nine-year-old Populist politician Marion Butler. His once-promising political career, after all, seemed dead.¹ Born in 1863 near Clinton, Butler quickly built a career as a Democrat in Sampson County and North Carolina politics. In 1890 Butler became one of 110 members of the Farmers' Alliance to win a position in the North Carolina General Assembly. As the youngest state senator, he became a crucial voice for the Populists in the Democratic Party and the General Assembly. In 1891 the members of the North Carolina Farmers' Alliance chose him as their president. Rather than form a third party, he wanted to work within the Democratic Party to accomplish his reform goals, specifically the coinage of silver. By 1892 Butler had lost hope for an alliance with Democrats when they nominated fiscal conservative Grover Cleveland as their presidential candidate. In 1892 he became a leader in the North Carolina People's Party and served as chairman of the party's nominating convention and platform committee. The delegates also chose him as their presidential elector-at-large.

During the 1892 campaign season, Butler traveled from town to town to support Populists in their election bids, and his personal reputation suffered. North Carolina's Democrats knew him as MaryAnn Butler and characterized him as a gambler, drunkard, thief, and "bad egg." On November 14, 1892, North Carolina Democrats crushed Butler's Populists by dominating elections for national, state, and local offices.² The defeat of the Populists inspired Sampson County Democrats to hold an elaborate funeral ceremony for their former champion.

At 4:00 p.m., the courthouse bells rang out, and Democrats gathered in large numbers in the courthouse square for the funeral rites. The crowd marched around the courthouse two or three times while a brass band played funeral dirges. At the head of the funeral procession, a few marchers held

Marion Butler, who rose to prominence in North Carolina politics as a Populist, watched Clinton residents bury him in effigy from his office window. Library of Congress, Prints & Photographs Division, LC-DIG-ggbain-33241.

a white banner with black letters: "In Memory of Maryann Butler. He died young." After completing the procession, the crowd gathered around a short, deep grave to hear funeral orations from local politicians, who brought "an infinite amount of humor to bear on the subject" and "a rare bit of wit and satire." After the orations, "the grave was closed and a number of young men gravely laid upon the new-made mound bunches of old dried leaves tied with dirty rags" while the crowd continued to sing hymns. To conclude the funeral rites, they erected a headstone and then dispersed "amid yelling and laughing over the ridiculous spectacle." According to rumors, Butler watched his own funeral from a nearby office window.[3]

Although the Populists suffered defeat in 1892, Butler did not disappear from North Carolina politics, and he would continue to experience humiliation at spectacles like the one in Clinton. He reworked the Populists' political strategy around the silver issue. He reached out to North Carolina Republicans to form a coalition capable of beating the Democrats. He purchased the *Tarboro Farmers' Advocate* and rebranded the newspaper as the *Caucasian*, which he used as an organ to spread a Populist and white supremacist message. From the editorial pages, he devoted his newspaper to the "interests of the wealth producers of North Carolina," thus spreading a subtler form of white supremacy than the original newspaper, which committed itself to "pure democracy and white supremacy." He no longer served as president of the state Farmers' Alliance, but he did serve as chairman of the executive committee. After marrying the daughter of a wealthy plantation owner, he embarked on a speaking tour of North Carolina to revive the Farmers' Alliance and People's Party.[4]

On November 10, 1893, Butler spoke in Monroe, North Carolina, to rally local Populists. The event's organizers arranged a band of Black musicians to furnish music as the audience filed into the Union County Courthouse on Main Street. At 11:30 a.m., Butler commenced his speech, but he did not finish without interruption: about twenty minutes into the speech, a prankster put red pepper in the ventilator at the top of the courthouse, which caused "a vast amount of sneezing and coughing" and forced the crowd "to vacate and wait for the building to cool off." After exiting the building, the wheezing Populists encountered the Black musicians on the porch. They did not know that their local leaders had employed the musicians. Instead, they assumed that the musicians had shown up "out of ridicule or spite." They "kicked and drove the band out into the middle of the street" before realizing their mistake. After the fray, Butler continued his speech, and the Populists permitted the Black musicians to play from the gallery within the courthouse. After concluding his speech, he walked the streets of the city, but residents threw eggs at him.[5]

When North Carolinians buried effigies, threw eggs at candidates, and attacked Black musicians, they participated in a thriving, centuries-old spectacular political culture through which citizens expressed national and party loyalties but also agitated for revolution and reform.

From the end of Reconstruction in 1877 until the end of the nineteenth century, African Americans marched in parades, blasted fireworks, and attended rallies as part of a vibrant era of spectacular politics. As voting rights deteriorated, in part due to this influence, African Americans continued to express their politics with spectacular displays, sometimes in aggressive ways that would seemingly put their lives in danger. They participated on behalf of both major political parties, but they also exercised considerable influence on reform issues, which tended to split the white electorate.

THE REPUBLICAN PARTY

After the Civil War, African Americans tended to support the Republican Party because of its ties to the Civil War and the Emancipation Proclamation. In support of the Republican Party, they cast ballots, but they also often attended official party functions, such as nominating conventions, and performed at public spectacles such as parades and rallies.[6] They generated enthusiasm, made political statements, and enforced their community's political norms and boundaries. They also reinforced the connections between the Republican Party, Civil War victory, and emancipation.

African Americans frequently performed to commence or dismiss a rally, convention, or other party function. In 1880 the Young Men's Garfield and Arthur Club of Knoxville, Tennessee, held a rally in support of the Republican Party. Black musicians helped kick off the meeting.[7] Also in 1880, African Americans participated in a variety of ways at the nominating convention for South Carolina's Fourth Congressional District. In Chester, South Carolina, they gave speeches and carried out official duties. The Republicans chose Absalom Blythe as their candidate, who condemned the Democrats for the methods they had used to take back control of the state in the 1876 election. When he concluded his speech, Black musicians played music and the audience cheered.[8]

Republicans recognized how Black talent could make or break the success of their campaigns, so they employed Black musicians for their entertainment value and to win electoral success. During the 1870s, Mike Duffy, a postal worker and local Republican Party leader in Washington, DC, testified to the usefulness of Black musicians in attracting the votes of African Americans. According to one of Duffy's reminiscing colleagues, there "was a negro band here, and as Mike was something of a politician, and the colored voter was numerous in the Third ward, he thought it would be policy to hire that band for the parade."[9] To acquire the band's services, he composed a letter requesting the songs "Hail to the Chief" and "See, the Conquering Hero Comes." To Duffy's delight, the band agreed to play the music during the parade.[10]

African Americans performed to attract spectators to political rallies and help keep the Republican Party alive in the region.[11] In October 1880, the Republicans of Yorkville, South Carolina, gathered for a rally. When the Black musicians commenced the music, the locals took it as a sign to make their way to the courthouse. After everyone had settled, Nelson Hammond, a Black man, called the meeting to order. Among many speakers, Hammond expressed delight in the reinvigoration of the Republican Party and the civic activity of the Black community. According to Democrats, the rally testified that the Republican Party in the county, "though sleeping for the past four years, is by no means dead." Republicans had, instead, "lulled the Democracy into a sense of perfect security."[12] To observers, a healthy rally served as a sign of a healthy party, and Black performers helped make both possible.

In the South, African Americans could help attract audiences to Republican gatherings in preference to the Democratic meetings. On October 14, 1889, Democrats and Republicans in Staunton, Virginia, held competing rallies. The Democrats hosted their event at the courthouse; the Republicans staged their rally at the skating rink. Both political parties employed musicians to generate enthusiasm. The Republicans employed both a Black band and a white band for the evening's event. They "paraded the streets several times drawing out the crowd towards the skating rink."[13]

Based on the work of African Americans at political spectacles, the Republican Party continued to have a noticeable and energetic presence in southern politics despite the lack of electoral success. In 1889 Republicans in Anderson Court House, South Carolina, staged "the largest and most enthusiastic Republican or negro meeting" since "the days prior to 1876." For Democrats, the sight of energetic Republicans "brought back forcibly to the minds" of citizens "the scenes and incidents that often occurred when the thieving carpet-baggers would come around on their campaign tours." An observer characterized the event as "equal to a circus." Henry Kennedy, a Black man and chairman of Anderson County's Republican Party, organized the rally and sent out a call for the county's Black citizens to attend. They answered the call and came from all over to participate. A Black band led the raucous crowd to the east front of the courthouse. In addition to the large crowd of African Americans, white locals turned out to hear the speeches and observe the spectacle.[14]

In a region dominated by Democrats, Black performers drew large crowds of African Americans to political spectacles held on behalf of the Republicans. In October 1892, a Black band "discoursed what was evidently meant to be sweet music for the purposes of drawing a crowd" to an evening of oratory at the courthouse in Asheville, North Carolina. When they heard the music, the town's Democrats, who were "accustomed to the routine of meetings of this kind," filed into the courthouse and took their seats. White Republicans came to the courthouse as well. African Americans "poured in, filled up the benches on the right, swarmed in and filled up the jury box, straddled the railing, perched on the edge of the judge's stand and then stood themselves up in the aisles and everywhere where they could find room." They had high expectations for the event. According to the reporter, "They knew what they were to hear—and they wanted a full view of this man who was to fire them with his words." During the speech, Republican M. L. Mott spoke in favor of labor rights and in support of protections for Black voting rights, which earned him hearty applause from the Black audience. After Mott finished his speech, which the local Democratic press referred to as "profane, vulgar and inflammatory," the Black spectators erupted. They "mounted the benches, threw their hats into the air and howled and howled; prominent men of the colored race clambered over each other in their efforts to get near their champion and perchance shake his hand." Meanwhile, the Black musicians contributed to the enthusiasm as they "blared its enjoyment" with the "tinkling cymbal" and "sounding brass."[15] This event started with Black musicians and ended with Black Republicans showing their support for the party with outward jubilation. By choosing to highlight the boisterous nature of the crowd, the Democratic press hoped to portray African Americans as unfit for politics.

When the Republican Party succeeded on the national or local level, Black and white Republicans affirmed these decisions with public spectacles. In June 1880, Black and white Memphians celebrated the nomination of James Garfield as the Republican's candidate for President. At 9:00 p.m., they gathered at the bluff on a grandstand decorated with flags and banners. For the most part the crowd consisted of African Americans, including a Black band, which "discoursed music" for the occasion. Although Republicans had already nominated Garfield at the Republican National Convention in Chicago, Memphis's Republicans staged the meeting "for the purpose of ratifying" his nomination. During the ceremony, speakers who took the stage to stump for Garfield included William R. Moore, who explained that the Republican Party united people from "originally across the sea" and other sections of the country and the world: "whether the blood which courses through our veins be Anglo-Saxon, Caucasian or African—we are all tonight, thanks to the genius of the great Republican party, Americans, freemen and fellow citizens." Next, he condemned the Democratic Party for trying to split the nation during the Civil War but acknowledged, gratefully, that "old things have passed away."[16] At spectacles for the Republican Party, the Civil War remained a central talking point precisely because their party had led the northern war effort. By participating, African Americans could help strengthen the party's association with emancipation.

After victories in national elections, Black and white Republicans legitimized the result with spectacular democratic rituals on the local level. After Republican Benjamin Harrison's victory over incumbent Democrat Grover Cleveland in the 1888 presidential election, the Republicans of Woodstock, Virginia, participated in a "grand illumination and street pageant" to celebrate. Despite heavier rain earlier in the day and the constant threat of bad weather, the Republicans formed a procession on the south end of town. At the corner of Main and Court Streets they erected a "huge, cone-shaped pile of pine" for a bonfire, which "lighted up the heavens until a late hour." The procession featured numerous local party leaders and musicians, including some Black musicians. The five hundred marchers carried torches and banners through the city's muddy streets and eventually congregated in the courthouse square, where bands provided some entertainment and speakers delivered orations to commemorate the victory. The spectacle helped generate a sense of pride "of so manly a spirit" and testified to the strength of the party in Virginia. A reporter indicated that the Republicans would gather again in a year for "a monster celebration" when Republicans won the state's gubernatorial race.[17]

In addition to humiliating candidates and legitimizing results, Black performers could honor Republican candidates, who acknowledged them as political actors and presented impromptu speeches to the crowd. In 1880 Alvin Hawkins ran for governor of Tennessee as a Republican. On the morning of July 22, Knoxville residents congregated outside Hawkins's hotel room in the Hattie House Hotel. Outside the hotel, Tom Prince's Black brass band serenaded the gubernatorial candidate. In response, Hawkins emerged and gave some brief remarks, which "were well received by quite a crowd."[18] Hawkins had strong support from the Black community. As the election drew near, prognosticators expected that "at least thirty thousand negroes" would vote for Hawkins, who would then win the election. After the counting of the ballots in November, Hawkins had indeed prevailed.[19]

In March 1886, a Black band paid a visit to a hotel in Maryville, Tennessee, where they serenaded H. B. Lindsay, who emerged in January as the leading Republican candidate for attorney general. According to an endorsement from the *Maryville Times*, Lindsay had earned a reputation as an "honest, upright and able young man" and "good lawyer." Upon hearing the music, he thanked them for their support with "a few hearty words and a basket of apples."[20] African Americans rendered their thanks to public officials and candidates in the form of public serenades. When candidates and government officials recognized the presence of African Americans, they also legitimized their presence in the public sphere despite white society's opinion that they did not belong there.

African Americans made a statement with their presence, but they also expressed their politics with their choices in music, such as connecting the Republican Party with Union victory in the Civil War. They could keep sectional spirit alive for partisan purposes by choosing to play specific

During the Civil War, Henry Clay Work wrote the song "Marching Through Georgia," which became a popular song for Republican candidates at campaign rallies to remind their audiences of Union victory in the Civil War. It also became a favorite tune for Black musicians to play to harass Democrats in the South. Library of Congress, Prints & Photographs Division, LC-DIG-ppmsca-46691.

war-themed songs. In 1889 Republicans rallied outside their party headquarters in Richmond, Virginia, featured Congressman Charles N. Brumm of Pennsylvania, and the audience consisted mostly of African Americans. During the event, a Black band "discoursed side-show music." Brumm spoke for almost two hours about protective tariffs. After completing his speech, the Black audience erupted into their "most enthusiastic cheer" of the night when the Black musicians "tooted the tune dear to every negro." They played "Marching through Georgia," which recalls General William Tecumseh Sherman's destructive military campaign in Georgia, South Carolina, and North Carolina.[21] The song's author, Henry Clay Work, worked for a music publisher during the Civil War. At the firm Root and Cady, he helped write more than seventy-five Union anthems. A month after Sherman completed his campaign, Work published a song in Sherman's honor, and it became immensely popular in the North. In 1890 General Sherman reviewed troops at a Grand Army of the Republic parade, and he heard the song hundreds of times as the soldiers passed. It would also become a staple at Union veterans' reunions.[22]

On some occasions, white Americans employed African Americans to play songs to embarrass government officials, including the president of the United States. In 1887, President Grover Cleveland nominated a Black man, James Monroe Trotter, to the position of Washington, DC's Recorder of Deeds. Previously, the position had been filled by Black civic leader Frederick Douglass and temporarily by another Black man, James Campbell Matthews, who the Senate did not confirm. Trotter, who was related to the Hemings family of Monticello, was enslaved as a child. After fighting in the Civil War, he became a music teacher and historian of African American music. On March 4, the Senate confirmed Trotter as Recorder of Deeds. Unaware of the Senate confirmation, a local milkman employed Black musicians to stand outside the White House, where they played popular ragtime song "A New Coon in Town" four times. The song, composed by J. S. Putnam in 1883, became popular with audiences and told the story of a gambling, flirtatious Black man, who came to town and made "the boys all cry." Despite unflattering lyrics, songs like "A New Coon in Town" became so popular with white Americans that they brought this type of music into the national mainstream. In fact, Black musicians composed their own versions of "coon songs" to take advantage of ragtime's popularity.[23] The milkman, Frank Ward, employed the band to harass President Cleveland with stereotypical images of African Americans to mock the appointment of Black men to public offices, especially the Washington, DC, Recorder of Deeds, an office previously filled by African Americans.[24]

On rare occasions, biracial spectacles staged on behalf of the Republican Party turned violent and deadly. In 1894 Republicans in Elizabethtown, Kentucky, gathered in town for a procession. The crowd consisted of about two hundred African Americans and "a few white men." As they organized the parade, white Republicans refused to march behind African Americans and quit the parade. Led by a Black brass band, the Black marchers continued the parade until a law enforcement officer approached them. The Black marchers carried weapons to fire into the air during the parade. As the officer approached, a Black marcher "fired at him" with the "load of shot searing a hole in his coat" and hit a bystander, who died. The officer shot and wounded the Black marcher and took him into custody. At the trial, the officer tried to kill the Black gunman "but was prevented from doing so."[25] In this type of spectacle, Black performers sometimes exhibited behavior that white bystanders interpreted as aggressive. In this case, they gathered in large groups with weapons. At other times, they dressed in military garb. Usually, they could escape harassment from white spectators, but not all the time.

African Americans did not always support the Republican Party, so they sometimes used the opportunity to play for them as a chance to make a statement. In August 1882, Republicans and Readjusters in Richmond, Virginia, gathered for a night of oratory. When candidate S. Brown Allen took the stage, "the colored band struck up and he had to desist."[26] At this event, the Black musicians showed up to oppose the Republicans. In the post-Reconstruction South, African Americans created many alliances depending on local circumstances to improve their condition. While they remained mostly loyal to the Republican Party, their interactions with Democrats provided opportunities for economic improvement and, at times, political expression.

THE DEMOCRATIC PARTY

African Americans sometimes openly confronted Democrats in public to humiliate them, especially after electoral defeats. On November 9, 1887, "a large crowd of disorderly negro men, women and children, headed by a negro band," according to the Democratic press, "paraded some of the streets" of Alexandria, Virginia, to celebrate the electoral defeat of a local Democrat. As they marched by his home, the marchers yelled and jeered at him. They set off firecrackers. They continued to an empty lot by his home, where they buried his effigy. After this display, they went to the store owned by the victorious Republican candidate, who addressed the crowd and thanked them for their work on his behalf. He expressed pride in the "victory they had won in the hot-bed" of the Democratic Party.[27]

Similarly, African Americans used rough music and street theater to ostracize members of their own race who violated community norms. On the same night in Alexandria, African Americans burned one of their Black neighbors in effigy in an empty lot in the northeastern part of the city. They had learned that Henry Johnson, a Black well digger from Alexandria, voted the Democratic ticket, so they burned his likeness and paraded the charred effigy through the streets. The Democratic press condemned these events. They argued that white Republicans "must have felt humiliated after witnessing such proceedings" and argued that the crowd's actions "showed what they would do if their party should ever get into power again."[28] In this period of limited power, African Americans recognized that they wielded the most power as a voting bloc. Johnson allegedly had an independent position, so his neighbors condemned him and humiliated him for supporting the other side. When these episodes occurred, the press used them as evidence that African Americans did not have the temperament or decorum to rule.

African Americans made political statements with their musical selections to embarrass Democrats by suggesting death or destruction. In 1892 Black musicians gave Tennessee Governor John P. Buchanan a preview of his funeral. Buchanan, a Democrat, rose to power in Tennessee by supporting Populist platforms, such as the regulation of railroad rates and a tax exemption for farmers' cooperatives. In 1890 he ran for governor and won. During his campaign, he opposed federal legislation, such as the Lodge Bill, that protected Black voting rights in the South. In 1891 he took office and worked with Democrats and Republicans in the state legislature to ease the hardships of Tennessee's farmers and laborers. During the first year of his administration, the Tennessee legislature enacted laws recognizing Labor Day as a holiday, protecting Tennessee business from foreign competition, and establishing the state's Commission of Labor. In addition to these measures, Buchanan supported higher poll taxes. On October 17, 1892, Buchanan spoke to a biracial audience at the Farmers' Alliance Tobacco Warehouse in Clarksville, Tennessee. According to the *Memphis Appeal-Avalanche*, Buchanan encountered a "chilly" reception. In the morning, many of the spectators traveled from many nearby counties and from across the border in Kentucky to hear Buchanan speak. By 10:00 a.m., the crowd numbered about five hundred people. The crowd consisted of a few Buchanan supporters, but most of the crowd came just "to see the fun." Before the speaking engagement, Buchanan and his supporters paraded through the town to the warehouse. The procession included 128 men on horses, a few people in carriages, and 180 members of the Farmers' Alliance, who walked the parade route on foot. Notably, Buchanan rode in a carriage pulled by four white hearse horses. The parade featured two musical groups: the Clarksville Military Band and a Black band. During the parade, the Black musicians played funeral dirges, such as "She Is Sleeping in the Valley," "The Dead March," "We Are Few and Far Between," and "Our Days Are Numbered." After the event, Tennesseans debated the significance of the horses and the funeral songs. Whether intentional or not, the Black musicians had made a political statement and humiliated Buchanan.[29]

Tennesseans expressed similar opinions concerning the meaning of the funeral horses and the songs played by the Black musicians. In the *Memphis Appeal-Avalanche*, the reporter explained that no one seemed to know if the band played the music "by chance or not." Despite the uncertainty, they used the headline "Blacks Guy Buchanan," which insinuated that the Black musicians had purposefully represented the governor in effigy.[30] In Clarksville's *Semi-Weekly Tobacco Leaf-Chronicle*, a reporter argued that the scene of the hearses and the music had left an impression on the spectators. According to the reporter, the horses "suggested a funeral procession" with election day "as the day of internment." The reporter added that the "burial will take place promply [sic] on that day, and the oration will be delivered by the Democracy of the Old Volunteer State." Finally, the reporter concluded that the "pall-bearers will be named later, and everybody will be invited." When the Black musicians played the funeral songs, observers seized upon the opportunity for political commentary. With regard to Buchanan's procession in Clarksville, a local Republican penned a note to a reporter stating that he considered the music "whether by chance or intentionally" as quite "appropriate for the occasion" given that he expected imminent demise for the Populist-leaning Democrat.[31] In the newspaper coverage of the event, reporters do not hesitate to give white Tennesseans a political voice. They seized upon the music and the horses and made numerous quips about Buchanan's likely demise. The reporters did not acknowledge any political awareness on behalf of the Black musicians. By portraying them as clueless musicians, the partisan newspaper reporters perpetuated the stereotype of the feckless Black musician without a political conscious. Whether or not the Black musicians acted intentionally, they set the tone of the day's events.

At political events, African Americans did not always harass Democrats but often played their roles as scripted by campaign organizers in the same ways they performed for Republicans. In October 1878, Black and white South Carolinians prepared massive demonstrations for the upcoming midterm elections. On October 12 Democrats and Republicans held competing rallies in Sumter, South Carolina. At 3:00 a.m., Democrats fired a cannon to signal the start of the day's festivities. At 5:00 a.m., more artillery fired and "kept it up all day till after the meeting." African Americans set up a stage at Emanuel Church for speakers. In the center of town, more than three thousand Black and white Democrats congregated in the city and "two splendid bands furnished music for the occasion." Simultaneously, Sumter's Republicans had their own meeting. According to observers, the Republican meeting consisted entirely of African Americans who "marched through the town." Although a "collision" seemed imminent, General Johnson Hagood "rode slowly to the spot with six hundred mounted Democrats." With this "show of force and the personal exertions of a few determined citizens," a potential riot fizzled out.[32] In these local political spectacles, Democrats and Republicans exhibited a high level of militaristic spirit and emotions ran high. African Americans could participate at the events of either party, but they could face harassment for their continued support of the Republican Party in South Carolina. When the parties competed, the threat of violence persisted.

On the same day, Republicans and Democrats gathered near Chester, South Carolina. The Chester Democratic Club held a rally featuring numerous speakers who bickered with one another. Major Julius Mills condemned a fellow candidate, J. A. Bradley Jr., for his alliance with the Republican Party. On the same night, Bradley had spoken at a Republican Party rally in the nearby town of Lewis' Turnout, which consisted of a small audience, thus demonstrating "the little interest taken by negroes in politics." At the Chester meeting, Bradley spoke again and defended his alliance. He could not "stand the denunciation" and left the event "amid great Democratic cheering." Although it was a midterm election year, the event "partook somewhat of the spirit of the campaign of '76 in its fervor and enthusiasm," including the Democratic Colored Band, which "furnished music for the occasion."[33] As Republicans, African Americans faced harassment and intimidation from the local press. As Democrats, they earned praise from local press for creating a festive atmosphere. In this time of party competition in the South, both sides competed for Black support and wanted it all for their own.

When African Americans participated at these events, they sometimes encountered violent racist terrorist organizations. In 1884 the Democrats of Chester, South Carolina, welcomed key party leaders with "the booming of artillery and warmest demonstrations of enthusiasm." The residents of Chester closed their shops and went to the rally, which featured a grand procession and numerous orations. The Sandy River Band and two Black bands "dispensed music on the thrilling occasion" as Democrats marched through the town in red shirts. Throughout the South, white Democrats formed paramilitary organizations, such as the Ku Klux Klan and, in this case, the Red Shirts. These terrorists intimidated non-Democratic voters, especially Black voters. In South Carolina, Red Shirts helped Wade Hampton III, who had served as a Confederate cavalry officer, win his gubernatorial and senatorial campaigns.[34] Six years earlier, Democrats and Republicans had held competing rallies in this town. With organizations like the Red Shirts, Democrats had taken firm control by this point. On a "beautifully decorated stage," the speakers engaged a massive, enthusiastic audience with oratory that sizzled with all "the patriotic fire of which their souls were capable."[35] With these newspaper reports, editors portrayed party rallies as unprecedentedly enthusiastic. They wanted non-attendees to wish they had been there, and provided an account of the events to help fellow partisans relive the events.

During the 1880s, Black and white Democrats, like Republicans, continued to view street spectacles as vitally important to the party's health and to ratify political decisions. In 1888 Democrats in Shelbyville, Kentucky, organized a flag-raising ceremony in support of President Grover Cleveland, who ran for reelection against Republican challenger Benjamin Harrison. In the early stages of the 1888 campaign season, the town's Democrats "wanted to be the first to float a Cleveland and Thurman flag from a hickory pole." On July 9, the Democrats realized their goal and town residents "witnessed the culmination of this patriotic desire" amid flashes of lightning, crashes of thunder, and heavy rain. The weather kept at home many people who otherwise would have participated in the "jollification." Despite "drenching rain," the flag-raising ceremony attracted a crowd of "hundreds from the surrounding country." The event organizers erected a "stout, shapely" 108-foot white pole. Amid the festivities, a Black band "paraded the streets in uniform" and played "furious music" to the crowd of nearly two thousand. After some speeches, the Democrats raised the thirty-foot-long flag while "the band played a selection of patriotic airs." After raising the flag, a salesman "with lungs like bellows" attempted to interrupt the next set of speakers. He took advantage of the large crowd to market his wares with a "voice uncommonly loud and harsh." "It was no use for an orator to dispute the field with him—that fellow was screeching and thundering loud enough to frighten the most aggressive kind of opposition," explained a reporter. After a short conference of the events' organizers, they agreed that the Black musicians "should play and drown the fellow out," which they did "until the man with the wares was forced to abandon his task." A reporter characterized these campaign spectacles as "not important of itself" but nonetheless explained that most people viewed this type of event "as an attractive campaign adjunct." At the event, a speaker made sure to comment that the Republicans, despite their best efforts, could not "get up a counter demonstration." Judge W. H. Anderson encouraged his party "to be up and doing" and help make sure that Kentucky votes Democrat in the upcoming election.[36] By staging these events, the people legitimized the Democratic National Convention's nomination. African Americans participated in this American tradition and helped erect the Democrats' pole, which served as a sign of the party's prowess in the area.[37]

With their musical selections, African Americans could link the Democratic Party to southern nationalism. In March 1892 Senator David B. Hill, a Democrat from New York, toured Georgia by train as he campaigned for nomination as his party's presidential candidate. On March 17 he arrived in Savannah to a spectacular reception. The Hill Club of Savannah marched by the hotel in columns of fours. In front of them, a Black band played "Dixie" for the northern Democrat. When they had assembled at the hotel's veranda, the Black band struck up "Hail to the Chief."[38] Despite having northern origins, Hill condemned "carpet-bagging vultures" who swooped "down on Southern capitalists." He praised the reunification of the country and claimed that the American form of government "represents an imperishable union of indestructible states." With these comments Hill was reaching out to southern Democrats. With the music, the Black band, most likely at the behest of the Hill Club, connected southern nationalism with the Democratic Party. By choosing "Hail to the Chief," the band made a prophecy, albeit likely at the request of the campaign.

After leaving Savannah, Hill traveled to Augusta to continue his tour before heading back to Washington, DC. On his way to the national capital, he stopped in Columbia, South Carolina, where a "colored band played a lively air" at the train station. In Columbia, he expressed his gratefulness that the state had been freed "from the control of carpet-baggers."[39] Although Hill's tour of the South seemingly helped reconcile the nation and connect Democrats across regional lines, the *St. Louis Post-Dispatch* editors chose the headline "Marching from Georgia" to remind readers of northern victory in the war.[40] For northerners and southerners, the Civil War and its legacy played out in spectacular fashion at campaign rallies and in newspapers, and African Americans had a role in this conversation with their choice in music by helping keep sectional spirit, and therefore partisanship, alive.

At events held on behalf of the Democratic Party, Black performers took on stereotypical roles reminiscent of the Old South, thus connecting the party with an idealized image of the master-slave relationship. In 1895 the residents of Fort Worth, Texas, prepared for the municipal elections by hosting a massive event featuring the many candidates for Alderman of three Fort Worth wards. The campaign committee developed a program for the campaign that featured "oratory and music and other adjuncts that follow Democratic enthusiasm." At this program, spectators could also expect to enjoy "a negro band with banjos playing and singing old plantation songs." The campaign committee had high hopes for the event because the city does not "lack of good speakers." The newspaper helped generate enthusiasm for the mass meeting at the city hall. A reporter explained that "there is great enthusiasm among Democrats and hundreds have signified their willingness to attend." The campaign committee advertised the meeting in the streets and anticipated a heavy crowd. The program featured a ball, as well.[41] By employing African Americans and requesting plantation songs for the occasion, Democrats tapped into postbellum nostalgia for the Old South, where masters enjoyed plantation songs rendered by enslaved African Americans at elaborate balls.

When African Americans attended Democratic events, Democrats used their presence as evidence that they were the friend of the race. On October 19, 1892, vice presidential candidate Adlai Stevenson, a southern Democrat, spoke to an audience of more than five thousand white and Black spectators in Decatur, Alabama. "Never before in the history of this section has there assembled so many Democrats as were here today," commented a reporter. The crowd consisted of people from across the Eighth District, and they gave Stevenson a "royal welcome." To entertain the crowds, musicians came to Decatur from nearby towns and cities, such as Huntsville and Cullman. The musicians "made the welkin ring with music" and the speakers "enthused the Democrats throughout the district." A reporter for the *Memphis Appeal-Avalanche* credited the enthusiastic audience for proving that "the district is safe for Democracy" and infusing "new life and hope into the party." The organizing committee characterized the massive gathering as a "splendid success" because Stevenson "made the strongest speech" of all his time in Alabama and his associate "captivated every one with his logic." Stevenson opposed the federal elections bill proposed by Henry Cabot Lodge in 1890 to protect Black southerners' voting rights. Later that month, Stevenson argued that it "would threaten the liberties of the entire people" and "would incite in many communities race troubles." He called it "un-American" and argued that it would "destroy popular representation and the purity of local self government."[42] Among the spectators, a "great many colored people" came to the gathering to "pay their respects to the General H. A. Skaggs," who had served as a county executive and as "a faithful worker to make a success of the meeting."[43] Like Stevenson, Skaggs had a local reputation as a loyal Democrat.[44] Although it seems unlikely that African Americans would attend an event staged on behalf of these two men, African Americans did have a notable presence, which Democrats highlighted to solidify their image as the true friends of Black southerners.

African Americans often greeted politicians and celebrities, including former Confederate generals, at train depots, which meant that they were among the first members of the public sphere to have contact with politicians. In August 1882 General William B. Bate, who had served in the Confederate Army, toured Tennessee as the Bourbon Democrats' gubernatorial candidate. In Carter's Creek, Tennessee, Bate and more than three thousand supporters ate barbecue and rallied. Spectators came to town on trains "from both directions." When Bate arrived at the train depot, a Black band from Columbia, Tennessee, furnished music to welcome him.[45]

In some cases, white southerners critiqued the presence of African Americans at Democratic events. The white residents of Winston, North Carolina, expressed disgust at the presence of Black musicians at formal and informal political spectacles as a waste of party and state funds. In 1893 a Black band entertained the guests at the inauguration of Governor Elias Carr, a Democrat, in North Carolina. At the inaugural ball held in Raleigh, organizers arranged to pay $150 for music. According to a constituent, the "gallant young men" and the "fair young ladies" accompanying them reacted with surprise "when it was discovered that the music was furnished by a negro band." He wondered "how it was so essential" to the dancing that the state had to "appropriate money to pay the fiddlers." The author, known only as R. Penstock, suggested instead that the funds should have gone to help soldiers and orphans. He asked readers and the editors to think about "how many little orphans" could have been "made comfortable and happy had that ball money been tendered the Orphan Asylum."[46]

Columnists continued to bring up this expense and critique the employment of Black musicians. A year later, North Carolinians still lamented the expenditure. A. M. Self, who had served in the state congress, wrote a letter to the same paper in which he explained that if the legislature of his youth "had been as liberal with the people's money as the last legislature was and had given to the public schools instead of giving to a negro band to play at the inauguration of Gov. Carr, I might have been able to have written my name."[47] After some time, as it happens with political talking points, the author exaggerated the sum.

Two years later, another author made a similar argument. In response to a column suggesting that politicians should not pay speakers for their appearances, George E. Hunt of North Carolina wrote a letter in which he referenced past abuses of public funds and suggested that paying speakers represented a wiser and more honest use of funds than using the money "to buy votes and bribe judges." He also referenced the inaugural ball, in which the state legislature appropriated "$500 of the people's money to have a big dance and hire a negro band from Richmond, Va., to make music for them to dance by."[48] At times, white southerners resented the employment of African Americans for entertainment purposes at political events, especially when white entertainers could have been procured. Rather than framing their objections in political terms, they portrayed the problem of employing Black musicians in economic terms. They wanted to restrict Black economic opportunity, especially when white talent was available.

When African Americans serenaded a Democratic candidate, they earned scorn from competing Democrats. In 1880 in Georgia, Thomas M. Norwood challenged incumbent Governor Alfred Colquitt for the Democratic nomination in the race for the governor. On the evening of August 29, a Black band under the direction of a "weazly [sic] looking young man" with a "squeaky voice" arrived in front of the Kimball House on Pryor Street in downtown Atlanta. There, the band "played a tune or two" to attract a crowd. Soon it became clear to spectators that the "object of the music was a serenade for Norwood." As the crowd grew restless waiting for their candidate to appear, a public official permitted the band and crowd to enter the building. When they arrived in the reception room, Norwood "fully realized that he was the object of the musical infliction and appeared upon the steps." At this time, evangelist and prohibitionist Samuel Small introduced Norwood as the next governor of Georgia, which elicited a wild applause.

Editor Henry Grady of the *Atlanta Constitution* supported Colquitt against Norwood. He claimed that Norwood "made the same old charges against Governor Colquitt in the same old way, and with the same old absence of proof." Then, he blamed Norwood for a "cheap bid for the colored vote" and blamed Colquitt "for not preaching to the convicts as well as the other negroes."[49] As two candidates competed for the Democratic nomination, it appears that a white musical director employed Black musicians to generate support for the candidate most likely to protect Black voting rights. As the Democratic Party returned to dominance in the South, African Americans often switched their alliances to the candidate most likely to protect them. As the challenger, Norwood would likely need Black votes to overturn the Democratic establishment.

In many cases, Black participation in Democratic meetings angered Republicans, who expressed entitlement to Black support based on their work for emancipation. In 1888 Democrats held a torchlight procession in Neosho, Missouri. During the parade, a Black band and a large number of African Americans joined the Democrats. The Democratic press stated that their presence "enraged the Republican leaders." The local Republicans were "determined to carry out their well known tactics of bulldozing the negroes." After the procession, white Republicans attacked Joe Ferguson, who had participated in the Democratic event. The attackers demanded Ferguson to explain himself. In response, Ferguson explained that "this was a free country and he had a right to do as he pleased." After he explained that he intended to vote for the Democrats, Republican leader Walter Ames seriously injured Ferguson with a hatchet. Upon learning of the attack, the town's Democrats became "very indignant" and had Ames arrested for his attack on a Black man. Across the town, Democratic attorneys volunteered their services in Ames's prosecution.[50]

Although African Americans ate and drank at campaign events staged by the Democratic Party, they sometimes had to participate in segregated ways. On October 18, 1892, the Young Men's Democratic Club of Brookhaven, Mississippi, staged the "largest barbecue ever given in the South." They hosted more than seven thousand people, including African Americans. The barbecue consisted of a mile-long procession of Democrats on foot and horseback. The event included banners, brass bands, and "booming of cannon." Democratic candidates spoke to the massive audiences. A Populist speaker spoke as well, but "he looked as lonesome as he would be in Congress." Instead, the audience consisted mostly of Democrats, who "cheered the Democratic speakers to the echo." In addition to the speeches, a "fat man's race was a humorous feature of the occasion" and provided a temporary distraction from the politics. For the meal, the Democrats slaughtered and barbecued seven cows, fifteen sheep, and forty goats. They also ordered six hundred pounds of bread from New Orleans to help feed the massive crowd. The white spectators ate first. African Americans participated in the event, but they did not eat with the white Democrats. Instead, the event organizers distributed "several hundred pounds of meat" left over "among the negroes."[51] With these paternalistic gestures, Democrats tried to attract Black voters.

For the most part, Black performers could access spaces otherwise off limits to African Americans, but they did encounter some hostility. According to a reporter for the *Washington Post*, the white residents of Rock Creek in Mitchell County, North Carolina, boasted that African Americans cannot live among them. On one occasion, according to the reporter, "a negro band was taken there from Asheville during a political campaign, but the bandsmen had to flee for their lives."[52] In general, white southerners reserved this type of harassment for Black voters whose political power threatened Democratic control over the region. The Black performer typically infiltrated the Democratic Party by manipulating white stereotypes of Black performers and southern nostalgia for the Old South, but not in every case.

Toward the end of the nineteenth century, Democrats gained increasingly more power over southern state and local governments with intimidation and disfranchisement. African Americans performed and paraded for these candidates. While they may not have had much of a choice in the candidate, they could choose whether to support or oppose the candidate with street theater, rough music, and public performances. As the Republican Party lacked power in the South, many African Americans also considered the numerous third parties and reform movements that either split white Democrats or challenged their unilateral control over politics.

AFRICAN AMERICANS AND REFORM MOVEMENTS AND THIRD PARTIES

In the late nineteenth and early twentieth centuries, reformers such as prohibitionists, labor advocates, and third-party leaders like the Populists continued to rely on the vibrant spectacular political culture of parades and rallies to spread their message and mobilize voters. They agitated the established political order with pamphlets and generated popular approval for their reforms with spectacular demonstrations. Reformers and third-party leaders depended on pamphlets and newspapers to differentiate their vision from the traditional political order. They did not, however, make educational literature the centerpiece of their campaigns. They based their political style on spectacle. They wore badges and uniforms to the polls, organized parades, raised banners and flags in city squares, and performed other ceremonies to create a sense of community. The Populists portrayed themselves as enlightened intellectuals with informed opinions who condemned spectacular displays, but they hosted parades, formed glee clubs, marched banners through the streets, and blasted fireworks into the sky.[53]

In addition to the need for spectacle, these reform movements and third parties required Black votes to succeed and overthrow the entrenched parties. Although reformers, like other white southerners, tended to have fears of Black political power, they needed creative alliances to mobilize enough votes. African Americans proved receptive to new political alliances as they became more disillusioned with the Republican Party, they provided considerable support to these movements, especially in local and statewide elections. African Americans held the balance of power when white southerners could not agree. At the spectacles staged on behalf of reform movements and third parties, African Americans often had a public, visible role in politics.

PROHIBITION MOVEMENT

Across the region, the prohibition issue divided white southerners. Prohibitionists generally drew their supporters from rural, native-born, evangelical Protestants by tapping into their frustration and cynicism toward immigrants and other urban dwellers. Catholics, Germans, and urbanites tended to oppose prohibition. Within the city, prohibitionists could claim support from the middle class but not the working class.[54] When voters went to the polls to decide the issue, they did not vote as Democrats or Republicans but rather as drys or wets.

In countless local-option and statewide referenda throughout the South, Black Republicans could vote as a bloc and tip the balance in whatever direction offered them the most promise. They seized these opportunities to make tangible gains in their conditions, but proceeded with caution because of their precarious condition.[55]

During the 1880s, African Americans formally contributed to prohibition campaigns at the voting booths and as leaders and managers for both sides of the issue. In 1881 and 1884, Black and white delegates gathered for the State Temperance Convention of Alabama. At the 1884 event, the biracial delegation moved to support the National Prohibition Party. In 1882 North Carolina's anti-prohibitionists formed the Liberal Anti-Prohibition Party and held a convention, where the 150-person delegation included thirty African Americans. The new political party ran Black candidates for the state legislature and secured a couple victories. In 1887 about 90,000 Black voters cast ballots in Tennessee's vote on a statewide prohibition amendment, which failed.[56] These Black voters and officeholders influenced the outcome of prohibition referenda.

In 1883 Black and white residents of Greenville, South Carolina, engaged in a spectacular contest over the future of the city's eighteen saloons. African Americans made up almost half of the town's residents, so they would play a major role in the outcome of the election because the issue split white voters without regard to party lines. On election day, Black men cast their ballots while Black children paraded and sang in the streets and Black women served lunch to prohibition supporters. At the conclusion of the voting, the wets had won by a slim margin. Black and white men affirmed the decision by partying in the town's streets, launching fireworks into the sky, and harassing leading prohibitionists by marching near their homes. In many prohibition elections, African Americans held the elections in their hands as they did in Greenville, where they leveraged their power into meaningful gains, such as improved schools and municipal appointments to the police and fire squads.[57]

In 1887 Democrats dominated Texas politics, but the prohibition issue split them. Progressive Democrats supported moral reforms, including prohibition, to ameliorate social conditions and promote better government. Conservative Democrats opposed prohibition because it threatened individual liberty.[58] With this split in the party, both drys and wets courted Black votes with public events.

African Americans did not agree on the prohibition issue either, but they did view it through a lens of racial improvement. On the one side, Black prohibitionists tended to view the issue as a chance to prove their respectability to middle-class white Texans. On the other side, Black anti-prohibitionists tended to associate the freedom to buy and drink alcohol as an issue of individual liberty, and they rejected any attempt to limit freedom.[59]

Across the state, drys and wets held rallies and barbecues for crowds of four to six thousand Black and white voters. At these events, the prohibitionists featured religious leaders to speak with moral authority against alcohol. Black voters wanted political leverage rather than salvation. They also wanted freedom and power. In a series of speeches against prohibition, ex-bondsman Melvin Wade embraced the theme of individual liberty. He promised to Black and white audiences that freed people would vote the wet ticket because they appreciated freedom.[60]

On July 26, 1887, anti-prohibitionists gathered near Fort Worth. The 500,000 participants from across the state created a festival-like event, which featured nine bands to furnish music. In the morning, they formed a procession and marched for forty-five minutes through the city's streets. The parade featured "colored voters from all over the State," who "marched with their delegations sandwiched between their white friends" with "no distinction made in regard to them." After the march, the massive crowd of Black and white voters feasted on poultry, goat, veal, and pork while listening to a series of speeches by prominent anti-prohibitionists. The program continued deep into the night.[61] By participating in this event, these Black voters became part of the anti-prohibition community, which welcomed both Black and white supporters. They helped forge a temporary yet important political and racial alliance that the prohibitionists could not overcome at the voting booths.

On August 4, 1887, the "fight culminated in a day of intense excitement" as the anti-prohibitionists and prohibitionists pleaded for every vote but with the white female temperance workers gaining most of the attention and headlines. "The thermometer was high, but not higher than the feeling between the parties," commented a reporter, who proceeded to chronicle the feverish events of the day. In Galveston, the prohibitionists "were out in full force" and set up booths by each polling place. At these booths, "women attired in a uniform similar to that worn by Salvationists" provided voters with lunch and marked ballots. The women employed their children in the work, as well. The prohibitionists rolled wagons covered "with various devices calculated to inspire a terror of rum and the liquor traffic" through the streets to energize voters. Prohibitionists, especially women, made their way through the streets and pled with voters to save their sons. They also met in churches, where they prayed with one another. In Denison, "women worked as hard at the polls as did their sisters in Galveston." The Women's Christian Temperance Union (WCTU) women met at the local church and descended upon each of the city's polling places, where they remained all day. Led by a drum corps, the city's children marched through the city and sang temperance hymns. On floats, young women sang temperance hymns.[62]

Likewise, anti-prohibitionists mobilized voters with a series of stump-speakers, who urged voters to avoid fanaticism and condemned the work of the women at the booths. In Laredo, the anti-prohibitionists staged an impressive procession complete with bands and carriages, which they used to transport the city's voters to the polls. In Tyler, the anti-prohibitionists outmaneuvered their opponents by taking possession of every major public space in the city, which relegated prohibitionists to private, smaller spaces. In Fort Worth, the anti-prohibitionists staged a rally for Black voters and read the letter penned by former Confederate president Jefferson Davis for the campaign. He emphasized personal liberty as the foundation of the United States. Despite its origins, the letter's message of freedom resonated among Black voters "with good effect."[63]

Amid the election day spectacle, voters did cast ballots. The wets benefited from the support of about 74 percent of the state's Black voters to win the campaign. Based on the success of the alliance, Black Texans would sporadically work with white voters to defeat establishment tickets at the polls in future elections, but the power wielded by Black voters strengthened opposition to Black voting rights.[64]

During the 1887 campaign for a statewide prohibition amendment in Tennessee, African Americans, as they had in Texas, were a constant presence at campaign events for both sides. In Tennessee, the prohibition also split white voters but in some different and unique ways, which created an opportunity for Black Tennesseans to have a determinative voice. The two sides made intellectual appeals. Prohibitionists argued that a town's incarceration rate correlated with its number of saloons. The anti-prohibitionists argued that they could not enforce the amendment and that prohibition would hurt the economy. This argument resonated with many Tennesseans. In rural areas, whiskey had been a product distilled and sold to recoup some of the financial losses of the Civil War, so the amendment faced stiff challenges.[65]

On September 14, a wagon carried a Black band through Nashville's major streets to announce a prohibition speaker at the Olympic Theater. A grocer and baker responded, "Vote for beer and pretzels," and promised: "If the state goes dry, goodbye my pretzels, good-bye."[66]

On September 24, about four thousand Black and white prohibitionists assembled in Nashville's Public Square to listen to Black minister J. C. Price of North Carolina speak in support of the proposed amendment. During the speech, he argued that prohibition would lead to harmony between the races, safer and more intact Black families, more educational opportunities for African Americans, and less criminal behavior. After the speech, a local Black minister gave a "short and earnest address" and "urged his people to throw themselves with energy into the great fight now before them."[67]

At the polls, Black and white men and women hit the streets. A reporter for the *New York Times* advised his readers that, from the beginning, "it was clearly apparent that the contest at the polls would be unusually interesting." Tennesseans brandished white badges for prohibition and blue badges in opposition. According to the reporter, the "hundreds of white and colored men" in Nashville with blue badges on their coats "moved here and there," with "the intermingling of the colors" an interesting sight. Businesses shut down for the day. Church bells rang. The drys and wets ran vehicles through the streets with campaign slogans, scripture passages, and images.[68]

After the polls closed the crowds grew larger in Nashville, as citizens debated the outcome as they collectively awaited results. On both sides, supporters knew where in the state they had advantages and disadvantages, and they watched results to confirm their expectations. "As the night wore on," observed the reporter for the *New York Times*, "the crowds became larger, and thousands congregated about the newspaper offices to learn the results." As results became known, "cheers were given by first one side and then another."[69]

Prohibition also failed in Tennessee. The wets had received 145,000 votes, and the drys had only secured 118,000. In the newspapers, African Americans received most of the credit for voting as a block against the prohibition amendment. They had assembled clubs in opposition to prohibition and, despite efforts by the drys, few Black voters had switched sides. Once again, the issues had split white voters, so Black voters held the balance of power.

In 1890 the Black and white residents of Lynchburg, Virginia, participated in a spectacular campaign on the issue of prohibition. The local-option prohibition contest stirred the town from "centre to circumference as it has seldom, if ever, been stirred before." With the excitement at a "fever heat on both sides," men and women rallied in the streets. On January 9, prohibitionists and anti-prohibitionists each staged a parade through the city's major streets with Black musicians at the head of the march. These two parades met near Main Street, where the "colored bands that headed the two processions came together, mingled momentarily in what seemed inextricable confusion, but finely separated without a serious collision." After the incident, the prohibitionists proceeded to a meeting at the city's opera house, and the anti-prohibitionists "marched on to the Madison Street armory, where an immense meeting in favor of 'moisture' was held."[70] In many of these events, the spectacle took the form of combat with opposing sides seeking to outmaneuver and disrupt one another. In these battles, African Americans sometimes led the charge.

When African Americans opposed prohibition, they often conflicted with white women before a public audience, which could result in trouble. In 1888 a local-option prohibition campaign in Versailles, Kentucky, caused quite a stir because of the interactions between Black and white street demonstrators. An Oregon-based newspaper reporter characterized the town as "in the very heart of the Blue Grass region" and "the hottest hotbed of Kentucky aristocracy." On election day, the city's female prohibitionists occupied booths near the polls and provided "free lemonade and winsome smiles" for fellow supporters. They sang temperance songs and spoke with voters in an attempt to influence the election. In reaction, "the chivalrous opposition sent away and secured a negro band to drown the voices of the ladies, and by that and other similar means carried the day." The reporter commented that despite "all the talk about chivalry in the South," bourbonism forced chivalry into the back seat.[71] In situations across the South, a confrontation between Black men and white women may have put Black men in danger, but aside from the criticism in the newspapers, these Black musicians escaped unharmed.

In the post-Reconstruction South, southerners had designed segregation to mark Black people as inferior but portrayed these measures as a desire to protect white women. They crafted laws to maintain distance between middle-class white women and Black men in crowded public spaces.[72] To similar ends, white southerners passed anti-miscegenation laws to maintain separation of the races in sex and marriage.[73] When Black men threatened the separation of the races, they could face severe punishment in the form of arrest or lynching, especially if a middle-class white woman made an accusation of rape.[74]

In Versailles and elsewhere, the Black musicians defied white supremacy by challenging the pedestal upon which southern society put white middle-class women by harassing them with music. Unlike many unfortunate Black southerners, these musicians escaped harassment because the spectacle required white women and Black men to act out their respective roles for consumption by spectators. According to the reporter, the Black musicians' unchivalrous, or rude, behavior starkly contrasted with the behavior of the white female prohibitionists. Upon witnessing the scene, white observers may have felt satisfied, to an extent, by seeing Black men act just as like the playful, perhaps even mischievous, characters in minstrel shows, which justified their white supremacist worldview.[75]

During the 1880s and 1890s, African Americans influenced the campaigns and elections concerning the prohibition issue because it split the white electorate. As Democrats strengthened their hold on the South, African Americans made an impact on other issues and supported many other third-party movements, which likewise split the white electorate. African Americans worked for and against many third parties, who often welcomed them.

THE READJUSTERS

After Reconstruction ended, white Democrats faced challenges to their dominance in the South because of factions within their diverse coalition. Many white southerners chose to leave the Democratic Party for any number of third parties. These third parties, including the Readjusters and People's Party, relied on popular spectacle. These third parties reached out to Black Republicans because they needed these votes to dislodge the Democrats. Often, these alliances did not amount to much because they required universal support from Black Republicans. When they did succeed, these parties mostly benefited white southerners, but African Americans did gain political influence and tangible results. During the 1870s and 1880s, African Americans lent their support, in similar ways as they did for the prohibition movement, to third parties with their ballots and with their participation in popular spectacle.[76]

In 1879 disillusioned Virginians established the Readjuster Party to challenge the power of wealthy white planters, and they relied on African Americans for their brief success.[77] During the 1870s Virginia Democrats, who had retaken control of Virginia government and started undermining Reconstruction-era policies, aimed to pay off the state's debt, so they cut public schools and other services, which tended to benefit African Americans and poorer white voters. In response, lower-class Black and white Virginians supported William Mahone, a former general in the Confederate army, for governor. Faced with the threat of bankruptcy and social and economic turmoil, the Readjusters intended to readjust the state debt and increase funding for public schools and facilities.[78]

Like most third parties, they actively courted African Americans to their ranks. After initial hesitancy, African Americans responded. They maintained loyalty to the Republican Party but recognized that an alliance with white Readjusters gave them a shot at electoral success and patronage positions. After the 1879 election, the Readjusters controlled sections of state government, including both the state house and state senate because thirteen Black Republicans had won seats. When these Black Republicans supported Mahone in his bid for the US Senate, they successfully forged an alliance that offered hope to Black Virginians. Immediately, the Readjusters offered patronage positions to African Americans. In state matters, the alliance seemed to work, but African Americans still owed their national allegiance to the Republican Party. Black Virginians did not yet know if the Readjusters would affirm their alliance with the Black community or compromise with the Funders of the Conservative Party, or Democrats. From the Black perspective, the Readjusters needed to guarantee that African Americans could access the polls on election day, which they both needed to protect their alliance and achieve electoral success.[79]

During the 1881 campaign, Readjusters made frequent use of spectacle, which had a militaristic element to it, and African Americans played a role in the fight. From the beginning of the party system, party leaders often created highly organized teams of campaign workers that resembled military units. Dressed in military-style uniforms, these teams went out to canvass voters and to encourage men to vote.[80] The Readjusters used similar means to mobilize voters in Virginia. In Petersburg, Mahone set up his campaign headquarters and directed "his forces with his usual skill." He appointed Black canvassers to travel around the state to rally voters, address audiences, and organize events. For each county, Mahone appointed Black and white lieutenants to manage the election-day work. They organized supporters into squads of ten voters and assigned Black and white squad captains, who had the responsibility to distribute ballots and march voters to the polls.[81]

Virginians debated the significance and utility of popular demonstrations on election day. On the morning of the election the *Petersburg Index Appeal* editors argued, "Elections are the curse of this country—not the principle, but the methods." They asked voters to cast their ballots quickly and quietly and then return to "daily business." The editors condemned "promiscuous gatherings about the polls" because these displays "breed confusion and disorder, and lead often to collisions and bloodshed." They argued that success did not result from having "the largest number of idlers about the polls" but instead insisted that "ballots only count." They pleaded for "a peaceful election."[82] In the late nineteenth and early twentieth centuries, middle-class white Americans increasingly made these arguments to remove spectacle from politics as an attempt to reform elections and restrict them to more educated participants. Although some people condemned electoral spectacle, they could not stop it or undermine its significance.

The political leaders of the Funders and Readjusters did not heed this advice. On the same editorial page, Superintendent of the City Central Committee Richard B. Davis encouraged voters to "vote early" and "remain at the polls, as far as practicable, all day" for the "welfare of the country." He instructed votes to "be not deterred by the weather from the discharge of your plain duty at the polls" because their "very presence will influence some vote and swell the certain majority" for the Funders. He concluded, "Up! Virginians! Do your duty to-day and save your State from the coalition."[83] Similarly, C. B. Raine, who served as the superintendent of the Republican Party, instructed his fellow Republicans, "Go to the polls and vote early, and stay there all day, rain or shine." He explained, "You will never know what vote you can influence until you try, and there is no better way to get votes than to be at the polls prepared to do your whole duty." He concluded, "There was never a battle fought on the soil of Virginia, or an election held in the State upon which depends so much good for us, and the whole country as the election today."[84] To party organizers, the spectacle had political significance because it could lead to electoral success, and they considered it an essential part of the campaign.

On election day, Virginians braved terrible weather to collectively participate in the spectacle. In Richmond, crowds gathered outside of the *Daily Dispatch* office to see updates from election officials. In the windows of the building, they hung pictures of the major candidates with the vote totals. It rained heavily at times, so the crowds found shelter in nearby doorways. Despite the rain, "the street was never wholly deserted, as there was about half an acre of umbrellas on hand, or rather in hand, and beneath these the enthusiastic Democracy stood cheering good news and growling at bad." Throughout the day, the crowd experienced mood swings as the election results remained in doubt. As conflicting reports reached the audience, the crowd would swing from moments of "great exultation" and quickly relapse into discouragement. During the day, rain may have dampened enthusiasm for the election day spectacle, but the weather turned favorable. In Petersburg, residents came alive at night and celebrated that the election "passed off in a quiet and orderly manner."[85] The newspaper reporter considered this a quiet election despite the presence of large crowds, who rallied all day and night.

Amid the spectacle, African Americans set the tone of the day by taking control of the polls. The white voters at the polls "had a realizing sense of the nature of the contest when on Tuesday morning they beheld long lines of ignorant negroes standing in solid array at the strong negro precincts ready to cast their votes."[86] By not only voting but through their visibility, African Americans demonstrated their power. Based on the sight of African Americans at the polls, white Virginians knew who had control.

In the 1881 election, Readjusters won all their statewide campaigns, but they did not stay in power long. They had come to power by forming a coalition that disregarded previous party allegiances and secured the Black vote. When Republicans had power on the national level, including Republican Chester Arthur as president, Mahone could distribute the patronage positions that made the alliance work. By 1885 the party had ceased to exist because Democrats had taken control on the national level, which cut off access to appointments. In their short existence, the Readjusters had proven that Black Republicans would consider alternatives to the Republican Party, especially on the state level. With these alliances, third parties could succeed, if only briefly.

THE LABOR MOVEMENT

African Americans participated in the labor movement of the late nineteenth century by lending their support to labor-oriented third parties. In these third parties they had massive membership, which they publicly flaunted at spectacles, massive meetings, and conventions. In addition to the support of labor parties, African Americans participated in the labor movement's many other public events, such Labor Day, which had a political charge. African Americans had a high level of visibility in national and local labor movements.

Among many labor parties, the Knights of Labor effectively aligned Black and white working-class southerners to agitate for labor reform. During its reign, the Knights of Labor, the most prominent of these labor parties, had a massive enrollment of Black members because of its emphasis on egalitarianism. During the 1880s, Black and white men and women joined this order to fight on behalf of eight-hour workdays, the abolition of convict labor, child labor laws, and equal pay for equal work for women. When the organization reached the South, it had a presence in the region's industrial centers but soon spread to the rural counties of the South. By 1886 the Knights of Labor had fifty thousand members organized into two thousand local chapters in ten southern states. They drew their support from the ranks of skilled and unskilled labor without regard for "party, race, and sex."[87] African Americans participated in many events hosted by the Knights of Labor.

In October 1886, the Knights of Labor gathered in Richmond, Virginia, for a convention. On October 11, the delegates enjoyed a day of festivities. In honor of the day, Richmond's mayor ordered all city offices closed, and many shops and factories followed suit. At 10:00 a.m. the Knights of Labor formed a procession of "four and five thousand men" and marched through the city. Amid the massive crowd, Black men and women marched and rode in carriages and numbered as many as 1,600 of the few thousand gathered. The Black members of Pioneer Assembly 3572, which consisted of Black members of the Knights of Labor, marched alongside their white comrades. Led by Black musicians, thousands of people lined the streets, especially in the eastern part of the city. Among the spectators, "the entire colored population" seemed to have "turned out to witness the parade." After the procession, the Knights of Labor gathered at the fairgrounds for games, including bicycle races and various tournaments. At the conclusion of these festivities, the delegates enjoyed a banquet and "white and colored delegates sat together at the tables," including Black women as well.[88] At this event, African Americans participated as marchers and members, but also as spectators in the crowd. In all these capacities, they crossed racial lines.

With these biracial activities, the Knights of Labor made a significant statement on behalf of racial equality and cooperation. With regard to the march, one of the Knights of Labor delegates explained, "It was a demonstration which showed the large numbers of the Knights in this vicinity" and "the practical equality of the races in action plainly before all eyes." The delegate added, "When assemblies of white men and a white band, and assemblies of colored men and a colored band, march in the same procession, each assembly coming into line just where it happened to be, the color line was to that extent rubbed out."[89] According to the *Hartford Daily Courant* editors, the Knights of Labor's biracialism in Richmond demonstrated that wage-earners "have declared that color has nothing to do with the rights of laboring men."[90] Many southerners disagreed.

In southern states, newspaper editors expressed disgust at the actions of the Knights of Labor, specifically their choice to have African Americans placed in honorary positions. During the convention, Black delegate Frank J. Ferrell introduced Grand Master Workman Terrence V. Powderly, which displeased many newspaper editors in the South. According to the editors of the *Mobile Register*, the Knights of Labor insulted Virginia Governor Fitzhugh Lee with this breach of protocol. They explained, "Mr. Powderly tries and condemns the southern people, and sets himself up as an exponent of the laws of God and man." The editors of the *Memphis Avalanche* stated that southern states did not appreciate "the meddling of Mr. Powderly or of anybody else" with their affairs. In the North, newspaper editors criticized these racist viewpoints espoused by their southern counterparts. The editors of the *Hartford Daily Courant* concluded their opinion piece with Robert Burns's poetic refrain: "A man's a man for a' that / And twice as much as a' that."[91]

In addition to labor parties, African Americans belonged to labor unions, which put on Labor Day programs with a militant, political message. In the

The Knights of Labor repeatedly broke the color line at their October 1886 convention in Richmond, such as when Black delegate Frank J. Ferrell introduced Grand Master Workman Terrence V. Powderly. Library of Congress, Prints & Photographs Division, LC-USZ62–120765.

1870s and 1880s, biracial labor unions had formed across the South, including cities like Richmond, Birmingham, and New Orleans. Labor leaders used Labor Day celebrations and spectacles to form a community of labor supporters, advocate for labor rights, and demonstrate the group's political power. In 1882 New Yorkers celebrated the first Labor Day, but the event soon spread throughout the nation with an endorsement from the American Federation of Labor, which hoped to turn the day into a three-day event. During Labor Day parades, working-class Americans expressed class consciousness while reveling in festivity, food, and drink with people of different ethnicities, sexes, races, and religions.[92]

For these events, labor leaders called upon playwrights, composers, directors, and campaign managers to create interesting demonstrations that would capture the attention of Americans yet spread a militant and aggressive class-based message. They organized speeches, performances, parades, and picnics, which became almost sacred elements of the Labor Day ritual. They created floats and banners and rehearsed skits and songs. By staging these events, working-class Americans forced local and national politicians to express their esteem for their wage-earning constituents. At the very least, they forced employers and the state to recognize a day off from work and gained the attention of millions of Americans.[93]

Labor Day became a major event, and newspaper editors covered the parades and festivities by reporting the intricate details with special attention to the crowds and the marchers and their dress and slogans. Before a national audience, laborers could reflect on the past year in the labor movement and state their goals and intentions.[94] With these rituals, labor advocates forced labor issues into the national mainstream political debate. For labor leaders, these celebrations became the primary means by which American laborers articulated an aggressive class-based message yet appealed to a wider audience of middle- and upper-class Americans.[95]

African Americans marched and played alongside white southerners in Labor Day celebrations throughout the South. On September 7, 1891, people "of all ages, sizes and conditions, men, women and children, white and black" arrived in Nashville, Tennessee, for a Labor Day celebration. Under a perfect, bright sky and brilliant sunshine, an immense crowd of 12,000 laborers celebrated and formed a procession for a long march through the city. Throughout the parade, musicians filled the air and "gay coloring brightened every portion of the long procession." The members of the various trade unions wore remarkable uniforms. At one point, a Black band from the Independent Order of Immaculates, which became locally famous for its "sho' 'nuff" music, marched by the grandstands and struck up "Dixie," which the Nashville crowd appreciated. In 1894 these musicians would make another appearance at the city's Labor Day festivities.[96]

Although many labor leaders tended to emphasize and celebrate biracialism in Labor Day spectacles, some African Americans encountered resistance. In 1896 the working men and women of St. Louis had a Labor Day parade, which featured a Black band at the head. In response to the Black band in this position of honor, many unions refused to supply bands for the parade, which created a "noticeable scarcity of union bands in line" because the white union men "say that they would not march in the same parade with the colored men."[97] In the biracial activities of Labor Day, Black and white laborers continued to participate in segregated ways.

Although the labor parties did not last long, African Americans continued to perform on behalf of the labor movement in the twentieth century, when they had been disfranchised. They found an opportunity in the labor movement because, like the campaigns around prohibition, it relied on popular spectacle and Black support to shake up the establishment. The era's most successful and revolutionary third party, the People's Party, also relied on spectacle and Black support.

THE PEOPLE'S PARTY

The Populists had a short-lived but highly successful insurgency during the 1890s that blended educational tactics with popular politics. The People's Party offered poor and rural Black and white Americans an alternative to the Republicans and Democrats by advocating for an energetic government to extend loans, build warehouses, regulate railroad rates, print paper money, and coin silver. As a third party, the Populists needed to display intellectual rigor to differentiate themselves from the more established parties, yet they had to mobilize voters with popular politics to achieve success at the voting booths. They distributed an immense amount of campaign literature. They filled newspapers with sophisticated arguments on politics and economics, in which they frequently referenced reports and statistics. They studied the plans of other nations and noted these ideas in their speeches and pamphlets. They made these arguments, however, without alienating common voters. In speeches, political cartoons, and other media, Populists had a knack for reaching out to poor and rural Black and white voters.[98] Like other third party and reform movements, Populists also made frequent use of spectacle to mobilize supporters to their cause.

The Populists frequently used spectacular tactics with a revival-like atmosphere to attract voters. In July 1896, Populists gathered in Sutherland Spring, Texas, for a meeting where the speakers pumped "political salvation into the ears of their admiring followers." At the climax of the weeklong affair, which consisted of Populists from nearby counties, Jerome Kearby, who the newspapers referred to as the Populists' "idol and their political Moses," arrived to speak and "lead them out of their night of darkness into the right sunlight of a subtreasury."[99] They generated a religious fervor for their issues with the public events.

In the South, white Populists shared Democrats' disgust for Reconstruction and fear of Black civic leaders, but they needed Black votes if they had any hope of defeating the dominant Democrats at the polls.[100] During the 1880s and 1890s, African Americans started to look beyond the Republican Party for a better political alliance. They formed their own Populist movement, which shared many of the same principles as its white counterpart, such as better wages and fairer credit conditions, but also advocated for measures to attain racial equality, such as the end of the convict lease system and the inclusion of African Americans on jury pools.[101]

African Americans also allied with white Populists to create fusion tickets between the People's Party and Black Republicans.[102] As a new party, the People's Party had the opportunity to practice their rhetoric and find a language that would win these Black votes without alienating white voters. In all the southern states, the Populists did not hesitate to openly appeal to Black voters, and African Americans appeared as frequent guests and speakers at Populist rallies.[103]

On July 26, 1892, the Populists of Greenville, Alabama, hosted a rally on the grounds of the Greenville Collegiate Institute. The program featured speaker Peyton G. Bowman, who campaigned on behalf of gubernatorial candidate Rueben F. Kolb. For the event, the Populists hired a brass band to "drum up a crowd of colored voters as the speech was made principally to capture their votes." Newspaper reporters estimated that the crowd of around five hundred people consisted of two hundred African Americans, which forced the speaker to acknowledge them.[104]

During the speech, Bowman focused on disfranchisement and told his audience that the Democrats intended to disfranchise both Black and poor white voters. He explained that Democrats intend "to win this vote by fair means if they can" but by "foul means" if necessary. He condemned the effort to disfranchise voters and characterized the man "that will undertake to swindle his neighbor out of his vote" as a "thief of the lowest cast." He appealed to every resident to "stand up as one man" and guarantee that each vote counts. Black voters responded by turning out for the Populists on election day.[105]

From 1892 to 1898, African Americans demonstrated visible, public support for the Populists, especially in Georgia, where African Americans had a highly visible role in the Populist movement. On July 31, 1894, a biracial crowd of five hundred men and women gathered in Waycross, Georgia, to hear Populist leaders Tom Watson, James K. Hines, Tom Morton, and S. I. Bishop speak. Watson had a successful speech, in which he "abused the democrats" with his "witty sayings and humorous anecdotes," which "elicited much cheering."[106] On September 5, 1894, Georgia's Populists gathered in Louisville, Georgia, for a rally, which featured numerous speakers, who commented on a variety of subjects to an audience of three hundred Black and white spectators.[107] On October 2, 1896, Tennessee gubernatorial candidate A. L. Mims spoke at the courthouse in Clarksville before a small crowd of two hundred Black and white Populists.[108] On November 4, 1898, fusion congressional candidate James Wilkinson "invaded Congressman Brantley's home county" and held a rally at the city hall in Brunswick, Georgia. The audience consisted almost entirely of African Americans. He directed his speech almost exclusively to the Black members of the audience and shook hands with the Black voters that had come to hear him.[109]

In the short lifespan of the People's Party, the 1896 campaign season represented a climactic, if unsuccessful, moment. They had been gathering strength for years and nominated candidates across the country. In 1896 they nominated for President a nationally well-known politician William Jennings Bryan, whom the Democrats had also nominated. He embarked on a vigorous campaign schedule across the country to make his case, which focused on the coinage of silver. On the Populist ticket, Georgia politician Tom Watson remained the vice-presidential candidate for Bryan although Democrats had picked Arthur Sewall. Bryan's energy trickled down to the state races, especially in Georgia, where Watson and others campaigned for national and local offices. The 1896 campaign season had many notable biracial moments in Georgia.

At Populist rallies in Georgia, Black speakers sometimes took the stage for the party's revival-like meetings. On July 9, 1896, Georgia Populists met in Montezuma to hear a series of speakers, including an African American.[110] On July 24, 1896, a crowd in Murfreesboro, Tennessee, gathered at the courthouse to hear prominent Populists speak, including Populist gubernatorial candidate Robert L. Taylor. Before the rally, a massive procession occurred with 1,500 horsemen, two bands of music, and countless banners and signs expressing their support. After the hour-long parade, the crowd assembled at the courthouse and in Public Square, where Taylor "stirred the crowd to the greatest enthusiasm." Upon completion of the program, African Americans took the stage. Elder P. W. Christian emphasized the need for the free coinage of silver. He encouraged his Black audience to "affiliate with the best element in the community in which they dwelt." He "captured his hearers completely" and "made a good impression."[111] When African Americans took the stage, they assumed prominent and extremely visible roles in third party movements.

On August 17, 1896, Georgia Populists gathered on Stone Mountain for a "big populist rally." The crowd had gathered to hear prominent Populist speakers, including gubernatorial candidate Seaborn Wright, but these speakers did not attend. Instead, less celebrated Populists emerged to speak and generated "little enthusiasm." During one speech, orator Azmon Murphey directed his attention "to a crowd of twenty or more negroes in the audience" by speaking at length on the subject of convict labor and lynching.[112]

Two days later, Wright officially opened his campaign with a meeting of Black, white, female, and male supporters at the Moody Tabernacle in Atlanta. During his speech, he reached out to the Black spectators with comments on violence at the ballot boxes, education, and prohibition. He recalled a story in which "helpless negro men were whipped and beaten until they were unconscious" and "bound and thrown upon their backs and that water was thrown into their faces until they were strangled and that blood gushed out of their lips." Later in the speech, he spoke on education: "They laugh at us and our promises to furnish the children of this state, white and Black, with primary school books. . . . the masses of the poor people must be educated and there are hundreds of poor people, white and Black, who are not able to buy their school books and send their children to a common school." He reached out to the Black members of his audience by speaking on the issue of prohibition. With regard to an anti-barroom bill, he explained, "I say to you Black men that your young men are being debauched and ruined in these abominable holes of vice" and encouraged them to vote for him in an attempt to eliminate taverns and saloons.[113]

In August the Populists staged a massive event in Alpharetta, Georgia, that featured numerous speakers and lasted for three days. People traveled as far as fifty miles on "horseback, mule back and in vehicles of all sorts and descriptions" to attend the event, plus many more "trudged many miles on foot." Entire families made the journey. While "men and boys listed to the political talk," the "women sat in the shade and devoted their attention to keeping the babies quiet—a futile task." On each day of this "genuine camp meeting," a major speaker engaged the audience, including vice-presidential candidate Tom Watson. On August 14, 1896, Watson spoke to the crowd and made a direct appeal to the hundreds of African Americans in his audience. He emphasized the need for penal reform, specifically the need for a reformatory to teach skills to young Black criminals to enable their return to useful lives rather than being "turned loose after long associations with the most hardened of criminals." He concluded, "You colored men owe us your votes. It was the populist party which first demanded and secured for you the right to vote."[114] Watson's expectation of loyalty and focus on reform had a paternalistic tone to it, but according to the reporter, the audience responded with applause. Unlike many Populists, Watson reached out to Black voters and made them a central part of his plan. For the most part, he argued poor Black and white Americans shared common enemies in government and business. Watson and his allies condemned the Democrats for their constant whining about "negro domination" and "negro supremacy."

Until the closing days of the gubernatorial campaign, Wright engaged Black and white audiences. On September 29, Wright spoke in Newnan before an audience of about seven hundred Black and white spectators. In the speech, he emphasized his independent position and committed himself to "pure methods in politics and pure men in office." On October 7, Wright spoke before an audience of Black and white populists as he closed his campaign for governor at the Moody Tabernacle in Atlanta.[115]

Despite all the energy and expense, Populists did not fare well in the 1896 elections on the federal or state level, including Georgia. Wright did not defeat the incumbent Democrat William Yates Atkinson, who went on to serve another two-year term before handing the office over to another Democrat. Bryan did not fare well in the presidential election. Although he earned about 46 percent of the vote, he only carried the southern states and the sparsely populated western states, and Republican William McKinley easily defeated him the Electoral College. Nevertheless, in its brief existence the People's Party had become one of the most successful third-party movements in the nation's history.

As the possibility of a biracial alliance threatened Democratic control over the South, Democrats accelerated the issue of disfranchising Black and poor white voters. Although the movement to disfranchise these voters had already started, many states responded to the People's Party with their own laws and amendments. In Georgia the inability to create a biracial alliance capable of overthrowing the Democrats proved frustrating. By the end of the 1890s, Watson, among others, had become especially hostile to Black voting rights, but they could not stop Black participation in the state or the region's culture of spectacular politics.

CHAPTER 2

"A CONTEST IN MUSIC"

Election-Day Spectacles in the Central Georgia Temperance Campaigns, 1885–99

"EARLY IN THE MORNING, BEFORE THE USUAL WARD WORKERS AND ELECTION bystanders had gotten to their accustomed posts" to oversee the December 1, 1898, local-option prohibition election in Macon, Georgia, "an army of five hundred of the wives and mothers and daughters of leading citizens . . . marched through the principal thoroughfares of the city" to each of the city's polling stations. At each station, they divided into choirs of thirty to fifty women and sang temperance hymns accompanied by church organs. As some women sang, other white female prohibitionists distributed sandwiches and coffee.

The anti-prohibitionists challenged the white female temperance choir by arranging for Black musicians to set up across the street from the women and play ragtime. In appearance and tune, the musicians stood in stark contrast to one another. Outside of Macon's City Hall, a procession of fifty white women marched down First Street and sang:

We are coming, we are coming, for the light has dawned at last.
Hark, hark, the battle cry is ringing, and our line is lengthening fast,
For God and home and native land our ballots shall be cast.[1]

Simultaneously, a band of Black musicians led a parade of African Americans to the voting booths "as though to challenge a contest in music." When the band arrived, white spectators cried, "Shame!" and forced the band to march away. As they left, they commenced an original composition set to the popular Civil War tune "Battle Cry of Freedom" by George F. Root. In their version, they encourage their wet friends:

Oh, rally round the jug, boys,
Rally round the jug,

*Let us drink our beer, boys,
From over-flowing mug.*

By changing the lyrics of this famous song, which has traditional verses about brotherhood and emancipation, the Black musicians connected their emancipation and the Union cause with drinking, camaraderie, and, above all else, individual liberty.² Undaunted by the "discord of the negro bands and the jeers and shouts of their opponents," the white women continued to sing for their cause, as well.³ By focusing on the Black band as disruptive and discordant, the reporter linked them to the centuries-old practice of rough music employed by seemingly powerless people to express themselves. In the end, the Black musicians marched away without causing any harm, but they had made their political statement.

From the 1880s to the 1920s, central Georgia residents monitored a series of prohibition campaigns, which dominated the region's political affairs. In 1885 and 1887, Atlanta residents carried out their own local-option election. In 1898 Maconites also put the issue to the test. During these campaigns, prohibitionists and anti-prohibitionists, regardless of race or sex, staged elaborate political spectacles in the region's cities, especially in Atlanta and Macon.⁴ On election day in both cities, Black men voted with white men as Black women and white women watched, rallied, sang, and paraded on behalf of their causes.

By 1898, however, Georgia's racial politics had changed. With racial tensions at a fever pitch because of the riots resulting from mobilization of Black and white soldiers for the Spanish-American War and the deadly insurrection in Wilmington, North Carolina, Macon's white voters had become much more hostile to Black voting rights. Also, in an era of lynching, these Black musicians openly confronted white women on the streets to make a political statement and escaped unharmed.

THE PROHIBITION MOVEMENT COMES TO GEORGIA

During the Civil War, temperance reformers felt a sense of urgency to accomplish their goals, so they appealed to the local and national governments to help them. Worried about temptation, reformers encouraged their governments to protect their fighting sons from alcohol through regulatory and even prohibitory measures. In both the United States and the Confederacy, people felt that the survival of their respective nations depended on the ability of fighting men to carry out their duties with sober minds and healthy bodies. Due to the expansion of federal power during the Civil War and the high stakes of the fight, temperance reformers insisted on using the government to enforce their version of morality, thus shifting the movement from personal pleas for temperance to state regulation and prohibition.[5]

On the national level, prohibitionists did not make much progress in the postwar period. Republicans set a precedent on moral legislation with the Emancipation Proclamation and Thirteenth Amendment. After Reconstruction ended in 1877, Republicans had little power in the South and little power to do anything about the prohibition issue. In the South, Democrats did not tend to support prohibition because of their party's rhetoric of staying out of personal matters. These roadblocks postponed national prohibition legislation, so reformers turned to local-option and statewide votes to pass prohibition laws.[6]

Southerners distrusted the national government and tended to oppose national legislation on prohibition, but they favored the new decentralized approach of statewide and local-option referenda. Many New South businessmen viewed prohibition as the means to facilitate obedience and diligence among their workers and as vital to the South's economic growth and development. In the Black community, middle-class African Americans advocated the merits of temperance to demonstrate their conformity to the dictates of middle-class respectability. In North Carolina, Tennessee, and Texas, voters considered statewide prohibition. In hundreds of other towns, cities, and counties within and outside of these states, citizens confronted the issue in local-option referenda. Prohibitionists believed the local-option strategy would mean that the communities that passed these laws would likely enforce them.[7]

Georgians took up the matter of prohibition, and reformers achieved a few important victories to make drinking less attractive and, eventually, eliminate it. During the 1870s, Georgians banned gambling in taverns and saloons. They also outlawed the sale of liquor to minors and banned its sale on election day. They also taxed liquor dealers. In Georgia counties could pass local-option prohibition laws, but only through a complex process involving state approval. By 1885, nonetheless, eighty rural Georgia counties prohibited the sale of alcohol. In twenty other counties, citizens regulated alcohol with high licensing fees and local-option laws on a town-to-town basis.[8]

On September 9, 1885, the Georgia legislature scaled back the processes by which counties could stage local-option prohibition referenda. They allowed any county to put the issue on the ballot if one-tenth of its county's residents signed a petition supporting it. According to Henry Grady's *Atlanta Constitution*, "this is the local option bill which represents the climax of a

Henry Grady, who from the pages of the *Atlanta Constitution* advocated for the New South, which had many tenets, one of which included prohibition in Atlanta. Library of Congress, Prints & Photographs Division, LC-USZ62-93574.

long prohibition campaign." The newspaper reporter predicted "that under its provisions nearly 100 elections will be held in this state between now and the end of the year." In late November, Atlanta and Fulton County residents would go to the polls to decide the future of liquor in their community, but not until they conducted exhaustive spectacular campaigns for and against the issue.[9]

THE 1885 AND 1887 ATLANTA LOCAL-OPTION PROHIBITION CAMPAIGNS

Atlanta had become the Georgia epicenter of the prohibition movement because of its influx of northern reformers and former bondpeople and because the city had Black and white leaders who sympathized with the cause.

After the Civil War, formerly enslaved people and northern philanthropists and missionaries both moved to Atlanta for new opportunities, which made it a hotspot for temperance work among African Americans. Although Atlanta did not have a large Black community before the Civil War, African

In 1881, Women's Christian Temperance Union President Frances Willard spoke in Atlanta to persuade the city to adopt prohibition. Library of Congress, Prints & Photographs Division, LC-DIG-ggbain-02864.

Americans moved to the city in droves after emancipation. By 1870 they made up 45 percent of the city's population. Meanwhile, northern reformers felt the need to educate formerly enslaved people in work ethic and manners, so they moved to Atlanta to work among emancipated people. Atlanta attracted some of the country's leading prohibition activists. In 1880 WCTU leader Eliza D. Stewart spoke before a crowd at Trinity Methodist Church in Atlanta. In 1881 WCTU president Frances Willard toured the South and delivered speeches in more than fifty southern cities, including Atlanta.[10]

Atlanta's prohibition reformers included many of the city's leading men and women. As the editor of the *Atlanta Constitution*, Henry Grady advocated a particular vision of the New South, which included prohibition. The movement enrolled other New South businessmen, politicians, and religious leaders in pursuit of their cause, such as minister Atticus G. Haygood, preacher Sam Jones, and politician Alfred Colquitt. Colquitt viewed prohibition as a means to reconcile the war-torn nation and encouraged the passage of local-option laws.[11] Haygood, who served as president of Emory College and held various political offices, published a book on the subject of prohibition. In *Lose the Saloons: A Plea for Prohibition*, Haygood provided statistics regarding alcohol manufacture and consumption in the state and relayed observations from Georgia judges concerning alcohol and criminal behavior.

Given the energy of the prohibition movement in the area, Atlanta became a focal point for prohibition reformers to meet and work. From 1881 to 1885, Atlanta hosted a series of state conventions, such as the annual meetings of the Georgia WCTU and the Georgia Prohibition Association. These organizations, among numerous others, published temperance newspapers for distribution among citizens.[12]

In postwar Atlanta, African Americans heard the temperance message from northern reformers and white neighbors. Northern reformers preached the value of temperance in Black neighborhoods with temperance literature, such as *The Temperance Tract for the Freedmen* published by the American Temperance Union, and columns in the *Freedman* and the *Freedman's Journal*, which both had large circulations in the city. In schools founded to educate formerly enslaved people, teachers instructed their students in temperance and asked students to take the Lincoln Temperance Pledge. The temperance reformers reached people outside of the school system by canvassing home-to-home to educate formerly enslaved people in the virtues of temperance.

African Americans also spread the temperance message among themselves. Upon arrival in Atlanta, African Americans founded their own Baptist and Methodist churches, which would play a leading role in the future temperance movement in the city. African Methodist Episcopal ministers made temperance a constant subject in sermons, and church leaders organized conferences on the issue. Minsters Joseph Wood, Henry McNeal Turner, Wesley J. Gaines, and E. R. Carter emphasized that only temperance could lead to true freedom. They also linked individual behavior to the common good and argued that an individual's intemperance hurt the entire Black community.[13]

In addition to the clergy, Black civic leaders advocated for prohibition. They believed it would help Black people prove their conformity to the norms of white, middle-class respectability. They recognized the prohibition movement as an opportunity to form an alliance with white Georgians through which they could prove their worth. For the sake of the Black community, they advocated for prohibition because they assumed it would help cut back on Black incarceration rates.[14]

By the end of September 1885, Atlanta's prohibitionists had been energized by the new local-option bill and commenced the battle. Based out of Good

Templars Hall in Atlanta, prohibitionists established a chain of command and bureaucracy to facilitate their work. They assembled a biracial coalition consisting of the city's existing temperance reformers, especially the members of the WCTU, and "a good number of the best colored men of the city." They immediately set out upon the city with twenty petitions to collect the requisite number of signatures, which they accomplished in a few short weeks. They also set up a committee of three representatives from each city ward and four representatives from the rest of Fulton County to oversee the campaign. It consisted of three Black men: Nick Holmes, R. J. Henry, and J. M. Jones. As soon as the campaign began, prohibitionists assumed the Black vote would go with them.[15]

The anti-prohibitionists had a cruder organizational structure composed of a motley coalition of businessmen, liquor dealers, and high-license advocates. Unlike the prohibitionists, the anti-prohibitionists did not have a nationwide network or years of established organization to act on their behalf. Despite their rudimentary organization, the anti-prohibitionists had plenty of financial support from the business interests of the city. "There is no doubt that there will be funds sufficient on both sides of the fight to make it lively," observed a reporter from the *Atlanta Constitution*, who expected the campaign to become "red hot" by the first week of October.[16]

From the beginning, newspaper editors from across the country closely followed the election, publishing sensational updates from the campaign. In their coverage, they hinted at potential violence and conflict but ultimately predicted victory for the prohibitionists. The editors of the *Chicago Tribune*, the *New York Times*, Nashville's *Daily American*, and other significant newspapers reprinted articles from the *Atlanta Constitution* for their local audiences. "The prohibition wave has struck Atlanta," explained a correspondent to the *Daily American*, who observed that "the excitement in Atlanta is intense over the election to occur here."[17] A reporter in Atlanta for the *New York Times* added that the local option law "revived the temperance crusade here in a wonderful degree" and that Atlanta had become "the scene of violent agitation" on prohibition's behalf. The reporter explained that "the agitation has extended to other cities, and prohibition in Atlanta will be followed by prohibition in Savannah and Augusta" despite the presence of German and Irish immigrants in these cities. The reporter concluded, "Before Winter is over there will not be a drop of liquor sold in Georgia under legal sanction."[18] Through the newspapers, Americans could participate in the campaign spectacle whether they resided in Atlanta or not.

In Atlanta's newspapers, prohibitionists and anti-prohibitionists waged informative campaigns to appeal to undecided voters with reason and argument, thereby practicing the type of educational politics that became notably prevalent at the end of the nineteenth century. Given the significance of the question at hand, one writer for the *Atlanta Constitution* asked, "Would it not be well to consider the subject fully, in all its phases moral as well as financial, in order to arrive at a proper conclusion before acting in the matter?" After "hearing and reading a great number of arguments," he informed the readership that prohibition does not tend to work. Instead, he encouraged them to support high licenses and moral persuasion. To his followers, he instructed, "Make drunkenness whether existing among the high or low, so offensive that no man will indulge in the repulsive vice; make the habitual drunkard feel that he is an outcast, by shunning it as you would a leper."[19] Many anti-prohibitionists adopted a high-license position. Julius L. Brown, an anti-prohibitionist, argued that it "is lawful to use firearms, but if crime results it is punished. It is lawful to desire and acquire property, but if crime results it is punished." Based on this reasoning, Brown advocated high license and better enforcement of laws against drunkenness instead of total prohibition.[20]

On the other side, prohibitionists countered with their own arguments focusing on the problems alcohol posed for women and children. They explained that business gained in liquor resulted in losses in other sectors. According to one prohibitionist, the "truth is the liquor traffic as carried on is debauching many of the young men in the city—making drunkards of many husbands and fathers, depriving many women and children of the comforts and often of the necessities of life."[21] Specifically, the prohibitionists focused their attack on a local brewery because they wondered if it had been taxed appropriately. They asked, if "the brewery company has made $200,000 so quickly, who has lost it?" To answer, they suggested, "Did all that money just grow, or have wives and children suffered from the need of the millions spent for beer, of which it is the net profit?" The prohibitionists argued the "liquor traffic does not make Americans of the Georgia variety more industrious—thrifty—economical—intelligent—peaceable—respectable or happy."[22]

Although drys and wets made appeals to logic and emotion in the city's newspapers, they both relied on spectacular popular politics to generate enthusiasm and mobilize voters on behalf of their respective causes, often including celebrities in the programs to draw massive audiences. They infused the spectacles with educational arguments. The anti-prohibitionists advertised that people should "come out and hear facts and figures."[23] They held their meetings throughout the city but tended to focus their rallies around the courthouse. The prohibitionists used the De Give's Opera House for their massive meetings, and also met in churches. During the campaign a group of workers erected evangelist Sam Jones's tent behind St. Philip's Church on Hunter Street, which became the key site for revival-like prohibition meetings.

On November 2, the "greatest crowd that ever filled the opera house" met to hear Jones and Colquitt speak on behalf of prohibition. Jones had a reputation for speaking on behalf of prohibition throughout the South. His supporters characterized him as "fearless before mankind." He preached on the principle that "people need to be startled to get them to act" and used language to arouse people "from lethargy and indifference" to action.[24] Before the program began, crowds cheered as the Young Men's Prohibition Club paraded from their headquarters on Broad Street to De Give's Opera House.

During Jones's speech to three thousand male and female spectators, he praised the city's temperance workers for putting prohibition on the ballot. He encouraged them to maintain the fight. He explained, "Whisky men get into much trouble and they are always fighting, but I never yet heard of a whisky man whipping a prohibitionist." The campaign rhetoric often entailed overtones of violence, contributing to a militant atmosphere.

He also emphasized the role of women and the Black community in the prohibition movement. He drew attention to the issue for African Americans by laughing off suggestions that prohibition would hurt the Black community. With regard to women, he asserted, "I can never go wrong so long as I stand on the side of God, and the angels in heaven, and the mothers and sisters and wives on this earth." With these statements, Jones recognized the power of people who had traditionally been shunned from formal politics.

Jones believed that Atlanta's decision would set the tone for the prohibition movement in the rest of the state and the region, and characterized the *Atlanta Constitution* as "the greatest power in Atlanta." He estimated that half of "the men and women of Georgia are on their knees every night praying that the great capital city of the state may redeem herself from this curse." He understood that prohibitionists around the state, region, and country followed, and indeed participated in, Atlanta's campaign through its coverage, so the *Atlanta Constitution* helped forge the prohibition community.[25]

In addition to Jones's fiery speech, Colquitt took the stage to relay the facts and figures, thereby adopting a more intellectual style. He highlighted prohibition's effects on the local economy, specifically property values, because he believed that Atlantans did not want taverns near their homes. The audience cheered in support.[26]

As they did throughout the speeches, the spectators at political rallies did not passively listen to the evening's speeches but instead cheered and applauded, even to the policy discussions. The speakers did their part to include the audience, asking them to cheer or stand up in support. At the end of the program, Atlanta Mayor George Hillyer asked all the prohibitionists in the audience to stand. Upon request, the "hundreds upon the stage rose as one man, and the great crowd in front and in the galleries rose with almost equal unanimity."[27] With actions like this one, these men and women publicly demonstrated their allegiance and claimed membership in the prohibition community.[28]

On the same night, the anti-prohibitionists held a competing rally at the courthouse to stake out their position to Black and white voters. Despite short notice, the anti-prohibitionists attracted "an enthusiastic" audience of eight hundred Black and white spectators. For the most part, the speakers argued that prohibition would have disastrous effects on the city's economy. W. A. Pledger, a successful Black lawyer, civic activist, and editor of the *Atlanta Defiance*, expressed his fear for the hotel and saloon employees who would lose their jobs if prohibition succeeded. Despite his position in the Black middle class, which tended to support prohibition, he opposed prohibition by arguing that the lack of money from a tax on liquor would entail higher tax burdens for the poor and worse schools. To support his positions, he quoted at length from residents of Athens, who had initiated prohibition in their city. Athens resident Madison Davis testified that prohibition hurt the city because of heavier tax burdens and lost business. Pledger's speech put African Americans and women at the center of the campaign. He believed that prohibition in Athens resulted from a fear that students would drink and harass women and children. In Atlanta he argued that the college's rules would prevent the city's Black students from drinking and rabble-rousing. If the college's rules failed to prevent trouble, he explained, Atlantans already had methods, suggesting lynching, to deal with the problem. He said Black students "are too well acquainted with what their fates would be to go around raising thunder with white women and children." In 1885 white Georgians had reasserted a line between Black men and white women, and Pledger pointed to that line as a reason to oppose prohibition.

At the conclusion of the meeting, the white anti-prohibitionists reached out to the Black spectators. They passed a resolution to "invite the special cooperation of our colored friends who are employed in the various bars and restaurants of this city, and who would, in the event of the closing of such places, be at once deprived of their daily earnings and thrown upon an already overcrowded labor market."[29] Although prohibitionists had assumed Black support for their cause, anti-prohibitionists did not resign themselves to defeat. They knew that the side who could win the Black vote would carry the day. The two sides competed for Black votes despite having passed laws restricting Black voting.

In 1885, W. A. Pledger, as one of Atlanta's leading Black civic leaders, advocated against prohibition in Atlanta because of its feared consequences on working people. Library of Congress, Prints & Photographs Division, LC-DIG-bellcm-13376.

In Georgia, Black voters faced numerous restrictions on their ability to vote. After emancipation, African Americans energetically participated in Georgia politics. As early as 1867, 70 percent of adult Black male Georgians showed up and voted. In 1867 Tunis Campbell won a seat in the Georgia state senate, which he assumed in 1868 before white senators forced him out of office because they had refused to guarantee Black men the right to hold office. In 1870 Georgians elected a Democratic majority to the state legislature and effectively returned white citizens to power. At the state's 1877 constitutional convention, Georgia's delegates passed a cumulative poll tax, residency restrictions, and registration requirements, which drastically reduced Black voting power on the state level. They apportioned the state legislature to temper the control of districts with a large Black community, as well. Within Atlanta, municipal elections changed from ward-based contests to citywide campaigns, thus making it difficult for the minority of African Americans in the city to overcome white majorities, even in Black neighborhoods. If these measures did not suffice, the Republican Party had no power in the state, thus making the vote an uninspiring and ineffective tool for Black Georgians. By the end of the nineteenth century, less than

10 percent of the otherwise eligible Black population voted.[30] Despite these restrictions, African Americans became a focal point of the campaign for the 1885 prohibition referenda in the city.

On November 17, Atlanta's Black and white prohibitionists gathered at the prohibition tent for a series of speakers. Evangelist Sam Small spoke "with good humored bits and stirred up a great deal of enthusiasm and applause" from the biracial audience. Once again, the speech focused on the racial elements of the issue. Small applauded Black efforts to uplift their race and hoped that they would use their votes to pass prohibition. He focused on the troubles alcohol posed to the Black community. With paternalistic condescension, he explained, "The tax books showed that the colored people have accumulated nearly eight million dollars. It would have been eighty million if the other seventy millions had not been squandered in barrooms." In conclusion, he spoke directly to the Black spectators in his audience and encouraged them "to be temperate, save their money and educate their children and to secure more of the comforts of life for themselves and their families."[31] After Small's speech, a quartet of Black musicians rendered the hymn "Awake, Awake." The hymn references the call of a master, presumed to be God. In the opening line, the song's character urges, "Awake! Awake! The Master now is calling us." This line of the song may have struck a different tone with formerly enslaved people.[32]

In addition to Small, two Black religious leaders from Philadelphia spoke before the audience. Bishop J. P. Campbell expressed satisfaction at the sight of "the two races united on such an issue as temperance" and encouraged them to continue the fight. Joining him, Dr. B. T. Tanner, an editor of the *Quarterly Review* of the African Methodist Episcopal Church, also spoke for a bit. The rest of the meeting consisted of hymns and other speakers.[33] The Philadelphia contingent had come to Atlanta for a conference, but they remained in town for a week to "help make the last battle for prohibition." On the night of November 23, the Philadelphia clergy gave "a wonderfully powerful speech."[34]

On November 24, prohibitionists made their final plea to the voters of Atlanta and prepared for the battle. The prohibitionists opened their headquarters at 6:00 a.m. for an entire day of campaigning and programming. By using their highly structured organization, which one reporter described as "military in character," they hoped to carry the election. The prohibitionists organized their supporters into companies and assigned a series of officers, including a captain and sergeant, to each club to command them into line, march them to the polls, and to guarantee that each voter correctly and legally cast his ballot. According to one prohibitionist, "We will have one thousand earnest workers at the polls tomorrow that will neither be bulldozed nor misled. They know the law, and they know their duty, and they are going to live the one and do the other. We will march over two thousand voters to the polls in line."[35] With a militaristic spirit, partisan voters and poll workers set out onto the streets to persuade voters and awe spectators.

To reward voters for supporting prohibition, female workers arranged to provide lunch at two locations: North Atlanta on Broad Street and another in South Atlanta at the corner of Pryor Street and Mitchell Street. There "was a busy scene at each of the lunch rooms" on the day before election. Twenty female prohibitionists worked all day to collect donations and prepare the meals. They relied on contributions, which varied from "the modest half dozen rolls to great baskets filled with viands worthy to be set before the daintiest epicure in the city," to feed all of the voters, including African Americans (albeit in a segregated lunchroom). The women devised this plan to keep people at work and in line as long as possible. They did not want voters vacating the lines to find dinner.[36] Although these women could not vote in the contest, they lent their efforts to help the cause by adapting their domestic duties for political purpose. They believed these activities would have a direct result on the outcome.

At 6:00 p.m. on the eve of the election, the prohibitionists started to organize outside the Young Men's Prohibition Club meeting house on Broad Street, and they marched from this site to the tent at St. Philip's Church to listen to speeches and hear music. In a long line, the voters paraded through the major streets of the city with "great crowds" on both sides of the street "heartily cheering their marching allies." Leading them, four musical bands inspired the voters with their "martial strains." The marchers met a crowd of Black and white spectators, which had already gathered at the tent, took their seats, and enjoyed the program deep into the night. The procession seemed the "most remarkable demonstration ever seen in Atlanta on the eve of an election."[37] After the parades, the Black prohibitionists went to their churches, which the temperance women had stocked with food. They stayed at the church all night. In the morning, they would march to the polls together.[38]

In the final moments, the prohibitionists made Black voters their primary concern. "We have an unquestioned majority of the white vote," declared one worker at campaign headquarters. He added, "I think nobody denies that the calculation of the antis has been that they would get one thousand majority of the negroes, and that we would perhaps get this down to four or five hundred with the white vote." He argued, however, that the prohibitionists had expected a massive majority in the white vote and had plenty of African Americans registered to vote on their behalf. The Young Men's Prohibition

Club offered a reward of $200 for the largest Black-led organization to show up and vote for prohibition.[39]

Although not quite as organized as the prohibitionists, the anti-prohibitionists efficiently prepared for the next day's election. At headquarters, "there were no loungers, and every man who dropped in had business, and when had transacted it he took his departure." The workers had done their jobs, and the "opening of the battle was being patiently awaited."[40] Like the prohibitionists, the anti-prohibitionists marched through the streets of the city on the eve of the election setting the streets "ablaze with the torches" and filling the air with cheering and music. By 7:00 a.m. parades from numerous parts of the city had gathered at the post office on Forsyth Street. The anti-prohibitionists wore red badges in the procession. By 8:00 p.m., the crowd started to move as one through the city. The banners received quite a bit of attention. On one banner, the artist represented a dying child with its mother crying at the foot of the bed. The doctor advised, "A drop of brandy will save your child." The mother lamented, "Alas, doctor, I have no jug." The other banners emphasized the economic impact of prohibition by depicting people leaving the city and the closing of schools.[41] With these banners, the popular demonstrations had a notably argumentative bent. After the parades, the anti-prohibitionists enjoyed barbecues that lasted until morning.[42]

Across the country, people followed the campaign in Atlanta and even came to the city to witness it, as they would a major sporting event. The news of the spectacle reached the Northeast and Midwest, and local newspapers relayed information about the "unusual state of affairs" in Atlanta.[43] They reported that musicians arrived from elsewhere in Georgia and as far away as Cincinnati, Chattanooga, and Nashville to partake in the last night of the campaign. In addition to the musicians, "hundreds of visitors" and northern newspaper correspondents arrived from outside the city to take in the drama.[44]

On the cold and blustery morning of November 25, election day in Atlanta arrived. Before dawn a few prohibitionists, including the police chief and one of his subordinates, had taken their place in line at the polling station at the Pryor Street courthouse. For more than an hour, they kept warm by blowing on their hands between bouts of idle chatter. Soon, thousands of voters prominently displaying red and blue badges would hit the streets. The editors of the *Atlanta Constitution* anticipated an "orderly and quiet" election but admitted that "some fear" remained that "there may be a collision between rival clubs as they march en masse to the polls" and "perhaps a squabble for the precincts."[45] They expressed an uneasiness akin to soldiers on the eve of battle.

An hour before the polling stations opened, a wet band marched through the streets and trumpeted its political allegiance with a rendition of Stephen Foster's famous drinking tune "We Won't Go Home 'til Morning," definitively ending the morning silence and commencing the battle. Captain Moses Bentley adorned himself "in truly gorgeous array" to lead the procession through the streets to the Pryor Street courthouse. Behind the band, George Yarborough, a Black barber, adorned himself in a red sash and red feather in his hat to lead a procession of African Americans. At this point, more than three hundred African Americans made their way to the polling booths "with military precision." The officers wore red sashes around their waists as they led the voters. At the voting booths, they divided the crowd into three detachments, which each took a position in line behind each of the three voting boxes. In the earliest moments of the election day contest, the antiprohibitionists seized control of the Pryor Street courthouse.[46]

At 7:00 a.m. voters rushed to cast their ballots but had to wait until police officers could manage the crowd. At first, the clerks had trouble with the mass of people and following the procedures, which resulted in as few as "two votes to the minute" polled at the Pryor Street courthouse, but the pace soon quickened. As voters started to cast their ballots, a band hired by Macon temperance workers led the Third Ward Colored Club, which consisted of fifty-two members. As they marched, the band played "We Won't Get Drunk Any More." They also divided into three companies and pushed their way toward the front of the lines. Nearby, prohibition's supporters cheered the arrival of the Black voters because their "hopes were evidently revived" by these reinforcements. At this point, red and blue voters mixed together and quickly cast their ballots.[47]

On the outskirts of town, the engine house became another key battleground. At this location, the female prohibitionists dominated the scene before dawn. They had made their preparations to provide the poll workers and voters with lunch and drinking water, which needed constant attention because it froze every few minutes. By 7:15 a.m. more than one hundred voters had already arrived. Within the hour the three lines extended across the street a distance upwards of fifty yards. The voters waited and chatted with one another in the freezing weather. Unlike at the courthouse, blueribboned dry voters and supporters dominated the scene. At 8:00 a.m. the windows of the polling station opened "and the rain of ballots began" with the prohibitionists in firm control.

By 10:00 a.m. the tide had turned against the drys at the engine house as the red-clad wet voters fired their ballots "hot and heavy" into the box. At this point, the prohibitionists appeared overwhelmed by voters in red badges. At 11:00 a.m., another group of anti-prohibitionists arrived. Marching down Marietta Street, the employees of the Atlanta hotel Kimble House carried banners and flags that cheered the cause of liberty. Facing defeat, the prohibitionists seemed emboldened by the presence of their enemy, and "for an hour they did good and effective work."[48] The momentum swings at each polling station contributed to the excitement and anxiety over the outcome.

The crowds and spectacle never ceased. It seemed that everyone in Atlanta had taken to the streets to participate in the election. The lines continued to grow even though voters moved quickly toward the ballot box. "As fast as one man deposited his vote and dropped out of the way another slipped up," explained a reporter, who added, "all along the line there was a forward march movement." For the most part, "every man held his ticket in his hand, and no effort was made to influence or change him."[49] The two campaigns focused on the few undecided voters, especially Black voters, who arrived at the polls.

At the engine house, any voter who approached the polls "in an indifferent manner" and "without a badge pinned on his manly breast" became a target for workers from both sides, who would grab him and attempt to persuade him. Black preachers appeared on the scene, and they would identify undecided Black voters and "cabbage on to the darkey and pour words of convincing argument into his unwilling ears" until he had made up his mind.[50] The drys and wets knew that Black votes would determine the outcome. They both courted Black votes, but they did not necessarily forget their racist views in this moment.

Many white Atlantans sneered at the Black voters and challenged their legitimacy. A reporter praised voters for taking their places in line and remaining there despite the undesirable nearness of Black voters. The Black voters who cast their ballots at the engine house polling station, according to reporters, "never did fail to take a chance at the free lunch table," where they enjoyed a meal of chicken, sandwiches, biscuits, and pies. In fact, reports circulated that "several red badge negroes got a good square lunch by hiding the crimson and pinning on the blue badge." At the courthouse, an elderly Black man arrived and announced that he intended to sell his vote. Immediately, a mob descended upon him and presented him with both red and blue tickets. "The old man was pulled and hauled about quite roughly" by the crowd, which lifted and carried him across the street. Eventually, a police officer arrived on the scene and secured the elderly man's release from its grasp. At the Collins precinct, an African American approached the polls with the intention to vote, but the crowd challenged the legitimacy of his vote because someone in the crowd claimed that he had not paid taxes in two years. The aspiring voter explained the circumstances to the satisfaction of the crowd and "was allowed to prove his liberty by casting his wet ticket."[51] The newspaper reporters shared these derogatory stories of Black men characterized as unprincipled freeloaders to reinvigorate racist stereotypes.

For the most part, the antagonism toward African Americans centered on the 'possum festival held at a Black church. Despite numerous stories in the newspapers about Black men asserting their rights, newspaper reports also spread stories about uninterested, disengaged Black voters to justify their exclusion. In the story about the 'possum festival, a Black civic leader, identified as Howard Horton, arranged to prepare two hundred opossums to feed the Black community at one of the churches as a reward to Black prohibitionists. According to the reporter, an "unregenerated anti, without the fear of the Lord" spread the rumor that Horton had instead provided cats, not opossums, for the meal because he had personally seen Horton "skin the cats." The Black voters "refused to touch the 'possums and threatened to withdraw their allegiance from the cause" until Horton "proved to their satisfaction" that he had not cooked cats. Then, the Black voters resumed the feast "amid genuine applause" and filled their bellies with "'possum and peace."[52] With this story, the newspaper reporter helped paint a picture of freeloading Black voters, which stood in stark contrast to the white women at the polls and, notably, the Black voters who seriously considered the issues and demanded their rights. In this story, Black voters sold their votes, found free meals, and fluidly changed their allegiances.

The white female poll workers and prohibition activists received quite a bit of positive attention from the press and the crowds, most notably for their own lunch service. "The ladies, too, have taken up the contest with vigor," explained a reporter.[53] The newspaper reporters praised them for their excellent service throughout the day and their ability to feed "hundreds of souls." At local churches, they gathered and prayed all day. They sang songs and made some remarks on behalf of prohibition. After the closing of the polls, prohibition activist J. W. Anderson thanked numerous people for their work in the campaign, especially the white female workers, who "were the inspiration of the movement, prayed constantly for our success, encouraged us to be hopeful and earnest, fed us on the day of election and contributed in every possible way" to the campaign.[54]

At the polls, the crowds hoped to spot local and national celebrities as the polling stations became the sites of spectacular displays of wealth. At 1:00 p.m. Senator Joseph Brown arrived at the polls to vote, "and the mob began cheering loudly," which became "louder and more furious as the carriage drove up and through the crowd." At other polling stations, private carriages with blue ribbons arrived to drop off voters. One wealthy man arrived via horse and carriage with the "silver mounted harness of the horses arrayed with blue ribbons and a large blue bow caught half way up to the driver's whip." The crowd received him with generous applause.[55]

The crowds watched the battle of the ballots unfold at each of the polling stations. Despite the wintry weather, people engaged in a contest that "was literally a craze on both sides." Back at the Pryor Street courthouse, a band led a long prohibition procession, which energized their supporters, who "jumped, pranced, danced and yelled themselves hoarse." During the fracas, the "air was full of flying tickets and hats, men climbed up each other's shoulders to see the advancing column and when the band passed through the throng the music could not be heard." The anti-prohibitionists gathered strength from this display, and with "renewed energy they searched the approaching crowds for voters."

Atlantans showed up at the polls with signs and banners containing bits of cunning commentary. At 4:00 p.m., a Black man appeared with a large pole draped in red, which he had topped with a live rabbit, which may have referenced the trickster Brer Rabbit from Black folklore, and a straight flush poker hand. Under the cards, he wrote, "You can't blame me. Liquor wins." He suggested that Atlanta's liquor interests, like a gambling house, would trick their way to victory. He believed that, like Brer Rabbit, liquor would find a way to defeat a seemingly more powerful opponent. He also suggested that prohibitionists should not blame African Americans, specifically him, for the results of the local-option election if it did not go their way.[56] At this point, the voting came to an end, but the spectacle had barely begun. People moved to each polling station to await results and circulate rumors about the outcome.

Leaders and spectators on both sides of the campaign gathered and eagerly awaited updates from each of the polling places across the city and Fulton County. Upon hearing the results from each polling station, they checked the reality of the results against their predictions, sending the audience into successive waves of optimism and pessimism. The crowd moved to each polling place as it closed to watch the counting of the ballots.[57] The announcement of results became a key feature of the election day spectacle because it provided prohibitionists and anti-prohibitionists a chance to share a collective experience and strengthen the bonds they had made during the campaign.

Outside of the city, a crowd gathered at the engine house and watched the counting of the votes through frosty windows. The spectators could not hear updates from inside the building, but they guessed and debated with one another. Prohibitionists had hoped for a 250-vote majority at this specific location, but the vote count appeared much closer. At one point, a "rumor stole out from a broken pane that where was not fifty votes difference." Soon, prohibitionists started to worry that the anti-prohibitionists had defied expectations and prevailed outside the city. Uplifted by the news, the anti-prohibitionists felt quite confident in an overall victory. At 6:43 p.m., poll workers declared that the prohibitionists had won the vote at the fire station by five votes.

After the news at the engine house, the spectators braved a brisk wind to await the results at the Pryor Street courthouse. Discouraged by previous results, the fearful prohibitionists hunted for information. They knew they had a 537-vote lead. They also suspected that the anti-prohibitionists would carry this location. The crowd buzzed and wondered if the anti-prohibitionists would make up enough votes to win the election and, if not, whether the prohibitionists would challenge the results. They "besieged" the windows with "frantic inquiries." To accommodate the desires of the crowd and feed their enthusiasm, the clerks announced the results after they had counted a set of 1,000 ballots. After the first thousand votes, the anti-prohibitionists led the courthouse vote by only seventy-eight, which alleviated the anxieties of some of the crowd because it indicated that the anti-prohibitionists would not make up enough votes to carry the day. After counting two-thirds of the votes, the anti-prohibitionists had a lead at the courthouse of 220, which left them behind the prohibitionists overall. At 10:13 p.m., the manager of the polling booth announced that the anti-prohibitionists had carried the courthouse by 326 votes, which did not erase the majority the prohibitionists had secured at the other polling locations throughout Fulton County.

Upon learning of the victory, the prohibitionists rejoiced and sealed their victory with "a procession that seemed endless."[58] The drys paraded "the streets by thousands, and torches and bonfires light the heavens."[59] Atlanta's voters had supported prohibition with their ballots, and its Black and white residents legitimized the result with their popular demonstrations in the streets.

Across the country, newspapers carried the news of the election. "After the most exciting election ever held in the State, Fulton County has adopted prohibition," announced the *New York Times*, and provided details of the election day spectacle as it had done over the course of the entire campaign. "At 6 A.M. the colored voters who had been locked up in the various halls were marched to the different polls, and the battle of the ballot began in dead earnest," explained a reporter. Reporters repeated the stories of African Americans at the polls, the opossum lunch, and the sighting of celebrities and dignitaries at the polls.[60] They became especially enchanted by the activity of

African Americans. They described how the anti-prohibitionists "provided barbecues, a big possum supper and an all-night frolic for the negro voters" and that the prohibitionists "sent a barrel of oysters and dozen boxes of oyster crackers to each of the negro churches, to be converted into stews for their own swarthy recruits."[61] By carrying these types of disparaging stories, newspaper editors strengthened negative attitudes toward Black voters as unfit for the ballot.

In Black newspapers, editors applauded the passage of the local-option law in Atlanta and emphasized the collective effort of Black and white prohibitionists. In Philadelphia's *Christian Recorder*, an editor regarded the law as "a mighty movement in favor of civilization and Christianity." He took the "union of Black and white men on both sides of this fearful moral struggle" as a "hopeful sign" of reconciliation between the regions and the races. In this contest, he explained, there was not "democrat nor republican, federal nor confederate, white nor Black." Instead, he portrayed this election as a righteous triumph in a "struggle between right and wrong, life and death."[62] By focusing on the Black–white alliance, Black newspaper editors hoped to separate themselves and their race from the derogatory stories found in the mainstream white press. The dry voters, who the Black press highlighted, had conformed to white middle-class norms on the issue and cast their ballots in a likewise manner. The wet voters, per the reports in the newspapers, had behaved differently.

Newspaper editors hypothesized that prohibition's victory in Atlanta would galvanize a massive movement, especially in the South. "Naturally, too in the first flush of this success, they are looking about for fresh cities to conquer, and are announcing that the war will now go on without any let-up until the last licensed liquor-saloon disappears from the social map of Georgia," explained *Hartford Courant*'s editors, who predicted that the prohibitionists would tackle Savannah, Macon, and Augusta next.[63] Encouraged by success, the prohibitionists declared "that not until the state is absolutely prohibition territory will the fight be stopped."[64] The editors of Nashville's *Daily American* added that if "a national election were to take place this week, the State would vote the Prohibition ticket," and explained that the African Americans "are all actively committed to Prohibition and go arm in arm with their white allies."[65] With this language, the newspaper reports about the future of prohibition continued the militant language of the election-day spectacle and predicted a total victory.

Unlike these other newspapers, *Washington Post* editors expressed quite a bit of cynicism toward the result. They argued, the "fanatics of Atlanta, Ga., have voted for prohibition" and called it "the first and easiest step." They stated that Atlantans now had the problem of enforcing their law, which "they will never do."[66] On both sides, most people believed that the results in Atlanta entailed national implications for the future of prohibition across the country.

Despite the energy generated by the campaign, prohibition did not even last long in Atlanta. For two years, Atlanta stood as the largest city in the country that did not permit the sale of alcohol. The prohibitionists had won by an extremely slim margin, thus making it almost impossible to rally public support for enforcement. Within a week of the victory, people already had doubts about the law's utility. In *Frank Leslie's Weekly*, a reporter indicated that the law was "likely to be overthrown" by legal proceedings.[67] Although the local-option law survived a federal court injunction, it took an entire year to close all the saloons and liquor retailers in the city, but the law never stopped the distribution and consumption of alcohol.

In 1887 Atlanta's voters again contested the issue in yet another local-option election. For two years, the anti-prohibitionists organized and mobilized their forces to overturn the law. As in the statewide referenda in Texas, Atlanta's wets received support from former Confederate president Jefferson Davis, who portrayed personal liberty as the cornerstone of the nation and the South. In this election, Black clergymen no longer generally supported prohibition. For the most part, anti-prohibitionists successfully persuaded working-class Black and white Atlantans to overturn prohibition because the law privileged middle-class and upper-class white Atlantans, who could still procure alcohol through private clubs and importers. They expressed resentment at wealthier white Atlantans' patronizing position and argued that they could take care of themselves without interference from upper-class reformers.[68]

In the final week of the contest, both sides held nightly events often featuring local and national celebrities, similar to the events from the campaign two years earlier. Yellowstone Kit, who worked as a traveling salesman and showman, arrived in Atlanta to speak against prohibition. He attracted audiences of thousands of people, especially African Americans, and provided the anti-prohibitionists with plenty of energy. The two sides held separate rallies in the days leading up to the election. The rallies featured torchlight parades, drummers, outdoor meetings, and brass bands.

On election day, the spectacle reached its climax. As they had done two years earlier, Atlantans adorned their blue and red badges and hit the streets. The anti-prohibitionists led a procession with brass bands and banners. Once again, female prohibitionists served lunch to prohibition's supporters. On this election day, a group of women marched to each polling station to lead prayers. At one point, prohibitionists started to circulate reports that the mayor had voted the dry ticket, which energized the drys to keep up the fight. The anti-prohibitionists spread a rumor that a policeman had shot one of their Black supporters. At the end of the day, the anti-prohibitionists prevailed with 5,183 votes compared to only 4,061 votes for prohibition, which far exceeded the majority the prohibitionists had won only two years earlier.[69]

THE 1898 MACON LOCAL-OPTION PROHIBITION CAMPAIGN

Although Atlanta's voters defeated prohibition, the movement did not end in Georgia. In 1889 voters defeated prohibition in Floyd County after "a vigorous and exciting campaign of three weeks."[70] In 1891 Governor William J. Northen signed a law to ban the sale of alcohol within three miles of a church or school, except in incorporated cities, thus effectively outlawing alcohol in most of Georgia because, according to a reporter, "either schools or churches exist almost every three miles, and where they do not exist cheap structures will be erected."[71] In 1895 "a general awakening of the prohibitionists" resulted in a prohibition bill before the state legislature. Georgia's prohibitionists gathered in a series of conventions to mobilize support for the bill.[72] Despite the energy of the prohibitionists, the Georgia House of Representatives did not pass the bill because they could not muster the required supermajority.[73]

During the Atlanta campaigns of 1885 and 1887, Macon residents had paid particularly close attention to their neighbors. "The town talk in Macon at present is the prohibition movement in Atlanta," explained a correspondent for the *Atlanta Constitution* about the 1885 campaign. The correspondent added that residents "eagerly sought" the newspaper "every morning for the latest developments in the campaign." Macon residents gambled on the outcome of the election with "five dollars and boxes of cigars" as the typical stakes. Most people bet on prohibition, including one man who reportedly wagered $6,000 on prohibition's victory. A reporter observed that "occasionally parties who are known to have bets to that effect are caught hedging." Macon's residents tended to support prohibition in Atlanta because it "would give Macon a nice little boom."[74] Macon residents obsessed over the prohibition referenda in Atlanta because its decision would affect business in their own city.

With over seventy liquor dealers, Macon had a reputation among Georgians for its alcohol trade. Observers noted the "consumption of whiskey, in the past few years has been remarkable." In addition to its financial power, the liquor interest held "full sway in nearly all political measures."[75] Atlanta and Macon residents predicted that Atlanta's liquor retailers would move their businesses to Macon if prohibition prevailed. Based on these rumors, Atlanta's prohibitionists charged Macon's temperance workers for failing to force the issue in their own city. "If prohibition is carried in this city it will add many people and much more money to Macon," explained a writer for the *Atlanta Constitution*, who condemned leading temperance activist Walter B. Hill, who eventually became president of the University of Georgia, for his weakness in bringing prohibition to his city.[76]

In 1898 Macon's citizens staged a prohibition campaign in their own city, where the drama surpassed the same movement in Atlanta. On September 27, 1898, the civic leaders of Bibb County announced that the county's prohibitionists had collected enough signatures to hold a local-option election. "The election will no doubt be attended with great excitement and interest," explained a reporter for the *Atlanta Constitution*. Macon had always allowed the retail sale of alcohol, but Bibb County had not seen liquor sales since the state law of 1891, when the legislature banned the sale of liquor within three miles of a church or school.[77]

For the most part, the campaign looked and sounded like the previous contests in Atlanta and elsewhere. Celebrities came to present speeches. Macon activists debated one another in the newspapers and paraded through the streets, thus using informative and popular campaign strategies. In fact, the two forms crossed over. Evangelist Sam Jones made his way to Macon to entertain massive audiences with his temperance message. As he had done in Atlanta, he preached at the prohibition tent on numerous occasions to large audiences.

In the newspapers, the wets took on Jones's views and challenged the drys to respond. The debates raged along similar lines as they had in previous contests. Prohibitionists emphasized spirituality and crime whereas antiprohibitionists focused on the economy, liberty, and enforcement. In one letter, P. C. Rittenhouse challenged Jones: "I have asked you, Brother Jones, to point out prohibition in the Bible. You have not done it. You cannot do it." After chronicling a series of instances in which biblical characters used wine, Rittenhouse provoked Jones, "I maintain respectfully, reverently, and with a full knowledge of all that it means, that these things establish the moral right to manufacture, sell, buy and drink alcoholic liquors in moderation." Then, he added, "If not, then the Bible is false, or else I have misquoted it. Get your book and see."[78] During the campaign, Macon's residents had numerous ways to participate either by hitting the streets or keeping up to date with news from the campaign.

Despite the similar tone and spirit, the Macon campaign did differ from the contests in Atlanta because of changes in the relationship between Black and white people. During the 1885 and 1887 campaigns in Atlanta, African Americans had participated without much trouble. In fact, the drys and wets courted Black votes because they had the power to swing the election. For centuries, stereotypes linked African Americans to intemperance and insurrection. During the campaign, Atlanta's newspapers did not make this connection but instead reworked those old stereotypes.[79] During the 1885 campaign, *Atlanta Constitution* editors argued that "every negro liked his dram" during slavery "but when they were freed they did not become drunkards." In fact, they declared that African Americans had "developed an astonishing streak of sobriety" after emancipation.[80] The city's newspaper editors did not tend to carry stories about Black intemperance.[81] At the 1888 Georgia WCTU convention held at First Baptist Church in Atlanta, female temperance activists expressed their commitment to temperance among African Americans. They concluded that they must court Black voters for "the cause of morality, religion, and the right." They acknowledged, "much of the success of the prohibition victories is largely due to them" and praised them for "the decrease of drunkenness and crimes and imprisonment amongst them and in their improved condition in every way."[82] Despite the existence of derogatory stereotypes, Atlantans did not employ them and sometimes revised those stereotypes to praise the Black community.

By 1898 prohibition in Georgia had become a Black versus white issue. During the 1898 Macon campaign, newspaper editors carried numerous reports of drunk and disorderly African American, and these stories often adopted a mocking tone. In February an African American "reached Villa Rica last night loaded with mean liquor," and local residents found him dead the next morning because he had consumed too much "wood alcohol."[83] At a school meeting in Tweed, "whisky flowed in abundance and many of the colored 'gentlemen' appeared lively during the day." Amid the Black crowd, two African Americans started to fight and one of them stabbed his opponent in the hand.[84] The newspapers strengthened the association between African Americans and intemperance by sharing these and other stories.

By June 1898, central Georgia's residents had become quite distrustful of African Americans, especially the intemperate ones, and feared riots amid mobilization for the Spanish-American War. On June 7, 1898, Captain J. S. Jones from Georgia pursued and confronted an intoxicated Black soldier in Tampa, Florida. Jones decided to arrest the Black soldier using physical force. The Black soldier fought back until "the unruly negro realized that he was resisting the wrong man." Within minutes of the scuffle, more than a hundred Black soldiers arrived on the scene, and "soon the storm burst." They harassed the arresting officer and released the Black soldier from his custody. The Georgian soldiers in the camp convened and considered "annihilating the negro troops."[85] That night, the Black soldiers "broke loose" and had "a wild time." The Black soldiers became drunk and nearly destroyed the nearby neighborhood of Ybor City by firing "forty or fifty shots into some of the houses." During the riot, a Black soldier shot and seriously wounded a white officer. "While the negroes were at the height of their wild revelry a company of Southern white volunteers appeared and promptly attacked the rioters," which resulted in the death of seven Black troopers. To resolve the issue, the soldiers of the Second Georgia Regiment took over guard duty.[86]

The residents of central Georgia followed the riots closely. According to the editors of the *Atlanta Constitution*, the Black troops "have disgraced their own race, and have planted in the minds of thoughtful people new seeds of distrust, doubt and suspicion." The editors worried about the effects of the riot on the war effort and asked, rhetorically, "If these negro troops perform like wild beasts and demons in the country they call their own, and whose flag they are serving, what is to be expected of them when in Spanish-held towns in Cuba?" The editors concluded, "the violent and criminal antics of these negro soldiers (unparalleled in the history of our army) are comparable only to the rapacity and brutality of the Spaniards in their treatment of the Cubans." The editors added that the event only served to "revive all the gloomy views and lively apprehensions that once made the negro problem so vexatious an issue" and that military discipline had no "real effect on the negroes who have been subjected to it." Without white supervision, Black soldiers became "seized with the temper and rage of demons and savages" and "begin to rob and steal, assault women and perform all the acts possible to men with brute natures."[87] In response, at least one white citizen felt the editors went a bit too far. He lamented that the editors offered such a "sweeping condemnation of all negro troops because of the reported violence and drunken lawlessness of one company of negro troops" but admitted that these soldiers "cannot be too strongly condemned" and that they have "brought a stigma upon their fellow soldiers of the negro race."[88] As a result of these riots, white Georgians grew suspicious of Black intemperance and insurrection, and they reasserted claims that Blacks needed white authority.

The news of the Tampa riots reached Macon residents through the *Macon Telegraph*, the *Macon News*, and personal testimony. Robert Patillo, a soldier from Company D of the Second Georgia Regiment, returned to Macon on furlough after contracting typhoid fever. The *Macon Telegraph* praised him for his "active part in quelling the famous riot at Tampa, in which seven rioting negro soldiers were killed."[89] For Macon's anti-prohibitionists, the stories of drunk and disorderly Black soldiers could not have come at a worse time.

As the election drew near, the *Macon Telegraph* editors highlighted another case of drunk and disorderly Black soldiers. In November a riot in nearby Anniston, Alabama, resulted when a Black soldier interfered with the arrest of an inebriated Black soldier. After the arrest, "an angry mob of white soldiers" gathered around the jail "clamoring for his blood."⁹⁰ By the time of the 1898 campaign, Georgians had revived old stereotypes linking intemperance with rebellion.

In late November, the Black soldiers stationed in Macon caused quite a stir with their own behavior. "After loading up on whisky," the Black soldiers armed themselves with bayonets and rampaged through the city's suburbs with intention "to take possession of several stores." Upon arrest, the Black soldiers stated their intention to "make graveyards for some of the people before they left here" on deployment.⁹¹ A few days later, a rumor emerged that Black soldiers from Virginia intended to arrive in town to attack the camp. Although nothing materialized, the guards arrested and returned any Black soldier who did not have a pass and ordered that the Black soldiers "must behave or they would all be shot." It seemed that white officers could not control the Black soldiers.⁹² Around the time of the local-option election, Macon's white residents had become alarmed by Black unruliness and expressed a desire to reassert their control through white supremacy in politics and society.

Before 1898 white Georgians had not spent much time worrying the power of Black voters because they had already taken measures to disfranchise most of the Black population. In 1877 Georgians passed a cumulative poll tax. In the 1885 and 1887 campaigns in Atlanta, African Americans who could not pay the poll tax overcame this law because both sides had wanted Black votes. Campaign officials paid the poll taxes of otherwise disfranchised Black men, so white Georgians still controlled the Black vote. In 1892 they permitted whites-only primaries for nominating candidates. With these measures, Georgians nearly eliminated Black voting. By 1900, for example, only 8 percent of African Americans could cast ballots in Georgia. In Bibb County, even fewer African Americans could vote. These measures had eliminated Black voting to such a degree that new disfranchisement legislation and amendments gained little interest from state legislators, but events toward the end of the nineteenth century inspired another round of calls for tougher disfranchisement.

Across the South, Populists formed alliances with Black Republicans, and white southern Democrats responded to the biracial alliance by clamoring for stronger disfranchisement legislation, but not necessarily in Georgia, which already had some laws on the books. The People's Party, which served as the official third party of the movement, had limited success in Georgia because of the effective disfranchisement of half the electorate. In 1894 Populists successfully polled about 40 percent of the total vote, but it only gained the party forty-seven seats in the 200-seat legislature. In 1896 Populists increased their tally to almost 45 percent of the total vote, but the party only managed to win thirty-six seats. After defeating the Populists, the Democrats assumed some of the Populists' most effective tenets, like the coinage of silver, into its own platform, thus immobilizing the party in Georgia.

Unlike in other places, white Georgians did not call for more voting restrictions in the wake of the Populist movement, but they did respond to the Wilmington Insurrection.[93] In November 1898, a coup d'état and massacre in Wilmington, North Carolina, renewed fears of Black political power among Georgia's white residents, who blamed Black office holding and voting for the violence and trouble in the Old North State. "The wave of negro outrages began soon after the republican government came into power in North Carolina," explained the *Atlanta Constitution*, which "would never have passed over the state, with all its horrors if the men who believe in white supremacy had remained in power in North Carolina." The editors lamented that "decent white people have little or no voice in the government in the Black belt counties" of North Carolina. They warned against the intrusion of Populists into the state government of Georgia. They declared, "This is but a reminder of what would occur in Georgia if the populists and republicans could successfully combine and lull the democrats in a state of over-confidence."[94] The movement sparked renewed interest in disfranchisement.

In addition to anxieties about Black political power, central Georgia residents worried about the dangers of "Black ruffians." In North Carolina, a Black woman allegedly confronted a prominent young white woman, insulted her, and "struck her with an umbrella without the slightest provocation." In another case, a Black man stole a bicycle from a white woman. Reporter Frank Weldon argued that African Americans "feel the most bitter hatred for the whites and when no white men are in sight are offensive in the worst degree" and added that Black women "are maddened at the sight of well dressed, respectable white women and seek opportunities to insult." These events had a transforming effect on race relations in the South because it heightened distrust in Black voters but also any Black person. With these perceived injuries in mind, Georgians worried anew about the effects of "negro domination" in their own state.[95]

As the local-option election in Macon reached a fever pitch, white North Carolinian Democrats seized control of Wilmington's government. In North Carolina, a "genuine uprising of the whites" pledged "to restore white supremacy" after years of Republican and Populist power. On November 8, 1898, white Democrats overthrew the local government in Wilmington and drove a Black newspaper editor out of town. The city's white residents patrolled the streets of the city, which had a Black majority, to keep African Americans away from the polls. They killed many Black residents and forced others to flee the city. According to Weldon, North Carolina's Black population "had a dream of sovereignty, of Black statehood" and "hoped to gain absolute control of the political machinery" in the election, but white North Carolinians protected the state from Republican and Populist rule with their violent efforts. The federal government refused to intervene in Wilmington.[96]

Amid the turmoil, white Georgians pushed their agenda for Black disfranchisement and stressed the importance of lynching. Rufus B. Bullock, who has served as the governor of Georgia, praised the state's "improved systems of election laws" for removing the threat of "negro domination."[97] A few years earlier, Rebecca Lattimore Felton had spoken before an audience at the Georgia Agricultural Society on the subject of lynching, to which Wilmington editor Alexander Manly replied in his newspaper. Manly had been forced out of Wilmington during the riots, and Felton repeated her arguments in the aftermath of the Wilmington insurrection. She explained, "I saw that when you take the negro into your embraces on election day to control his vote and use liquor to befuddle his understanding and make him believe he is your man and brother" and "honey-snuggle him at the polls and make him familiar with dirty tricks in politics" that "lynching will prevail" because "the cause will grow and increase with every election." She encouraged lynching because of the "crying need of women on farms is security in their lives and homes." She specifically condemned Manly for his comments and argued that "the slanderer should be made to fear a lyncher's rope rather than occupy a place in newspapers."[98] The Wilmington Riot had a transformational effect on race relations in the South because it helped generate regionwide support for poll taxes, residency requirements, and other fraudulent methods.[99] Although Georgians had already adopted these measures, the Wilmington Insurrection cast a large shadow over the events in Macon.

By the time election day arrived, Macon's white voters feared Black voters, especially those with a tendency toward intemperance. On the eve of the election, prohibitionists channeled their newfound distrust in Black voters by charging their opponents with election fraud. They had become suspicious after a heavier-than-anticipated registration.[100] They accused the anti-prohibitionists with printing forged and fraudulent ballots and sending them to loyal prohibitionists, especially those "who were supposed to be so

Rebecca Latimore Felton became famous for her public support of lynching, and Wilmington editor Alexander Manly heard her comments and criticized her. During the 1898 Wilmington Insurrection, rioters forced Manly to quit town. Library of Congress, Prints & Photographs Division, LC-USZ62-109794.

unintelligent as to be deceived by the letter and ticket." The Bibb County Anti-Saloon League deposited $1,000 into a local bank for the purpose of rewarding informants who came forward with evidence to convict fraudulent voters. They explained that the anti-prohibitionists had registered a thousand illegal voters, which consisted of felons and tax evaders, and thereby had "insulted the intelligence and virtue" of Macon's citizens. With the color-blind language emphasizing illegal voters and fraudulent ballots, Macon's white prohibitionists certainly meant to imply that, given the recent events and the movement underway to disfranchise Black men, the presence of Black voters had damaged the election. Unlike the campaigns in Atlanta, the Macon campaign consisted of hatred toward Black voters and suspicions of election fraud undoubtedly elevated because of the recent riots and insurrection. By making these concerns public, Macon's white prohibitionists had already provided their excuse should they lose the election.[101]

As they portrayed the wets as the party of corruption and Blackness, the prohibitionists used the election-day spectacle to emphasize their whiteness and purity. The prohibitionists had informed the city's mayor that they "intended to avail themselves of every means to drive whisky out" and guaranteed him, despite objections, that "the women would surely be at the polls" to "exert a large influence" on people who might change their minds if exposed to "proper pressure."[102] In an era when people debated women's role in politics, Mrs. W. G. Solomon published a letter in the *Macon News* to justify women's activity on behalf of prohibition. She asked, rhetorically, "Is it not in woman's sphere to raise a protest against that which brings her down to wretchedness and poverty, and which makes her life a burden and misery which no tongue can describe?" She continued, "Does it not come within her province to seek relief from the curse which follows her husband, her son, or her brother like a dark shadow?" She explained that the temperance women had no intention to clamor for the ballot and preferred that voting remain a masculine endeavor. Instead, she simply wrote the letter to "catch the conscience of some man who will cast his vote in the place of some mother who has realized the misery of this traffic."[103] In the morning, the prohibitionists reminded everyone that the city's women and children could not vote, so "it will be the pleasure of every gentleman in this city to vote for them."[104]

Before sunrise on December 1, 1898, female prohibitionists Sallie B. Hill and Hattie Gibson Jobe Harris led an army, perhaps numbering more than five hundred, of Georgia's white female prohibitionists onto Macon's cold, windy streets to wage the battle of water versus wine. At 6:34 a.m., the polls opened throughout the city, which became the site of "the most remarkable election the people of [the] community have ever experienced."

When each male voter arrived at his designated polling site "to cast his ballot according to the dictates of his conscience," he encountered choirs of ten to twenty women, who had positioned themselves in each of Macon's precincts with "tearful eyes to make an impression" on undecided voters. By the time Macon's shops and offices opened, "the entire city was echoing beautiful church and temperance songs . . . often to the accompaniment of church organs, which had been moved to the polling places." The temperance women carried banners throughout the city, distributed coffee and sandwiches, and challenged opposing voters to change their votes at the last second. At one point, a leader of the prohibition movement confronted the city's fire chief and asked him, "Will you not be on the Lord's side today?"[105]

Throughout the city, Black men confronted these white female choirs on the streets. Outside of Macon City Hall, Black bands leading Black voters competed with a female choir singing temperance hymns. At the East Macon polling station, a similar drama unfolded. When the ladies commenced their rendition of "Vote as You Pray," another group of Black musicians countered with the ragtime tune "There Will Be a Hot Time in the Old Town Tonight."[106] With this choice of music, the Black musicians played a ragtime hit focusing on good times to counter the religious hymns. The song, written by Joe Hayden and Theodore A. Metz in 1896, had become extremely popular. In the first verse, the song suggests a Black revival meeting with the speaker claiming:

When you hear that the preaching does begin,
Bend down low for to drive away your sin,
and when you gets religion,
You want to shout and sing,
there'll be a hot time in the old town tonight, my baby.

By using this song, the Black musicians suggested that their religious beliefs do not necessarily require temperance and prohibition. In fact, they imply that their religion compels them to have a good time. The song also tells the story of a courtship, in which the song's speaker claims "there'll be girls for ev'ry body in that good old town," who will beg:

You're all mine and I love you best of all,
And you must be my man, or I'll have no man at all.

If the Black musicians sang the lyrics in addition to the music, they would have been suggesting that the white women stationed across the street preferred them to white men. Given the emphasis on attacks on white women in the reporting of the Wilmington insurrection, it would have been a dangerous argument for them to make in a biracial crowd. The Black musicians may have only played the tune. Without the lyrics, the tune nonetheless suggests marching and had become associated with militancy, which had significance given recently escalating fears of Black soldiers, especially intemperate ones.[107] During the Spanish-American War, soldiers played this song extensively because they found it an energizing and joyful marching and fighting companion.[108] They chose music that in terms of melody and timbre expressed joy, which contrasted with the solemn hymns sang by white women. With this song, they challenged prohibition and offered an alternative, in which everyone would have a splendid time.

After months of anticipation, people left work to vote and watch the spectacle unfold. Throughout the day, "business was practically suspended, while professional men, bankers, merchants, clerks, all gathered to watch the battle of wine and water." The scene enchanted the spectators because the drama seemed real. The roles of the Black musicians and white choirs appealed to their gender and racial prejudices. White women had gained a reputation for their domestic virtue and piety partly through their association with the prohibition movement. From the perspective of the city's white residents, Black men had become a symbol of intemperance, foolishness, dishonesty, and corruption. Throughout the day, Black and white Maconites played out these stereotypes on the streets.[109]

The white female prohibitionists resorted to emotional persuasion and emphasized their domestic duties with their work at the polls. In the voting lines, female workers appealed with sentiment rather than "materialism of worldly things" to aid their cause and persuade voters.[110] The "undaunted and hopeful" women made their way to the polls to pin white bows on the lapels of voters and pleaded with them to prohibit alcohol.[111] For the most part, the female workers gained attention for their portrayal of piety. As the election started to swing in the favor of the anti-prohibitionists, the prohibitionists' cause was "upheld by the hands of fair women, who pleaded and prayed and prayed and pleaded for sons and husbands and fathers gone astray."[112] To this point, many wives and sisters followed their male relatives to the polls in a last-ditch effort to persuade them to vote for prohibition.[113] They carried banners with signs such as "God Save Our Boys," and sang hymns including "Vote for Jesus."[114] They sang in choirs, prayed, and fulfilled their domestic duties by serving sandwiches and hot coffee to the voters in line.[115] Newspaper reporters retold these stories, which enhanced the reputation of the women.

Across the country, the white female prohibitionists earned praise for their work. The *Davenport* [Iowa] *Daily Leader* explained, "At no time during the day did their work lag, and even toward the evening, when it became apparent that the antis would carry the day, they prayed and sang and pleaded harder than ever to turn the tide in their favor."[116] The *Baltimore Sun* reported that the female temperance workers "were not daunted by the discord of the negro bands and the jeers and shouts of their opponents" but instead continued to sing and plead with voters.[117] In the *St. Louis-Dispatch* the editors printed the headline: "Woman's Work in Politics: She Can Do Heroic Work for the Cause of Good, but She Can Also Be Mighty Cute."[118] In these accounts, the reporters pit the white female prohibitionists against the Black musicians and applauded them for sticking with the cause despite the harassment. They also praise the women for their hard work, piety, and beauty, in stark contrast to the descriptions of Black men and women.

In the streets of Macon, Black men and women appeared on the scene with red ribbons to oppose the white female prohibitionists.[119] "The almost simultaneous appearance of a body of brazen negro women, flaunting red ribbons attracted the attention of the leaders of both sides," commented a reporter of the scene. The Black female anti-prohibitionists "took their stand on the sidewalk," and "hummed occasionally songs with such expressions as "I am a rummy, I love my liquor, and I will have it, too."[120] Throughout the day, Black brass bands paraded through the city playing drinking songs on their instruments. By circulating these images, newspaper editors helped strengthen the link between African Americans, intemperance, and unruliness. By manipulating these stereotypes, Black Maconites took part in the spectacle and expressed their views. The brass bands mobilized voters and led the Black voters to the polls. They drowned out white women with their music. Unlike in Wilmington, African Americans survived the day and achieved victory.

Prohibition failed in Macon. In the aftermath of the election-day spectacle, Macon temperance reformers condemned Black voters for the failure of the initiative. Prohibitionists charged Black voters with selling their votes to the anti-prohibitionists. Leading the charge, Hill argued that the anti-prohibitionists had purchased their victory at the expense of honesty and "that their only salvation is in a corrupt and debased suffrage." He claimed, "No intelligent honest man in Bibb county doubts that the antis won the election by repeating negro votes, using the same men under different names, at the different precincts."[121] In response to the outcome, one Macon resident explained, "North Carolina taught us a lesson." He added, "We have lost through the negro vote, and if we do as they did in the Old North State, it will be found that white men can settle this difficulty without further ado."[122] In Atlanta, Black men had voted without this type of harassment, but the times had changed.

In fact, Black and white voters both helped defeat the prohibition initiative. Overall, white voters outnumbered Black voters by fewer than eight hundred votes, but the wets prevailed by a massive majority with a count of 2,678 votes to 1,280 votes. In Macon, Black and white voters did not vote on this issue as blocs as they did in some other times and places. At the Godfrey polling station, white voters had their largest majority over Black voters, outnumbering them 500 to 186, yet the wets carried the precinct by seventy-nine votes. At the Howard precinct, white voters had only a slight advantage in registration. Here, the prohibition ticket claimed its only victory of the day. The ninety-nine white voters and sixty-nine Black voters who cast their ballots at the Howard precinct resulted in a prohibition win by fifty votes. When the election concluded, Black people may have leaned toward the wet ticket but had not helped it prevail in any insurmountable measure.[123] Although neither white nor Black voters voted in blocs, white Maconites blamed Black voters for the result anyway.

In the aftermath of prohibition's defeat, central Georgia's white residents joined the crusade to more effectively eliminate Black voters. A few days before the election, white temperance leaders proposed electoral changes to guarantee that "the voice of the best people of the community" made the decisions about prohibition. These changes purported that future elections would run "on a perfectly clean basis" and "make the politics as clean as possible, free from all taint of bribery and anything else."[124] In reality, such changes intended to deprive African Americans of the right to vote in order that middle-class reformers could more easily get their way in local politics. The defeat in the prohibition campaign spurred white Maconites to create a white primary for local elections and white Democratic executive council to ensure white control in Bibb County, which a reporter deemed "one of the inevitables" of this election. During the campaign, both sides had paid the taxes of 1,700 ineligible or otherwise unwilling African Americans. A leading prohibitionist claimed that neither prohibitionists nor anti-prohibitionists would object to the changes and "that both sides look upon it as a necessity."[125] *Macon News'* editors chimed in on the subject, arguing that Black voters probably did not change the outcome of the election, but they did admit that the present system made it "absolutely impossible to have a perfect election." Journalists encouraged Macon residents to "condemn the present system of balloting" and suggested a new constitutional amendment to "eliminate that element whose vote at any and all times fails to secure the public's confidence and respect."[126] The editors of the *Atlanta Constitution* argued that African Americans "cannot take the fullest advantage of (practical and material opportunities) as long as he remains an active political partisan." They added, "It is true that negro domination is intolerable to the whites, but the affair at Wilmington would have had a different beginning if the negro rulers had been conservative, considerate and fair." Based on the events in Wilmington, and most certainly in Macon as well, the editors concluded, "we advise negroes to let partisan politics alone, and address themselves to the practical work of building up the material interests of their race."[127] Although white Georgians had been previously satisfied with their election laws, the Wilmington insurrection and the failure of prohibition in Macon rejuvenated the movement to eliminate Black voters.

Regardless of the cries of fraud and scandal, some Macon editors expressed satisfaction that the city's residents had conducted an orderly and quiet election. "Whatever else may be said of yesterday's election it was an orderly one," opined the *Macon News* editors. They praised the "perfect order and good feeling in the closely contested election" and commended the opposing sides for their efforts. Despite the incessant blaring of brass bands and the cries and prayers of female temperance activists, the newspaper reporters focused on serenity, peace, and order. It seems that the presence of the women caused the most stir at the polls. When the prohibitionists stated their intentions to use female workers at the polls, it seems to have bothered or worried some of the city's men. In the *Macon News*, the editors explained that "notwithstanding the ante-election talk of ladies at the polls and of 'crowding,' all fears of trouble in this direction proved to have been ill founded." Despite these anxieties, in other words, the election went off without any trouble. In fact, the *Macon News* argued that the presence of the female workers and spectators "allayed any turbulent spirit that might have animated a few and caused everyone to conduct themselves in that respectful, gentlemanly manner that always characterizes" Black and white southern men.[128] The Black musicians received only isolated criticism. According to the *Baltimore Sun*, the "band started to cross the street to the choir, but was stopped by a party of white men, acting in behalf of the women."[129] If this incident occurred, it represents a remarkable yet tacit admission on behalf of white men of Black men's political rights. By taking a step in the direction of the Black men, white men ceremoniously played their role as the protector of white women without violating Black rights to the polling stations. In contrast to the consequences usually reserved for Black political activity, especially in the wake of the deadly events in Wilmington, the musicians avoided trouble, yet they made a nationally recognized contribution to the spectacle and outcome. They marched Black voters to the polls and articulated their politics with songs and music. They gained access to the formal levels of power, which had been restricted in Georgia for decades. They confronted white women in the streets. Despite these seemingly atrocious breaches of protocol and the law, newspapers like the *Macon Telegraph* reported that the election "passed away without any disturbance worth mentioning."[130] With hostility reserved for Black voting, African Americans could participate in the spectacle without any repercussions.

After the election, the centuries-old stereotypes linking African Americans to intemperance, which had been not been present in the Atlanta campaigns but had been revived in Macon, persisted. At the 1900 Georgia WCTU convention, President Mrs. W. C. Sibley argued that the 'negro problem,' 'race troubles,' and trouble with foreign immigrants all resulted from the liquor traffic." She concluded, "Settle that question and the others will settle themselves." Georgia's female temperance activists continued to canvass Black schools and Black churches for support and educate Black Georgians about the evils of intemperance.¹³¹ In September 1906, white Atlantans responded to baseless claims of Black assaults on white women by rioting. They killed dozens of Black Atlantans. After the riots, Georgians pressed even harder to disfranchise Black voters and pass prohibition laws. In 1908 Georgians passed statewide prohibition and stricter suffrage laws.¹³²

Although white southern Democrats had started the process of disfranchising Black men as soon as the latter had gained the right to vote, their movement entered a new and more resolute phase in response to the biracial Populist alliance. Previously, white southerners had used methods to inhibit and restrict Black voting rights, such as voter manipulation and intimidation, which they had carried out through paramilitary organizations such as the Ku Klux Klan and others. With these methods, white southern Democrats operated on the assumption that Black men had the right to vote, so they did everything in their power to make sure that if a voter made it to the polls, the vote did not count as intended. In the 1890s and early twentieth century, white southerners started to eliminate Black voting. They aimed to make it insignificant if not nonexistent by denying access to registration. After toppling the Republicans in the campaign for state, local, and national office, they viewed the elimination of Black voting rights as the heroic final victory in their attempt to overthrow the political order established by Republicans during Reconstruction.¹³³

BRIDGE

"A STRICTLY SOCIAL FUNCTION"

The Contest of Black Labor and Confederate Memory at the 1903 UCV Reunion

"THE SPIRIT OF THE PEOPLE IS MORE INTENSE THAN IT HAS EVER BEEN ON any occasion," commented a journalist from New Orleans on the eve of the United Confederate Veterans' (UCV) annual reunion in 1903.[1] "In every feature and in every line of wonderful New Orleans, there were signs of joyous welcome. Laughter rose high above the tumult of trafficked streets. Flags waved from every window... in the thoroughfares men marched and instruments made music," described another observer, who added that "[not] except during the most crowded days of Carnival had the streets been as full nor the street cars crowded throughout the day."[2] The people of New Orleans anticipated the arrival of the Confederate veterans and the commencement of the annual reunion with great excitement, but the city's Black and white laborers threatened to destroy the celebration as a means to obtain equal opportunities for African Americans.

"A curious combination of race, labor and sentimental prejudices has arisen in connection with the Confederate reunion to be held here next month," explained a reporter from New Orleans to the *Baltimore Sun*.[3] The UCV required bands to lead their parade, which many considered the climax of the event. The Musicians' Union consisted of separate but cooperating chapters of Black and white musicians, but they could not meet the veterans' demands for twenty white bands and offered to supply Black bands to fulfill the request. According to a reporter, a "negro band would be like a red flag before an army of old vets who fought for four long years over the Black man," and many veterans do not "care for any colored bands to lead them in the big parade."[4] Some veterans, however, expressed their desire to have Black musicians lead the parade. Reflecting on the Old South, one veteran explained that the "old vets are willing for the sons of their old plantation darkies to make music for them anywhere."[5] In the struggle over music for the 1903 UCV reunion in New Orleans, Confederate veterans and white and

This unidentified Confederate soldier wears a membership badge for his service in the Army of Northern Virginia and his commemorative badge for attending the 1903 UCV reunion in New Orleans. Library of Congress, Prints & Photographs Division, LC-DIG-ppmsca-57064.

Black musicians fought against and among one another concerning issues beyond musical preferences.

During the reunion Black and white southerners struggled over historical memory of the antebellum period and the Civil War, which had implications for turn-of-the-century politics, specifically the labor movement, and revealed attitudes toward Black participation in spectacular culture. As Lost Cause mythology dominated southern interpretation of antebellum and Civil War history, the reunion committee refused Black musicians for their parade because they rejected their professional status and feared biracialism in the labor movement. Confederate veterans, nonetheless, manipulated the images of Black musicians playing for white masters to reinforce racist stereotypes and craft an idealistic image of the Old South. They expressed adoration for Black music as long as they were able to control it on their own terms and manipulate it to fit their image.

Although the veterans used the reunion to celebrate the Lost Cause, which romanticized slavery and reinforced white supremacy, Black musicians argued that they had the right to play at the event. For the Musicians' Union, the reunion represented an important opportunity to take a stand on behalf of the benefits of union labor. The Black musicians wanted recognition of their professional status and union rights from their peers, and to these ends, manipulated southern memory and advocated their own hopes for the future for the South. The debate forced both Black musicians and white Confederates to express their views on Black music, the Black musicians, and labor rights.

THE UNITED CONFEDERATE VETERANS

By 1903 the United Confederate Veterans had spread throughout the South and involved most living Confederate veterans. According to a reporter, the UCV made an effort to "organize camps in every town and district of the south." Despite high death rates of veterans, the "United Confederate Veterans have steadily grown in strength." At the time of the New Orleans reunion in 1903 the UCV consisted of 1,532 camps, with more joining the nationwide organization every day. Of the 100,000 estimated surviving veterans in 1903, 65,000 of them participated in the organization.[6]

The Confederate veterans gave the UCV a specific mission to care for and honor aging and deceased veterans. Before the founding of the UCV, earlier veterans' organizations and Ladies Memorial Associations had memorialized the victims of the war and cared for disabled veterans.[7] The UCV assimilated these goals into its own mission to create employment agencies for veterans, build soldiers' homes, disseminate pensions, tend tombs and graves, and fund monuments and memorials. By performing these tasks, these organizations celebrated the Confederacy and its cause.

The UCV advocated a regionally satisfying interpretation of the Old South and the Civil War. Among many efforts to spread the "correct history of the civil war that will do the southern cause justice," the organization edited textbooks to avoid teaching "the youth of this section erroneous ideas as to the war and the cause leading up to it."[8] With the Confederacy defeated in a military and political sense, white southerners created a regional cultural and intellectual identity rooted in their particular vision of the Old South, which they hoped would survive long beyond the demise of their beloved Confederate nation. The UCV, along with the United Daughters of the Confederacy formed in 1895, played a fundamental role in the project of creating the Lost Cause myth. Through control of the past, white southerners intended to influence the future of the South. They detested everything about the postbellum political and social order, especially Black voting rights, Black office-holding, and Black economic opportunity. The Lost Cause provided the foundation and justification for disfranchisement, segregation, lynching, convict-lease, and the rest of the social and political system designed to return the South to the antebellum status quo.⁹

The UCV and other veterans' organizations celebrated white southern identity and the Lost Cause at numerous spectacles, such as reunions, monument dedications, and Memorial Day events. At these events, former Confederates gathered with comrades, friends, and family for social purposes, which they infused with sectionalism. They decorated buildings and ballrooms with Confederate flags and banners. Veterans, women, and children paraded through the streets. Former officers and local leaders spoke of heroism and virulently defended the cause of the Confederacy. In these speeches, they emphasized individual liberty, state sovereignty, local self-government, and white supremacy. Despite military defeat, many speakers remained unrepentant over secession and promised to make the same decision if confronted with the choice. They argued that northern military might have overwhelmed Confederate soldiers on the battlefield, but military defeat did not make their cause illegal or unjust. Unable to realize their dream of an independent South, white southerners looked to conquer the present and future by taking control of the past. They separated their cause from the slavery issue, yet they portrayed slavery as a mutually beneficial institution by circulating stories of faithful slaves. Based on this imagined antebellum past, they condemned Reconstruction and Republican governments in the South. They abhorred enfranchised and office-holding Black southerners.¹⁰

THE FAITHFUL SLAVE MYTH

When Confederates gathered with one another, southern newspaper reporters found and disseminated accounts of faithful Black Confederates. By showing that African Americans had supported the Confederacy, they hoped to prove that the short-lived nation's cause had been just and that its racial hierarchy, which had been in place for two hundred years, had been natural and mutually beneficial. They worked these narratives into a critique of the modern industrial and political order of the post–Civil War United States.

On many occasions, white southerners staged events to relive the Old South and reconstruct racial hierarchy after emancipation. At the 1893 World's Columbian Exposition in Chicago, Virginians created a replica of George Washington's Mount Vernon Estate as the main display in the

Virginia Building. In the Virginia Building, bands played "Dixie" and crowds hollered the rebel yell. They included a portrayal of slavery in the Mount Vernon replica, including the employment of several African Americans as attendants. Sarah Robinson, who had worked for the Mount Vernon Ladies' Association, played the role of Sarah Washington, a descendant of a Mount Vernon slave. At the time, African Americans like Robinson provided tourists with their interpretation of the Mount Vernon site. In the Virginia Building, however, it seemed as if the Civil War and Reconstruction had never occurred. In this imagined reminiscence of a real time and place, African Americans gleefully served their distinguished white masters as part of a mutually beneficial arrangement. At the Mount Vernon replica, slavery had never ended. These slaves had never taken their opportunity at freedom. With this exhibit, the Virginians provided a markedly different portrayal of race relations from those of Frederick Douglass and Ida B. Wells, who used the Columbian Exposition as an opportunity to denounce racism.[11]

Elsewhere, white southerners staged events to relive the Old South and its race relations. In 1894 Confederate veterans gathered for a reunion in Birmingham, Alabama, and it featured a variety of entertainment. On two different nights, organizers arranged for dramatic reenactments of historical and cultural importance. Among these performances, African Americans took the stage to "sing famous plantation songs" and "render favorite and famous Southern melodies."[12]

At some of the most popular Lost Cause spectacles, African Americans had a notable presence. On May 29, 1890, thousands of people gathered in Richmond for the unveiling of the Lee Monument, including some of the most prominent Confederate veterans and formerly enslaved African Americans. Among the dignitaries, General Fitzhugh Lee, General Joseph E. Johnston, General Jubal Early, and General John B. Gordon marched in the procession. During the ceremony, "nothing but the best of feelings, not only toward each other but for all sections of the country, prevailed." In the speeches, veterans and dignitaries praised southerners for their undying love of the Confederacy. They praised Lee relentlessly for his service and honor.

Black men participated in the day's events. According to reports, these men had "followed the army from the opening of the war to its close." At the Lee unveiling ceremony, these Black men received many honors and special recognitions. Tarleton Alexander made the trip to Richmond from Charlottesville. According to the reporter, Alexander "always voted the Democratic ticket" and wore Confederate badges to the event. General Early brought two formerly enslaved people with him, whom he introduced to his friends as "respectable darkies" and not "scalawag niggers." When he introduced these

Black men to fellow veterans, the Black men would respond, "We is Mars' Jubal's niggers. We is, and we done cum over two hundred miles to pay our 'specs to him." Among the handful of Black men at the event, one Black man from Huntington, West Virginia, had made the trip thanks to financial assistance from "those whom he served so faithfully during the war." He had dozens of Confederate badges on his breast, which he had received as gifts from numerous veterans.[13] When news spread that African Americans had made the journey to Richmond to pay their respects to Robert E. Lee and fraternize with Confederate veterans, some Black journalists became incensed.

When African Americans participated at these Lost Cause events, they risked insulting Black leaders and Black neighbors. Editor William Calvin Chase of the *Washington Bee* heard a rumor that the local Black militia had filed an application to participate in the procession, which inspired heated remarks directed toward African Americans and the South. He lambasted local Black southerners for wanting to participate in a ceremony on behalf of Lee, "who attempted by force and arms to destroy a republic and to perpetuate slavery." He argued, "It is a most damnable outrage on civilization; it is a mockery to the memory of those many thousand union heroes that fell in defense of liberty." Although it turned out that the militia had not made an application, the editor did remark, "Every negro that participated in these ceremonies ought to have a rope around his neck and swung to the tail of the horse upon which the dead ex-Confederate is mounted." He berated these people for participating in "arch traitors ceremonies." He concluded the remarks by claiming that these ceremonies should raise the suspicions of the North because the South seems "just as ready to secede to-day as it was in '61." He warned, "Let the North beware and abandon its cowardice and strike for liberty."[14]

Several years later, white southerners dedicated another monument in Richmond. On July 2, 1896, thousands of people gathered in the city's streets under a bright, midday sun to watch Confederate veterans march toward Monroe Park, where veterans and freemasons laid the cornerstone for the Jefferson Davis monument. At the front of the procession, two hundred young people of the Children's Brigade adorned in red and white sashes presented themselves to the crowd as the next generation of ardent Lost Cause advocates. Following them, Gordon, who served as commander in chief of the United Confederate Veterans, had the honor of presiding as chief marshal of the parade, and he rode with many distinguished veterans and dignitaries, including multiple state governors. Among the Lost Cause celebrities, Varina Davis and a host of "lovely young ladies," who participated as female sponsors and maids-of-honor, rode in carriages immediately ahead of the veterans.

Despite old age and weakness, the veterans summoned their remaining strength and marched "with pride and pleasure" toward the site of the ceremony. The veterans wore coats torn with bullet holes and carried canteens, knapsacks, and tattered battle flags just as they had done in the war. The column of 15,000 marchers moved slowly. Although a faint breeze provided some relief from the unrelenting sun in "the azure skies overhead," the numbers dissipated along the parade route due to the heat.[15] When they arrived at Monroe Park, they formed a square around the park, where the ceremony commenced.

To many observers, Monroe Park seemed like an obvious choice for the Davis monument because of its past utility for the veterans and present proximity to the equestrian statue of Robert E. Lee. During the war, it had served as a campground of Confederate soldiers, who knew the space as Camp Winder. They "seemed charmed with the beauties of Monroe Park, and delighted that so beautiful a spot had been selected for the monument." There they honored Jefferson Davis, who one reporter characterized as "patriot, soldier, statesman, orator, stainless knight, and Christian soldier."[16] Then they ritualistically laid the cornerstone.

During the ceremony, General Stephen D. Lee's keynote address focused on numerous themes of the Lost Cause, specifically the question of slavery and the long odds of Confederate victory. First, he provided his perspective on the causes of the Civil War, which *Richmond Dispatch* editors believed he did with "great precision, clearness, and force."[17] In the speech, Lee emphasized the constitutionality of secession. He explained, "I should be false to the memory of the dead if I did not remind you that he, the man we all adore, battled for the constitutional right to dissolve the Union, not for revolution, not for slavery—that the war was fought upon a legal, not a moral, issue."[18] Then, he summarized the life of Jefferson Davis. He argued that people adored Jefferson Davis because he led his people bravely against an enemy "outnumbering them four to one in arms" and "incomparably better prepared for war." Reflecting on the Civil War, he declared, "When we look back now at the mighty contest, we wonder how we ever held out so long."[19] With these arguments, Lee shaped the way white southerners remembered the antebellum past and the Civil War. By emphasizing that slavery had not caused the war, he hoped to erase any moral judgment posterity might make on the Confederacy's cause.

Inspired by the ceremony, local white southerners praised reconciliation with their former enemies, but they gushed sectionalism and nostalgia for the Old South. The editors of the *Richmond Dispatch* observed at the ceremony that the "feelings of the people were profoundly moved" and that "old times came back again." They especially enjoyed seeing the battle flags and hearing "Dixie" and the rebel yell. In addition to the sectional spirit, they expressed satisfaction at seeing the Confederate battle flag flown alongside the American flag. They explained, "Our people are well on with the new love, but they are by no means off with the old one; nor will they ever be." They praised Richmond's citizens for their understanding and exhibition of an "intense love for the southern cause," of which they had become increasingly proud.[20] "It was a grand spectacle," commented a reporter, who added that spectators would likely not see this sight again for years.[21]

Amid thousands of white Confederate veterans, African Americans participated in spectacle in the role of faithful former slaves. According to a reporter, several Black marchers remained "true to their old masters" and accompanied them in the parade. Among them, Phil Valentine, who had been General J. E. B. Stuart's slave and had accompanied his master during the war, marched in the parade with the white soldiers of the Tenth Virginia Cavalry. He suffered a wound to his forehead during the war, but he remained by General Stuart's side as he died at the Battle of Yellow Tavern. After the war and emancipation, he went to work on a farm in nearby Henrico County. During the parade, he grinned and remarked that he was "certainly glad to be with the old boys again." The other former faithful slaves marched alongside their former masters. At the back of the parade, a dozen Black cooks marched, as well.[22]

African Americans had a notable presence at reunions immediately prior to the planned event in New Orleans, and Confederate veterans embraced the opportunity to celebrate these Black men. In 1899 the *Atlanta Constitution* reported that Clinton Rodgers, who went by the nickname "Jeff Davis," journeyed to the reunion in Charleston, South Carolina, because he "believes he has as much right to be with the veterans as any man who wore the gray." According to the report, Rodgers had followed his master during the war. He received a wound, and he showed the scar "as if it was the grandest trophy with which he could be possessed." When asked about his attendance at the reunion, Rodgers explained that he had seen battle alongside his master. He remarked, "Habn't de ole nigger bin wid massa all fru de smoke ob de battle and he'ped ter take ole massa's boy frum offer de field when he war shot mo' ter death?"

In stories about faithful slaves at Lost Cause events, white southerners described them as disdainful toward the younger generations of African Americans and intensely loyal to the Confederacy. Writing about Clinton

Rodgers, the reporter explained, "Like old-time darkies he, of course, has contempt for many things of the present time." When Rodgers saw Black soldiers on the streets, he would remark, "Nebber smelt gunpoweder and nebber will. Dese play soldiers sho does make dis ole chile tired."[23] Unlike contemporary generations of African Americans, Rodgers had reportedly had his loyalty tested in the trials of war, and he remained unrelentingly faithful to his master and the Confederacy

In 1900 Amos Rucker marched in a gray suit alongside fellow Georgia veterans at a reunion in Augusta, Georgia. According to the *Atlanta Constitution*, Rucker had followed his master and continued to serve him throughout the war. The editors claimed that Rucker had never wanted freedom. Instead, he "handled a musket whenever he got the opportunity" and suffered a wound at Murfreesboro, Tennessee. After the war, he joined the UCV's Camp Walker and followed the veterans to every reunion. Of the many so-called Black Confederates, Rucker remained a famous example celebrated by Lost Cause advocates deep into the twentieth and even twenty-first centuries.[24]

When African Americans showed up or otherwise supported Confederate events, white southerners portrayed them as living proof that the South should handle its own racial problems. In 1901 William A. Gordon, a white man, served as the president of the Washington, DC, camp of the UCV. He joined his fellow veterans at the annual reunion in Memphis. In a letter back to the *Washington Post*, he reported that a prominent Black citizen of Memphis named Robert R. Church had given the veterans a generous donation of $1,000 to make the reunion a success and to guarantee "real, genuine feeling between the races." According to Gordon, Church had lived his early life as an enslaved person in Mississippi. After the war, Church became wealthy by "frugality and thrifty attention to business." In fact, Church became a real estate guru, and he turned Beale Street into a center for Black businesses. By investing in real estate, Church became the south's first Black millionaire.

Although Church suffered a gunshot wound to the head during the 1866 Memphis riot, he expressed no ill will toward Confederate veterans or white Memphians. In a newspaper interview, Church claimed, "I want to see the veterans enjoy themselves, and I want to see Memphis do herself credit in the matter of entertainment." He praised white southerners for their treatment of him and his fellow African Americans. Specifically, he highlighted spending on schools and the abundance of opportunity. He declared, "No persons on earth are more disposed to help the former slaves than are the veterans of the Confederacy; those old men who yet remember the negro in slavery." Church believed that Memphians should put the war behind them. After all, Church had quite a bit to lose given his financial success, so it seems likely that he supported the Confederate reunion to maintain an alliance with white Memphians, who had already targeted him once. When Church donated the money, however, Memphis's Black community condemned him.[25]

Although these statements earned him scorn from the Black community, Church's sentiments appealed to Gordon and other Confederate supporters. He wrote, "The Southern people have not forgotten how devoted the former slaves were to the families of their masters during the war." He applauded "these faithful friends and servants" because they "remained on the plantations" and "provided food and raiment for the women and children" and "watched over and protected them from harm." He praised his fellow white southerners for their efforts to uplift the Black race. He concluded, "The race problem, and there is such a problem, can most safely be left to the people of the South, white and colored, who understand and mutually appreciate each other, and who will in time work out a solution of the question, which will be for the best interests of all." In this letter, Gordon explicitly stated how the image of the grateful, benevolent Black person supported white southerners' claims to govern their own racial affairs. The editors of the *Memphis Commercial-Appeal* expressed similar views by referring to him as a credit to his race.[26]

In these cases, the presence of these African Americans helped strengthen white southerners' version of the history of the Old South and the Civil War because it demonstrated that slavery had been a benevolent, mutually beneficial labor system. Although this event and similar spectacles strengthened white supremacy, African Americans had many of their own reasons to participate.

Some African Americans may have portrayed themselves as faithful to their masters to earn favors and rewards from former masters. In 1879 Jesse H. Drake of Missouri left his estate worth $10,000 to three formerly enslaved people. Calvin Drake, Aaron Drake, and Judah Drake inherited the entire estate. In the will, Jesse Drake emphasized that these men had served as "faithful slaves and had remained with him since freedom, nursing and caring for him in his old age." He bequeathed his estate, which consisted of about four hundred acres, to them to show his gratitude. Upon hearing the news, the Louisville *Courier-Journal* editors commented, "This should be noticed at the North to evince the fierce feeling of anger entertained by old slave-holders against their slaves."[27] In 1891, Jane Lewis earned "a large part of a fortune of $50,000" left by her former master, a Kentucky planter, who bequeathed large sums of money to his "faithful slaves."[28] To inherit a part or the entirety of a master's fortune, African Americans might have expressed loyalty.

Similarly, African Americans convinced white southerners, specifically their former masters, that they had served faithfully in the war to earn a pension from the state government.[29] In 1888 Mississippi passed a pension law to provide for Confederate veterans, which included a provision to assist "colored servants of soldiers and sailors who are disabled in like manner as soldiers or sailors by reason of said service."[30] Likewise, Tennessee's government provided pensions for Confederate soldiers, their widows, and former servants.[31] In 1907 veterans in Raleigh, North Carolina, passed a resolution "to make a new class of pensions" for "worthy negro servants who followed the fortunes of the Southern Confederacy and rendered service to their owners or others" during the war.[32] In 1923 South Carolina's legislators voted to provide pensions for "faithful slaves who stood by their masters during the Civil War" under "the same conditions as those now paid to Confederate veterans."[33]

To receive a pension or earn favors from former masters, African Americans would have had to prove their loyalty, so they would have had to do things like attending Lost Cause events. At the 1917 reunion in Washington, DC, Josh Robinson from Kentucky attended. Robinson had earned the Cross of Honor from the United Daughters of the Confederacy because he "shouldered a musket in 1862." Robinson drew a pension for his service.[34] The promise of a pension might have encouraged other African Americans that had involuntarily served the Confederacy to take on the role of the faithful slave. In 1922 a group of Huntsville women in the United Daughters of the Confederacy requested a raise in pensions for Confederate veterans and "to place the faithful negroes who served as company cooks or servants for their masters on the pension rolls to receive the full amount of pensions," as well.[35] Although they had involuntarily served in the Confederate Army, they might have played up their willingness to serve as a testament to their loyalty. In a period of limited opportunity, African Americans may have portrayed themselves as loyal, faithful slaves to earn extra income.

In some cases, African Americans gathered to celebrate their own fraternal bonds forged during the war, which they did without the participation of white veterans. In 1889 African Americans gathered in Jacksonville, Alabama, for a reunion. These men had served, likely involuntarily, as teamsters, servants, and cooks during the war. At the reunion, they played baseball and enjoyed a barbecue meal, and "good humor prevailed throughout." According to the reporter, the "negroes who were in the war and heard the bullets whistle are very proud of it." They did not gather to commemorate their former masters. The event featured no white people. Instead, the African

Americans staged a mock debate with regard to the best political party for the future of the race. As none of them supported the Democratic Party, a few Black men had to play the role in the debate.[36] The reunion of these Black Confederates demonstrate that African Americans who worked involuntarily for the Confederate Army did not have to support the cause to forge bonds with one another and, possibly, white soldiers, which represents one of the many reasons African Americans might participate in these events.

For some African Americans, the role of the faithful slave became a means to earn money. In 1897 a group of northern tourists to the South stopped at a railroad station and encountered an "old, gray-wooled darky" with his arm in a sling "made of faded blue bandanna." He came up to the train and passed his hat along for spare change. They asked him about his war service, and he explained that he had hurt himself in the war. He had followed his master to the battlefield. He told his audience, "I was right by Mars' Robert's side when I got hurt. Dem was sho' mighty troublous times." Upon hearing the story, the tourists dropped nickels and dimes into his hat, which the tourists passed throughout the train.[37] In the account of Clinton Rodgers, the reporter explained, "He is a pet of nearly all the old confederate veterans in Atlanta, and they humor him in all his whims." At Rodgers's recent wedding, a white judge performed the ceremony for free, and many white veterans paid the license fees. Rodgers attended as many reunions as possible. At a reunion in Texas, he reportedly met Varina Davis, who he considered "to be the greatest and the grandest lady in all the world." He attended the reunions without paying train fare. Instead, he relied on white veterans on the train to pay for him. On the train, he sang plantation songs, which earned him a few dollars here and there.[38]

Prior to the 1903 reunion in New Orleans, both white Confederates and African Americans had established a presence at Lost Cause spectacles, especially the reunions. When the debates over the reunion music broke out, both sides drew on these past events to make their respective cases.

THE REUNION COMMITTEE VERSUS UNION LABOR

In early 1903, the UCV announced that it would hold its annual reunion in New Orleans from May 19 through May 22. Gordon served as the General Commanding, later known as the Commander in Chief, of the UCV from 1890 to 1904, and had ultimate control over the reunion and most of the UCV's affairs. The Adjutant General, William E. Mickle, had primary responsibility of the reunion arrangements, such as the time and place.

From 1890 to 1904, John B. Gordon, who had served as a general in the Confederate army, became the first leader of the UCV. Library of Congress, Prints & Photographs Division, LC-DIG-cwpbh-04706.

On the local level, E. B. Kruttschnitt served as the president of the reunion committee. Kruttschnitt, a prominent man in New Orleans, worked as a lawyer and businessman. In 1898 he had served as chairman of the state's disfranchisement convention. He headed the state's Democratic Party and campaigned heavily among white labor unions in New Orleans on the party's behalf. As chair of the reunion committee, he had authority over the various subcommittees, such as the committee on music. J. W. Gaines served as the chairman of the Music Committee. In addition to the six members of the committee, J. C. Febiger Jr. served as an advisory manager.[39] Within this hierarchy, the UCV planned and executed its annual reunion to accomplish its business, social, and educational goals.[40] To make the reunion a success, they had to organize a massive parade of veterans, friends, and family.

For the veterans and the New Orleans community at large, the veterans' parade represented the most anticipated event of the UCV reunion. One reporter characterized the parade as the "climax of the reunion" and described it as "always inspiring." He acknowledged that spectators should not expect to see the old veterans march with military precision, but he assured them, "the confederate yell that goes up as the procession marches by recalls one of the striking features of the civil war."[41] Journalists estimated between 20,000 and 25,000 veterans would march in the parade. In Louisiana and Mississippi, public school officials canceled Friday classes to permit students to "witness what they will probably never have a chance to see again."[42] Journalists estimated that 150,000 people would come to New Orleans for the festivities, including "tens of thousands of school children" from Alabama, Mississippi, and Louisiana.[43] The business owners along the parade route, which stretched for four miles, had the responsibility to decorate their property for the parade with bunting, flags, portraits of Confederate generals, and Civil War relics. To the supporters of the Confederacy, the parade provided a memorable occasion and inspired sentimental and nostalgic feelings for the Old South. To the Musicians' Union, which consisted of Black and white musicians, the parade provided economic opportunity.

In the 1880s, New Orleans workers cultivated a radical, militant, and biracial labor movement. As a cosmopolitan city, New Orleans hosted people from around the world. These visitors brought their own ideas on labor politics, which radicalized the workers in the city. After emancipation, Black residents faced segregation in schools and public services, but they lived alongside white neighbors and fraternized with them, making biracial movements possible.

The city's Black and white workers organized the Central Trades and Labor Assembly (CTLA). In addition to the biracial Knights of Labor, which had a presence in New Orleans, the CTLA facilitated cooperation across racial lines. In 1881 the organization enlisted 5,000 members and grew to 20,000 members by the mid-1880s. In 1888 the CTLA folded, but biracialism did not fail. In New Orleans, it persisted into the twentieth century.[44]

In the early twentieth century, race relations deteriorated in New Orleans and across the South, but the working classes in New Orleans cooperated across racial lines in their quest for labor rights. In 1899 American Federation of Labor organizer James Leonard led the effort to create the Central Trades and Labor Council to represent white unions. In 1900 Black workers formed the Black Central Trades and Labor Council, which eventually became known as the Central Labor Union. During the 1900s and 1910s, these organizations consisted of 30,000 to 40,000 members. Although separate, these organizations cooperated with one another.

In a similar fashion, white and Black musicians in New Orleans formed separate unions but often supported one another to protect their labor rights and to maintain the city's proud reputation for musical tastes and talents. Many visitors to New Orleans recognized its residents' preferences for the fine arts, specifically music, and gave the city the nickname "Paris of America." Black musicians, according to observers, played an integral part of this music culture and contributed to its fame.

In 1902 white and Black musicians each formed their own local chapters of the American Federation of Musicians. The white musicians formed Local 174, and the Black musicians followed a few months later with the creation of Local 242.[45] In the constitution of Local 174, the founders explicitly limited membership to "all white male or female musicians recommended by the Examining Committee."[46] Despite this fact, the two unions cooperated with one another because, according to a journalist, the white musicians "thought it well to have [the Black musicians] in at Mardi Gras time."[47] The cooperation between white and Black musicians in New Orleans deviated from the norm. In New York, Black musicians could not join the local chapter of the AFM, which left Black musicians without much opportunity to play for white audiences in the city.[48] In New Orleans, white and Black musicians had taken steps to professionalize their industry, and white musicians recognized the proficiency of and demand for their Black colleagues and hoped to benefit from Black success through a labor alliance.

When it came time to negotiate with the UCV, the history of biracial cooperation in New Orleans, specifically within the Musicians' Union, presented the white musicians with a quandary. The reunion committee clearly indicated a preference for white musicians and a desire to exclude Black performers, so the leadership of Local 174 had to sacrifice either cooperation with the Black Local 242 and their stance against scab musicians or the opportunity to play at the reunion. In the founding constitution of Local 174, the union explicitly stated, with few exceptions, "[no] band or bands, belonging to the Union are allowed to play publicly in parades, concerts or other occasions within a radius of ten miles from the point of intersection of Royal and Canal Streets of this city, where non-union bands are engaged." In addition to the rule, the union offered to reimburse its musicians who lost engagements by following the rule. According to the by-laws, any "member finding non-union members employed at an engagement where he is engaged, and declines to play, shall, on personally notifying the Board of Directors of the fact, be entitled to the amount of the engagement" paid for on behalf of the union's funds.[49] The union's leaders expressly permitted the members of Local 174 to reach out beyond their own organization and cooperate with other union musicians.[50] According to one of Local 174's leaders, they could navigate the problem and participate in the union by temporarily disaffecting the Black musicians. He argued that the African Americans had their own union for protection. The leaders of Local 242, however, threatened to take the matter to the national headquarters of the AFM if the white bands alienated them.[51] Given the conditions prescribed in the constitution, the leaders and membership of Local 174 had an obligation to stand by fellow union musicians regardless of their race.

In a special meeting on March 30, 1903, the white musicians of Local 174 met and resolved not to participate in the UCV parade if nonunion bands also played at the event, which necessarily though not explicitly meant that they determined to stand with their Black colleagues. The chapter's leadership went to the reunion committee's headquarters within the city to deliver their ultimatum in person to music committee chairman Gaines. They explained to the chairman that they could provide fifteen bands, including some Black bands, for the parade, which still fell short of the committee's desire for twenty bands, but they argued that they could meet the committee's demands better than a combination of independent bands.

The reunion committee did not accept the position. In an initial response to this news, a UCV official, probably Gaines, lamented, "I do not think their proposition will be acceptable to the music committee. I think they might be more liberal in this matter. It is not an ordinary occasion. We feel that they could put aside these union rules for the day, as other unions have done."[52] On April 2, 1903, the members of the music committee unanimously rejected the Musicians' Union's proposal and stated its intention to fill their need with nonunion bands. Gaines expressed his regret that they could not use the union bands but that the music committee had rejected the offer because the union could not meet its full demand for music. He stated, the "very best they could do would be in the neighborhood of a dozen, and I understand some of them are negro bands."[53]

Journalists had speculated that the UCV would balk at the thought of having Black musicians at their parade. According to one reporter, the "old veterans are said to have plainly stipulated that there must be no negro bands heading their line of march."[54] Gaines confirmed these suspicions in his statement. He explained, "I made it very plain that we would not have a colored band in our parade. Therefore, it seemed the number of bands the Union could furnish us would not be over ten, at the most."

After making this statement, Gaines confidently asserted that many bands had already contacted them to play at the event. He informed the Musicians' Union that they would accept these offers and secure enough music for the parade on their own. After making the decision, Director General James Dinkins, a member of the executive committee for the UCV reunion, sent out a call to all the UCV chapters to bring their own bands.[55]

When the UCV rejected the offer to accept the Black musicians and decided to employ non-union bands from across the South, southern musicians came to their aid to play at the reunion and in the parade. The music committee hired the Memphis Drum and Bugle Corps to lead the parade, which local journalists characterized as "an elite organization" of forty-five members.[56] In addition to the Memphis buglers, the parade also featured the Atlanta Fire Department Drum Corps, which consisted of thirty-two of the 150 members of the firefighting brigade.[57]

In addition to these well-known bands, many camps of the UCV brought their own musicians to the reunion. A UCV camp based in Jackson, Tennessee, brought their own "splendid bugle and drum corps."[58] Executive committee chairman James Dinkins assured everyone that they would have enough music for the reunion.[59] Due to the number of bands brought by state delegations, the UCV decided to put a band in front of every state in the parade, which had not been done in previous years. More than a month before the reunion, the music committee had already employed sixteen of the necessary twenty bands with "more in sight." The UCV arranged to feed these musicians and pay for their accommodations.[60]

After learning of the UCV's decision to use nonunion bands, the Musicians' Union took a bold stand. On April 11, the leadership of the Local 174 took their case before the white-led Central Trades and Labor Council and requested the addition of the UCV reunion to the unfair-to-labor list because "of its attitude in refusing to employ only union bands for the big parade." In the case against the UCV, Local 174 president George De Droit specifically highlighted the UCV's unwillingness to "march behind negro bands." He characterized the UCV's actions as unfair and unprecedented. To these ends, he highlighted previous instances of Black participation at Confederate reunions, specifically highlighting the reunion in Memphis, where Church donated a generous sum to the reunion fund and Black bands had "taken a prominent part in the music." He also pointed out that union rules prohibited them from participating alongside nonunion musicians. After concluding his remarks, he requested a complete boycott by all the city's unions against the UCV, which had significant implications for the UCV's ability to carry out the reunion.

The leadership of the Central Trades and Labor Council had a difficult decision because they had to choose between supporting their nostalgia for the Old South and reaffirming their modern labor positions. Robert E. Lee served as the organization's president. Born amid war in 1863, Lee had come of age in the post-Civil War South and worked as a machinist. He had attended the 1898 disfranchisement convention as a delegate and had little contact with Black workers. Commenting on the plan to boycott the reunion, he explained, "[no] union labor could serve the Reunion if it should be declared unfair to union principles."[61]

If the Trades Council passed the measure to put the reunion on the unfair list, it would devastate the veterans' ability to stage the reunion because carpenters, painters, and other laborers would walk off the job. The Trades Council did not make a decision on the boycott at the April 11 meeting because "of the sentiment surrounding the Confederate Veterans."[62] The recognition of overwhelming feeling for the UCV within the Trades Council testified to the limits of the labor movement in the early twentieth century.

At this point, the Musicians' Union's struggle against the UCV gained national attention, and the Black musicians and Musicians' Union received mixed responses. When the news broke, some Confederate veterans and newspaper editors voiced their support for the Black musicians because the Black musicians appealed to their nostalgic memory of the antebellum past. According to one veteran, the Black musicians "will furnish more really inspiring music than all the other bands—composed of foreigners as they are—ever dreamed of, and more reaching after the Southern heart." He characterized Black music as the only true form of American music.[63] He remembered how white southerners "danced all night till broad daylight and gone home with the girls in the morning to the inspiring strains of 'Old Frank Johnson' and 'Pompey Long.'" Looking forward, he explained, "we old veterans can afford to march to the strains of 'Dixie,' or the 'Mocking Bird,' of the 'Suwanee River,' when rendered by our Southern darkies."[64] These memories, according to the veteran, had their roots in the experiences of slavery, but he assured the readers that the enslaved Black musicians they had known before the war had "successors who are quite as responsive to demands upon them."[65] This Confederate veteran was not alone in his support of the Black musicians.

Newspaper editors supported the presence of the Black musicians because their participation would revive a nostalgic vision of the Old South. From the 1890s to the 1930s, former Confederates disseminated hundreds of stories of faithful slaves, in which they emphasized the devotion and loyalty of enslaved people. Rejecting the contemporary social and political order, many white southerners also rejected contemporary blues and work songs and longed to hear old plantation songs played by Black musicians.[66] The editors of the *Washington Post* explained that before the Civil War, white southerners "danced to the fiddle, flute, guitar, and bass viol of the colored artist. No picnic was complete without a colored orchestra; no ball so much as dreamed of with the colored Orpheus left out." Commenting on the present, this editor explained that Black musicians represented the "most favored and sought-for" in the city. He concluded, "it seems to us that this squabble is beyond the reach of serious consideration."[67] Upon learning about the disagreement between the Musicians' Union and the Black musicians, the editors of the *Richmond News-Leader* remarked, "[this] is nonsense. Southern white people have marched behind Negro musicians and have danced to the music of Negro fiddlers all their lives."[68] The veterans continued this theme. In these arguments, the writer expressed an idealized vision of the Old South in which slaves willingly made music for their masters and white southerners enjoyed their music at social events.

The white supporters of the Black musicians wished to see the Black bands at the reunion because of their musical abilities, which they deemed a natural talent. In the letter, the veteran emphasized the talents of Black musicians as one of the reasons they should play. He wrote, "if any one on earth ever threw his soul into his music it is our Southern negro when he is glorying hallelujah, touching the light guitar or tooting a familiar Southern melody on a horn."[69] Similarly, the editors of the *Richmond News-Leader* explained, "[certainly] there is nothing involving social equality in the employment of one Negro or a band of Negroes to make music. This is folly number one."[70] By portraying musical ability as a natural talent, veterans could deny that African Americans had any political value at the reunion, reinforce white stereotypes of the feckless Black performer, and deny the political significance of their participation.

To ameliorate any anxiety over the presence of Black musicians, Confederate veterans and newspaper editors repeated the argument that the social elements of the reunion did not entail any political significance. In the earliest days of the UCV, Confederate veterans insisted that their reunions had no political significance. If they admitted that these reunions had a political motive, they would appear disloyal.[71] Nonetheless, the reunions did have a political bent to them because the imagery and oratory celebrating the Lost Cause had implications for contemporary race relations. Using similar reasoning, many people, including some veterans, expressed their support for the Black musicians by arguing that the musicians also had no political significance at the reunion, and therefore, should receive permission to play. "Where the objection to the colored musicians can come in we fail to see," opened the Confederate veteran in his letter to the *Raleigh Post*. He explained that the Black musicians "will only be employed for their music and nothing more."[72]

According to newspaper editors, African Americans did not belong at a political event, but they should play at a social event. In the *Washington Post* an editorial asked, "when did Southern people cease employing the colored band, string or tooting instrument, or both, for their strictly social function?"[73] From the perspective of some white southerners, Black participation at the reunion possessed no political significance, but their presence did have cultural value because their presence would reaffirm a picture of harmonious race relations in the Old South and revive nostalgia for southern traditions. For white southerners, the presence of African Americans at a social event, as they portrayed the UCV reunion, entailed no threat to white supremacy but instead reinforced it. It would also testify to southerners' abilities to handle racial matters on their own. As Musicians' Union president De Droit pointed out, UCV reunions had welcomed Black contributions and participation at past reunions. In fact, they had been fundamental to strengthening the image of the faithful slave in postbellum America. These particular Black and white musicians in New Orleans, however, had struck the wrong chord with the UCV music committee because of anti-labor sentiments and the ambitions of the reunions' organizers.

Old South apologists and New South advocates condemned the labor movement to allow their region to compete with established manufacturing centers in the North. After the switch to a free labor system, southern entrepreneurs and their elected officials portrayed low wages and anti-unionism as a regional advantage to help grow industry in the impoverished South.[74] In 1873 Americans suffered through an economic depression, which generated class conflict. As poverty and labor violence ravaged the country, labor unions became a public enemy, especially in the South. By the late nineteenth century, the Old South had become celebrated as an alternative to the chaos of industrialization and urbanization. For many Americans, the Old South seemed idyllic because of its lack of industry. In literature, writers depicted the Old South as a place of orderly race relations unencumbered by machines, urbanization, and labor unrest. Attracted by these themes, readers flocked to pick up books about the romantic Old South.[75] To many white southerners, biracial unionism was anathema to the imagined Old South and their visions for the New South.

In the post-Reconstruction South, many New South promoters and white workers hoped that cheap Black labor would attract industry and modernize the region, so they specifically attacked Black and biracial labor organizations. Industrialists hoped to revive the antebellum social order, in which white masters exploited labor from enslaved people. Similarly, these industrialists possessed a paternalistic view of Black laborers based on nostalgia for antebellum slavery. They emphasized a need for "cheap, docile, Black labor."[76] In fact, they referred to Black labor as one of the region's greatest assets because they could cheaply exploit it. Meanwhile, white working-class southerners argued that Black workers threatened their jobs because they worked for lower wages, so they launched protests and strikes to prevent the hiring of Black workers and the admission of Black laborers into unions.[77]

Within the Black community, many middle-class Blacks shared the same views. Booker T. Washington helped advocate on behalf of the New South, and he hoped that Black Americans would have a place in it as disciplined, cheap workers. In his famous 1895 Cotton States and International Exposition speech, he reminded his white audience that Black laborers, instead of using the term "slaves," had worked without striking.[78] In 1898 he repeated a similar argument and stated that Black workers did not want labor unrest because they preferred the open-shop policies prevalent in the South.[79] In 1903 he reminded readers of *Southern States Farm Magazine* that African Americans had given "peaceful, faithful service" during their enslavement.[80] By portraying Black labor as faithful and servile, Washington hoped to open opportunities for Black laborers.

In New Orleans, white residents had many of the same views toward African Americans in the labor movement and politics, which they expressed in local newspapers. One writer to the New Orleans *Sunday States* declared that the "time is to come when every effort should be made to discourage in every way an alliance between white and Black labor, because it not only menaces the peace of the South, but the welfare of every white workingman in the South." He warned against admitting African Americans into the trade unions of the city because they might perceive themselves as "the social equal of the white men" working with them. African Americans, according to the writer, put white workers in economic and physical danger, he explained: "by his willingness to work for less money [the Black man can] either drive the white artisans to the wall or cause a race war." After chronicling a list of reasons why African Americans can survive without much money, he argued:

> a great mistake was made when negroes were admitted to labor organizations in this city and unless a halt is called social equality between the working classes of the whites and blacks is inevitable. It is impossible for the two to work side by side and sit in meetings and conventions without the white man sinking to the social level of the negro.[81]

He explained that African Americans belonged in the agricultural sector, and he wanted them out of the city because they believed African Americans turned to laziness, crime, and vices such as gambling.[82] In a *New Orleans Daily States* editorial, the editors argued that the mixing of the races would lead to the downfall of both. They characterized enfranchisement of African Americans as a punishment to the South because "it was desired that the Southern whites should be subjected to the most abject form of humiliation that the most cruel mind could devise."[83] New Orleans had a long history of racial cooperation in the labor movement, which recognized Black professionalism and their right to labor protection, yet their inclusion in professional organizations sparked intense reactions.

For many white residents in New Orleans, the UCV reunion served as a vital opportunity to honor the veterans and the Lost Cause, so it must not encounter any obstacles, especially from labor organizations at odds with the idealized future New South. The reunion must succeed, according to *Daily Picayune* editors, because it represented the "only reward which the grand old heroes of the most tremendous warfare of almost any age get and can ever hope for in return for their magnificent devotion to the cause they had espoused and for their unsurpassed gallantry in battle in its behalf." In support of the reunion, the editors preached, "let us give them the best we have, the best the city affords." They described generous contributions as the "duty of the people of this good city."[84]

For the business and tourist industries in New Orleans, the UCV reunion provided an occasion to enhance the city's reputation among travelers, and they feared so-called special interests, such as labor organizations, could threaten its success. Some supporters of the Confederate reunion did not address the situation with the Musicians' Union directly, but they emphasized the need for a successful reunion. With thousands of people expected to attend the reunion, city leaders asserted, much "of the city's future depends on the reports they will take back to their people."[85] The editors of the *Daily Picayune* launched a massive campaign to raise funds for the reunion. In one appeal for financial support a supporter remarked, "the coming Reunion should be made one which visitors will never forget." They emphasized that everyone would benefit from contributing to the city's reputation. With regard to business interests, the editors argued that it "is even more important that everybody should go away praising the great port and its advantages."[86] The responsibility of upholding the city's fame for entertainment and hospitality depended on the support from all classes of the city's citizens, but especially those who "profit by the coming of the visitors."[87] For the cause of sectionalism and profit, the reunion must not suffer from anything, especially biracial unionism.

In New Orleans, many white residents and Confederate veterans opposed the Musicians' Union because of the anti-labor platforms vital to the success of the New South. Upon learning that the Musicians' Union threatened to destroy the UCV reunion by putting them on the unfair to labor list, some people attacked the union for putting their labor agenda ahead of the success of the reunion. The leaders of the city of New Orleans had put much effort into planning the reunion. In a letter to the editor of the *Daily Picayune*, one Confederate supporter understood the city's efforts to make this reunion a success and lamented that the union sought to destroy it. He explained that it "is to be regretted that there is an organization of men who are so much opposed to public enterprise that they will not only not contribute themselves, but would tear down and prevent others from making the Reunion a success." He specifically condemned their willingness to "stop the work on the auditorium and kill the enterprise" and for wanting "exclusive privileges over every one else." He proceeded to use the case of the Musicians' Union to make a larger point about civic awareness by arguing that if everyone in the city adopted the attitude of the union, the city "would be enclosed in little, narrow bounds, so measly and dwarfed that the outer world would never know we existed." He damned the Musicians' Union, stating that "the act deserves the contempt of every right-minded man and woman of this city. It should be cried down until those who thought of such an act should feel ashamed of themselves and hunt a dark spot to hide."[88] From the perspective of the musicians' opponents, the reunion required a high level of civic virtue and sacrifice, and the musicians had not shown any inclination toward either.

The union's opponents argued that the policies and actions of the Musicians' Union damaged the city's culture and reputation. In the same letter to the *Daily Picayune*, the writer explained, "a majority of the brass bands have left the Musicians' Union because of the rule or ruin spirit displayed in it." He explained that the union tried to destroy "every public benefit or enterprise" that had given them an opportunity to play. At previous city festivals, the Musicians' Union refused to play unless the managers only employed union bands. On two previous occasions, the Musicians' Union asked the Trades Council to put the city's festivals on the unfair to labor list. He also pointed out an episode in which the city of New Orleans hosted a relief campaign for the Louisiana Field Artillery, and the Musicians' Union boycotted the event because their rules prevented them playing for free. He concluded his attack on the union by noting:

> [this] is just a glimpse of the history of the organization that has now come so particularly to the front and demands that the Confederate Reunion be placed on the unfair list; that it be boycotted and blacklisted; that all union labor be pulled away from it and not allowed to assist in its enterprise, even though paid their wages demanded.[89]

Certainly, this writer condemned the idea that the reunion might suffer because of labor activism. He asked, "[is] it not a blot on our community that good, fair-minded and patriotic laboringmen and their organizations should suffer for the actions of one union?"[90] To support the Confederate veterans, the devotee emphasized the potential benefits for the city and its reputation in his argument that the Musicians' Union should set aside its rules and stop threatening to destroy the reunion. Amid the general disapproval of the labor movement, the Black musicians would have been especially unwelcome at the parade given the prevalent condemnation of biracialism in the labor movement.

New Orleans's labor leaders supported Black participation at the reunion by focusing on the benefits of unions to the city's reputation. In an initial defense of the union's position, Recording Secretary of Local 174 Frank Sporer explained to *Daily Picayune* that the union benefited the art of music and the culture of the city. He asked, "[would] it not be better to assist in elevating the art, than to crush it?—which surely tends to weaken the reputation which New Orleans claims as a musical center." He described the Musicians' Union as a movement to "sustain the quality and grade of music which is expected to be found in a city enjoying such a reputation as New Orleans for its love of good music."[91] Labor leaders viewed their organizations as beneficial to the community, and they used that premise to defend their rights to organize.

Outside of New Orleans, the editors of the *Washington Post* weighed in on the debate between the Confederate veterans and the Musicians' Union on the side of labor by stressing the need for Black laborers to have union protection. They explained, in "this controversy we think the Trades Council has the best of it. The negro musicians belong to the union, they pay their dues, and they are entitled to protection." They explained that the Black musicians have an equal right to the revenue and recognition of their talents.[92] By taking this stance, the editors of the *Post* advocated a future of biracial labor cooperation. From the perspective of labor leaders and supporters, the Black and white musicians had the right to organize and negotiate the terms of their contracts, and they did have to accept work on any conditions at any time. They also viewed the UCV reunion as a job, whereas the Reunion Committee members perceived the reunion as a social, public event. Although the Black musicians would perform a service that their enslaved ancestors had done, the postbellum generation of Black musicians and their supporters expected respect and recognition of their professional status.

African Americans across the country heard about the struggle between the musicians and the UCV through newspapers and expressed their support for the musicians. The editors of the Indianapolis *Freeman* reported that the "quarrel has assumed wide proportions, and so far the colored men seem to have the best of the situation if newspaper talk counts for anything." The editors proceeded to publish excerpts from two editorials in outside newspapers, the *Washington Post* and the *Richmond News-Leader*, and offered their own perspective on the dispute and its coverage in these widely distributed papers. They wrote that the "colored brother, however, is getting consideration and from excellent sources." They admitted that the Black musicians might not achieve their goals in this instance, "but he will lose nothing by the controversy." According to the editors, "the admirable stand taken by those sheets that are not particularly in love with colored folk is but another indication of an effort to get on—to have the races to get on with the least friction possible."[93] When the editors of the *Colored American* came across the story, they reported that the "ex-Confederates threw up their hands in holy horror and in indignant protest" and then praised the Trades Council for their support of the Black musicians. "While we are lamenting our wrongs in the South," concluded the editors, "it is well to point out an occasional ray of light."[94] From the perspective of Black newspaper editors, the controversy highlighted an effort by many white southerners to put racial issues behind them and move forward. In the story of the Black musicians and the UCV, Black newspaper editors found an opportunity to advocate their own vision for a future with racial equality and labor rights.

On April 13, Local 174 president De Droit went to the local union paper to present his argument on behalf of the musicians by focusing on the city's reputation for musical abilities. "The excellent music furnished by the union bands of New Orleans have been, on a number of occasions, a subject of comment, not only by residents . . . but by those visiting here from other sections of the Union," he explained in the *Union Advocate*. He compared the present circumstances to a previous Mardi Gras involving nonunion bands. He characterized that parade as "badly marred by the hideous noises made by a lot of Hayseeds and 'scabs'" and hoped that the UCV would accept union music and avoid a repeat of that apparent disaster. "It seems almost incredulous," he added, "that after that bitter and somewhat expensive experience that the committee on music of the Confederate veterans could not have adjusted the difficulty in a manner satisfactory to all concerned." He concluded his statement by appealing again to the city's pride in its music. He stated, "There are many reasons why home talent should be employed on occasions of this kind, and for the reputation of the city and its people, who are lovers of harmony, it is to be hoped that in the future it will be employed."[95]

On April 20, Sporer also came to the defense of his union's position and the Black musicians with a statement. He outlined the importance of labor unions to the musicians. He explained, "if the musicians of this city would fail to maintain this organization that he would advise that they break up their instruments and give up the business, as they would certainly starve." Sporer detailed a list of the benefits of the Musicians Union. He wrote, "I will mention: 1st, better music; 2nd, cheaper music; 3rd, the good will of the labor classes."[96] In addition to this list of general principles, he turned his attention to the present conflict with the UCV's music committee. He condemned them for passing a resolution that the musicians "accept unconditionally all such work as the committee chose in their supremeness to allot" and "that no discrimination be allowed" between union and nonunion music. With regard to the Confederate veterans he explained: "we do not consider that we are against them, but we claim to be against their Music Committee and their Advisory Manager. I should not mention the Music Committee, but should say their 'Dictator,' for it is he who signs all contracts for music for the Reunion."[97] Apparently, the Musicians' Union had a long history of trouble with a member of the music committee.

During a previous Carnival season, J. C. Febiger worked as the manager of the Rex Association, which still annually stages one of the most celebrated and elaborate parades of the season. He refused to employ the bands of the Musicians' Union unless they accepted "his proposition to do the work according to his views." When the union refused to yield, Febiger hired nonunion music for their famous parade. "The bad music, and the comments of the public on the same, at the different Carnival events, are history," sneered Sporer. To arrange music for the UCV parade, the music committee looked for expert advice because their committee consisted of volunteer veterans. According to Sporer, these volunteers "knew nothing of the work to which they are assigned." The committee hired Febiger, who Sporer jeered as "a noted Carpetbagger." From this position, Febiger resolved that each committee should maintain exclusive power over its own affairs, which meant that he had unilateral control over the hiring of musicians. With regard to the Black musicians, Sporer explained that the advisory manager locked them out of the reunion as "punishment inflicted on the Black man for refusing to aid . . . his schemes against our union."[98] In a hostile climate for biracial unionism, it seems that the personal vendetta of an anti-labor manager may have kept the Black musicians out of the reunion parade.

At the end of April 1903, the Musicians' Union withdrew its motion to add the UCV to the unfair to labor list, but they still did not participate. According to a reporter, the threat of boycott raised "a storm of indignation."[99] On April 23, 1903, the Musicians' Union voted to withdraw their request because "the musicians were friends of the old veterans and did not wish to hamper them in any way, and would waive all feeling in the matter in an effort to make the reunion as grand an affair as possible." Despite withdrawing their demand, they explained that the musicians "still felt that its position was right, from a standpoint of principle." They admitted, the "reunion was something in which everyone should feel a personal pride in making great." Although the Musicians' Union withdrew their request to add the UCV to the unfair to labor list, they refused to participate, which earned praise from the national office of the AFM.[100]

Although they withdrew their motion, they took pride in seeing the Confederate veterans struggle with nonunion bands but worried about the success of the reunion. A reporter working on behalf of the Trades Council wrote, the veterans "are so flush that they are willing to pay twice as much for unfair music as it would have cost them for first-class union music. It is hard to understand how a committee willing to treat organized labor in this manner should expect anything but expressions of loathing and disgust from that large class of our very best citizens." The leaders of Local 174 declared their intention to "furnish no music under any circumstances or for any price, preferring to leave the odium of employing scab labor entirely with the Committee and their adviser."[101] With the threat of the boycott eliminated, the reunion committee could complete its work over the following three weeks.

THE NEW ORLEANS REUNION

With this trouble out of the way, the reunion organizers still had much to accomplish, so the reunion organizers and newspaper editors appealed to sectional and local pride to help their cause in making the reunion a success. First and foremost, the reunion committee needed to raise funds. By April 18, the Reunion Committee reported that they had $23,000, which totaled only one-third of their goal. They called upon the railroad, hotel, and restaurant industries to contribute more money to the cause because the reunion enables them "to make a great deal of money."[102] They emphasized that New Orleans had put its reputation on the line to hold this reunion, and it required private citizens to help make it a success. They asked, "Is the faith of the South justified?" and "Can New Orleans afford to have a failure?" They pitted the city in a competition with the previous reunion held in Memphis, which raised $82,938 for their reunion. They asked, "How much more patriotic is New Orleans?"[103] In April the Committee on Parade and Review asked residents to donate saddle horses for the cause. They called upon citizens to help them make the reunion a success because they hoped to make it "a most notable event in the history of this metropolis of the South."[104] With these arguments, reunion organizers hoped to acquire the funds and help they needed.

New Orleans residents answered the call and gave their time, money, and possessions because it allowed them to participate in the reunion in a variety of ways. In response to the call for aid, eight New Orleans residents sent a letter to the reunion committee expressing their willingness to help "in any capacity." They explained, "It has occurred to us that you might need young men, who are familiar with the city, to give information and to assist in any other manner in providing for the convention of visitors during that time." If selected, they promised to provide teams of young men to help guide the city's guests.[105]

Across the country, northerners and southerners contributed to the reunion and expressed feelings of reconciliation. From New York, Confederate veteran H. O. Seixas sent $100 to the reunion committee because, "I hope through the efforts of all my comrades in New Orleans, that they may be able to entertain the veterans in a becoming way." New Orleans resident O. W. Chamberlain made a small donation, but he felt "as great an interest in the cause of the Reunion as others whose contributions are large." Born in Pennsylvania, Chamberlain's relatives fought for the Union army, but he explained, "I have lived in this delightful city for a number of years and have received such cordial friendship that my allegiance is wholly and unreservedly to the city of my adoption." He continued, "I sincerely trust that our people, so well known for hospitality, will not fail to meet the obligation which rests upon them: certainly no band of men deserve greater honors or better tribute than the Confederate soldier." He encouraged his fellow residents to contribute because the city "cannot afford to do less than other cities for their entertainment, and it should be the pride of every citizen of New Orleans to do more."[106] New Orleans residents and Confederate veterans recognized the need to make the reunion a success, and they contributed in large and small ways to the cause.

On May 17 and 18, New Orleans residents made their final preparations to welcome the Confederate veterans, which seemingly put everyone in New Orleans to work. "There is a spirit akin to that of the Carnival abroad. Everywhere in New Orleans that feeling of expectancy so familiarly associated with the approach of great public events permeates the populace," described a reporter from the *Sunday States*. The reporter continued, "If anything, the spirit of the people is more intense than it has ever been on any occasion."[107] Across the South railroad operators arranged for special trains to New Orleans to allow all veterans to make the journey. Based on the demand for tickets to New Orleans, these managers estimated that between 150,000 and 250,000 people would attend the reunion. "These are big figures and have appalled New Orleans and the reunion committee," explained reporter Norman Walker to the *Atlanta Constitution*. Walker praised the city of New Orleans for its "reputation of handling them well," but argued that the city had seldom had more than 90,000 visitors for any one occasion. To transport the veterans within the city, the New Orleans streetcar company arranged to have its 300 cars in operation, and its spokesperson claimed that they could handle 60,000 people an hour on these cars. To accommodate the veterans, the reunion committee kept a ledger of all available hotel rooms and arranged for private families to lodge veterans for the reunion. The reunion committee provided Confederate veterans that wanted "a touch of the army life again" with tents and bedding to sleep at the fairgrounds. To entertain the veterans, New Orleans civic leaders constructed a new auditorium that seated more than 10,000 people at the Crescent City Jockey Club fairgrounds, which served as the site of the reunion. "There could be no better place for the gathering," commented Walker.[108] In advance of the reunion, it seems that everyone in New Orleans had a role to play in making the reunion a success.

The reunion's organizers and civic leaders called upon every member of the community to show their pride for the former Confederacy. In the *Sunday States*, the editors expressed their utmost respect and "admiration for the men New Orleans is about to entertain." They explained that the reunion brought "to the surface in every true Southerner a feeling of splendid brotherhood for the old vets" because they represented the "remnants of that greatest of armies which fought for the cause which though lost, was none the less honorable."[109] In the daily paper, the editors called upon every male and female citizen of New Orleans to wear Confederate buttons "to show homage to the distinguished visitors within our gates this week." They encouraged everyone to decorate their homes and businesses with flags and memorabilia, "which will add much to the attractiveness" of the city and "cannot fail to

During the 1903 UCV Reunion, people flocked to see the Confederate veterans parade through New Orleans, which was decorated to celebrate the occasion. Alexander Allison Photograph Collection, Louisiana Division/City Archives, New Orleans Public Library.

make a pleasing impression on the veterans."[110] It was important to please the veterans because of the potential boom in business related to the reunion.

From the beginning of the planning process, the city's business interests had made a successful reunion a priority. "On sentimental grounds, the coming Reunion should be made one which visitors will never forget," explained the *Daily Picayune* editors. "On the argument of business interest," they continued, "it is even more important that everybody should go away praising the great port and its advantages."[111] New Orleans already had a fantastic reputation as a tourist destination because of Mardi Gras, but the *Daily States* editors argued that "the present reunion will result in more substantial good to New Orleans than a dozen Mardi Gras carnivals." They expected much larger crowds and explained that the reunion would attract visitors that would otherwise have no interest in coming to the city.[112]

On the night of Monday, May 18, the reunion unofficially opened with a large parade that reportedly featured Black men marching behind Confederate veterans. When seventy-five veterans from Tennessee arrived in New Orleans, they paraded through the streets before taking the streetcars to the fairgrounds. At the rear of the parade, "a number of aged negroes, old-time darkeys" followed the veterans. According to a *Daily States* reporter, these Black men plodded along like "faithful old souls" and paid no attention to the insults hurled at them by "the younger elements" of their race. The older Black men reportedly referred to these young Black men as "young trash" and kept in step with the former soldiers "with proud demeanor." By idealizing the older Black men, the newspaper reporter helped strengthen the white supremacist worldview that only younger Black southerners, who had not been through slavery, caused trouble between the races. Whether the Black men had marched or not, the story helped kick off the reunion, which would idealize the Old South and the relationship between masters and their slaves.

On Tuesday, May 19, the reunion commenced with a formal program to honor Confederate heroes and to welcome the veterans. Amid the joy of the occasion, the veterans gathered at 10:00 a.m. and held a morning memorial service for Jefferson Davis at Christ Church. At noon, General J. B. Levert of the Louisiana division of the UCV called the convention to order. Rev. J. William Jones, who served as chaplain general of the UCV, opened the convention with a prayer. Following the prayer, local executive committee chairman E. B. Kruttschnitt welcomed the veterans and their friends and family.

After this address, General John B. Gordon gave a short presentation. He hobbled across the stage with the help of Adjutant General William E. Mickle. As soon as Gordon sat down, "a fair young woman . . . approached and, bending down, kissed the general," which quickly reenergized him. After thanking the veterans, he turned the platform over local politicians, notably Louisiana Governor W. W. Heard, who gave the out-of-state veterans and their friends a formal welcome to the reunion.[113] After his speech, the reunion adjourned for a few hours.

In the afternoon of the opening day, Judge J. H. Rogers, a Confederate veteran and congressman from Arkansas, gave his keynote address. He explained that the veterans had gathered in New Orleans to honor their deceased comrades, show gratitude to the women of the Confederacy, and to "renew old friendships, forged in the white heat of common sufferings." These friendships, he explained, were "hallowed and sanctified by the conscious conviction that in the hour of trial and peril we were true to the Constitution as it was framed and handed down to us by Washington and his compatriots."

After listing these purposes of the reunion, Rogers proceeded to explain the process of secession and Confederacy's cause. He distinguished between the ideas of secession and rebellion by noting that the "South made no war on the States remaining in the Union" and that secession "meant disunion so far as the seceding States were concerned, but it meant neither war nor rebellion." He assured his fellow veterans that the "whole history of secession shows conclusively that in seceding the South had no intention of assailing their former confederates." He buttressed his argument with quotations from politicians, Supreme Court rulings, and examples of legislation passed by Congress. He emphasized the importance of the history lesson for future generations because their "children should know that the Confederate States, by the act of secession, made not war on the United States; that the war between the States was not rebellion."[114] In the keynote address, Rogers absolved the South of blame for the war and diverted it to the North.

During his speech, Rogers also tried to downplay slavery as the major cause of the war. Rogers repeated the familiar argument that thousands "and thousands of soldiers from every State in the South, perhaps not less than eighty percent of them, entered the army willingly and deliberately, and served through the war, who never owned and never expected to own a slave." While he admits that slavery had some influence on the southern states' willingness to secede, he argued that slavery represented a "bane of our social order" and a "chronic cancer which gnawed at the vitals" of the South's potential for future greatness. In the end, he praised God for the destruction of slavery and for reunification under a single flag.[115] In the address, Rogers attempted to separate slavery from the causes of the war and hailed the benefits of reunification, all of which epitomized the Lost Cause.

In New Orleans, the reunion inspired feelings of sectional pride and nostalgia for the Old South among the city's white residents, who expressed resentment toward northerners and the postbellum social and political order. The editors of the *Daily States* took the opportunity to rant about life in the post-emancipation South by expressing similar themes as Rogers but with harsher criticism for northern politicians and the federal government. The editors argued that the northern states made war upon the South to punish them. "With this purpose in view," they continued, "the emancipated slave was enfranchised, his former master disfranchised, and the reins of power were placed in the hands of the negro." [116] The spirit of the reunion overflowed beyond the boundaries of the reunion and gave commentators an opportunity to vent their frustrations. Given the chance, they continued to portray Reconstruction and the post-emancipation social order as the true crime, not slavery.

During the reunion, the delegates and their supporters worked on a series of committees to accomplish goals relevant to the veterans, including an attempt to write their own brand of history. On the first day of the reunion, these delegates went to their committee meetings and attended to the "routine business" of the convention while the rest of the veterans and their entourages had free time to visit the city's sights. General Stephen D. Lee served as the chairman of the historical committee, which oversaw the

UCV's attempts to "teach young men and women the true history of the Civil War and of the war itself" and "instill into the minds of the young in the South the truth of the conflict." Similarly, the Confederate Memorial Association, which consisted of women, met at the same time as the UCV. Led by President Kate Walker Behan, these women hosted the annual memorial service for the long-departed Jefferson Davis and spearheaded many of the memorial efforts for Confederate leaders and soldiers across the South.[117]

On the final day of the convention, the veterans took care of numerous business items to help strengthen the organization's message and help it prosper in the future. First, they unanimously reelected Gordon as commander-in-chief of the UCV and similarly reelected other department commanders. During the rest of the meeting, the veterans considered and resolved a series of motions. General Joseph Wheeler urged the delegates to provide help to elderly soldiers. General A. P. Stewart presented a report on the project to build a monument to southern women, which Gordon heartily supported. Focusing on his own mortality, Gordon explained, "Boys, I am willing to spend and be spent in your service," but "you boys must not die until you have built that monument to Southern women." He concluded, "Build it, white and pure, and let it tower to show what the men of the South think of the women." Similarly, Judge George L. Christian presented his report on the efforts to erect a monument to Jefferson Davis. In addition to these measures, the UCV took steps to perpetuate their organization from beyond the grave. General I. C. Walker worked to help strengthen the official relationship between the veterans and the Sons of Confederate Veterans. They agreed to give sons full privilege of the floor at reunions and conventions, but they did not give them the right to vote. The sons could wear grey uniforms in veterans' parades, but they could not wear military insignia and possess military rank.[118] Although the reunion's delegates had official business, they spent most of their time socializing with old comrades.

During the day, the delegates participated in business meetings, but they had their evenings free for spectacular social events that helped celebrate the Old South, especially its white women, and promote the Lost Cause. During the reunion, veterans and their entourages attended balls every night. On Thursday, May 21, the veterans went to the new auditorium for the grand ball. When the event commenced, sixteen "grizzled veterans" danced a quadrille with sixteen young white women, referred to as heralds, adorned in Confederate symbols. They danced to famous southern tunes, such as "Dixie" and "The Bonnie Blue Flag." Upon conclusion of this portion of the program, the veterans paraded behind the Memphis Bugle Corps in a grand march. By 11:00 p.m., the crowd of ten thousand veterans and guests commenced the dancing, which included up to a thousand people on the dance floor at a given time and lasted deep into Friday morning.[119] At night, many veterans camped at the fairgrounds, which became a sentimental sight for many of the younger visitors to the reunion. Every night, the veterans "gathered there as around the camp fires of the sixties" and bonded with one another and with their children and supporters. At these types of balls, Black musicians would have likely been a welcome presence, if not for the anti-labor stance of the music committee.[120]

During the reunion, the veterans and visiting southerners expressed pride in the South and its people to such an extent that symbols of the Union and federal government earned scorn and condemnation. Veterans and other visitors spread rumors that General Joseph Wheeler appeared at the reunion hall in the uniform of brigadier general of the United States Army. By showing up in a blue uniform, his reputation suffered and, according to veterans, most people treated General Wheeler as an enemy. When he rode in the carriage in the parade, he received no special attention or honor, which had been usual for him at previous parades. In fact, one Confederate veteran asked, "What do you think Lee and Jackson would say to your appearance at a Confederate reunion in that uniform?" The rumors spread that an embarrassed Wheeler spent most of the reunion locked in his room and left town as soon as the parade finished. When confronted, he explained that he wore his Spanish-American War uniform to show his old comrades that sectionalism had ended, but it clearly had not. Instead, the veterans resented the fact that Wheeler had worn the uniform of "the armies which the veterans of the South fought for four years."[121] In 1903 the reunion had reinvigorated intense passion and regional pride.[122]

In addition to the formal elements of the reunion, private entrepreneurs catered to veterans by offering entertainment options that appealed to the militaristic spirit and sectional sentimentalism. In New Orleans's West End, conductor Armand Veazey's military band entered "into the spirit of the reunion with great vigor" and played "music that smacks of war at every concert" at a local theater. For the entire reunion, they chose a series of songs "dear to the heart of every southerner."[123] Veazey, a notable musician in New Orleans, had traveled all the way to Chicago to assemble artists for his band. Although he belonged to Local 174 and did not seem to participate in the official work of the reunion, he still lent his military band to their cause.[124] At the Grand Opera House, singer Ada Hollingsworth-Watkins, a soprano from Louisiana who relocated to New York, presented her program "Three Centuries of American Ballads," which consisted of songs from colonial, antebellum, and Gilded Age America and earned rave reviews across the

In Louisiana and neighboring states, schools closed so young children could make the journey to New Orleans to see the Confederate veterans march in the parade. Alexander Allison Photograph Collection, Louisiana Division/City Archives, New Orleans Public Library.

country. According to New Orleans papers, "She possesses a splendid soprano . . . and sings the old ballads with particular charm."[125]

In the sweltering late afternoon of Friday, May 22, the UCV reunion concluded with a massive parade that awed people across the South. The parade, which started on Canal Street and moved south on St. Charles Ave, twice passed the Robert E. Lee Monument and lasted for four hours. In this parade, 10,000 men and women marched in a line that stretched more than four miles. In an editorial, *Daily Picayune* editors characterized the parade as "a remarkable spectacle presented to the world in the streets."[126] General J. B. Levert, who served as chief marshal, led the parade surrounded by his staff "beautifully mounted and presenting a brave appearance in gray and gold." Behind them, the Memphis Bugle Corps led Company A of the UCV, which consisted of Louisiana veterans, and both the musicians and veterans earned "great applause" for their "splendid marching." Then, a "beautifully decorated float" float made its way through the streets with sixteen seated female heralds representing the former Confederate states and Missouri, Kentucky, and the Indian Territory. "The young ladies, all in white," presented a "beautiful picture, surrounded by the gray decorations of their float." They earned an applause that had no equal save for the old veterans. Next, leaders of the Confederacy made their way through the parade route in carriages. Generals

While most of the veterans marched on foot, some soldiers, including this former cavalry officer, rode horses through the parade route. Alexander Allison Photograph Collection, Louisiana Division/City Archives, New Orleans Public Library.

A. P. Stewart and Joseph Wheeler rode alongside the widows of Thomas "Stonewall" Jackson, Braxton Bragg, and other Confederate generals.[127]

Finally, the veterans paraded through the streets followed by the Sons of Veterans and female members of other memorial and patriotic societies. They received a deafening applause throughout the parade route. Spectators honored these veterans, who had earned "first place in the hearts of the Southern people." As they marched, young women broke "into the lines to hand them flowers, to clasp them round the neck, to kiss their wrinkled faces."[128]

Numerous people described the parade as a remarkable and sentimental experience. A reporter from the *Daily Picayune* who observed the parade claimed: "old soldiers, inspirited by their great numbers, the fine weather, and the enthusiasm of the admiring spectators, marched with a precision and whim that would have done credit to young men." He concluded his observations by characterizing the parade as "one of the most memorable" events that the city had ever staged.[129] A female observer recalled, "when the parade was almost over, I ran up to my room, which overlooked the street, and it seemed, as I stood there and looked over the vast throng of people, that the whole world was suspended beneath my window, and every person was cheering."[130] To the massive audience, the parade certainly inspired awe, but it also inspired sectional sentiment, nostalgia, and political commentary.

Some veterans could not march anymore, so they rode in carriages along the parade route. Alexander Allison Photograph Collection, Louisiana Division/City Archives, New Orleans Public Library.

In their descriptions of the parade, many southerners boasted their pride in the South and the former Confederacy with militaristic spirit. During the parade, commented a reporter from Shreveport's the *Caucasian*, New Orleans "held close to her heart the incarnate spirit of the Confederacy, and for her it lived and breathed again." In the sectional gush, southerners emphasized a love for the flag of the Confederacy, the "white-starred cross of blue on the crimson field" that represented "the cause for which the heroes fought, and by whose blood it was purged and sanctified."[131] In addition to the emphasis on the flag, many observers portrayed the atmosphere around the parade as militaristic. To start the parade, "a bugle's shrill notes sounded 'forward march'" and the ranks moved forward. During the parade, "the martial airs of forty years ago born[e] upon the breeze" as "men of war" marched through the streets. The music, uniforms, banners, and "other warlike accompaniments" inspired "old-wartime memories" among the veterans. The spectators expressed heartfelt satisfaction when they heard the "rebel yell," which one observer characterized as "that southern cadence of the fighting cry of the fighting Anglo-Saxon race."[132]

In addition to pride in their former country, the parade's participants and spectators celebrated whiteness. Most notably, sixteen white female heralds near the head of the march "dressed entirely in white" rode aboard a float.

The unionized Black musicians of New Orleans attempted to secure their economic right to play for the UCV reunion, but the UCV reunion committee refused to employ Black musicians for the parade. Alexander Allison Photograph Collection, Louisiana Division/City Archives, New Orleans Public Library.

These women were "drawn from among the prettiest women in a land where all women are beautiful" and provided a stark contrast "with fresh vitality and youthful charm" to the masses of "withered yet staunch old men who had faced death in so many battles."[133] For the first time, the Confederate reunion featured these white women in the role of heralds. They had an honorable position at the head of the parade, and it seems unlikely that they would have taken this position had the music committee permitted Black bands to play in the parade.

In the wake of the parade, white southerners reflected on the parade's political significance for the South and the nation. The *Daily Picayune* editors defended the southerners' eternal right to "maintain their constitutional rights against outrageous aggression and invasion." They defended the constitutionality of secession and the honor of the soldiers fighting for the Confederacy. They contradicted the notion that southerners had changed since the war. Instead, they explained, "The country is the same that it always was, and the people are the same, only the institutions are changed." They condemned the term New South because it portrayed the Old South as "formerly inhabited by a nonprogressive race of slaveholders, who were always unfriendly to the Union." They argued that the older generation had fought against a superior foe to defend their rights, and the younger generation, with the same principles and fortitude, had worked hard to restore the South to prosperity and wealth after its destruction. "There was something truly inspiring to see the old and grizzled men who had fought a hundred battles, marching behind the fresh-faced youths who composed the escort of honor to the Confederate Veterans yesterday," they explained. By walking together, these two generations invalidated the concept of the New South. The editors argued that the younger generation of southerners shared the same values of older generations. They continued, "The spectacle was a declaration before the whole world that the sons and the fathers were united in the same principles as well concerning the past as the future."[134]

After the reunion concluded, veterans and other southerners characterized the event in New Orleans as one of the most memorable occasions in the history of the South. In the *Nashville American*, a reporter explained that the parade had concluded the "greatest reunion of Confederate soldiers held since the close of the civil war" and other papers repeated a similar sentiment.[135] By all accounts, New Orleans had met the daunting task and provided an outstanding experience to everyone who attended. According to a *Colfax* [Louisiana] *Chronicle* reporter, New Orleans put its famous "famous hospitality" on display for the thousands of veterans that gathered there. He praised "the ability of the city of New Orleans to furnish amusement for vast numbers" of people and highlighted the efforts of the streetcar workers, police force, hotel and restaurant managers, department store clerks, and street vendors. "They all seem to have mastered the knack of getting along with a big crowd," concluded the reporter.[136] In fact, some veterans started a movement to make New Orleans the permanent home of the reunion.[137]

For some southerners, the reunion achieved success precisely because it emphasized a regionally satisfying interpretation of the Civil War. By 1903 it seems that the history of the Civil War had become a primary concern among many southerners. In a column for the *Confederate Veteran*, Bettina Ruth Bush reminisced about the reunion. In it, she explained that the "most rousing and enthusiastic part of every speech" were the comments made about "the untrue histories of the Civil War that the young and rising generation now study."[138] According to many sources, the New Orleans reunion did much to calm their anxiety over being history's villains. According to the *Caucasian* editors of Shreveport, Louisiana, this reunion "was the greatest and most successful in the record of the organization" and "fairly eclipsed the reunion demonstrations in other cities." Not intending to insult previous reunions held in other cities, the editors explained that this reunion disseminated "to the world historical facts which are of priceless value as a legacy of loyalty and fealty to the sons and the daughters" of the veterans.

They praised the business work of the veterans and the social aspects of the reunion, but they emphasized the value of the reunion for vindicating "the stigma of Rebel and Rebellion which has been ascribed to them and with which they would be branded forever by the North." Specifically, they highlighted the keynote address from Rogers, who presented these so-called facts with "forceful awakening."[139] More than fifty years after the conclusion of the war, northerners and southerners continued to fight over its causes and its meaning because these memories had implications for contemporary politics and the labor movement.

At the 1903 UCV reunion, veterans, sons, daughters, and other southerners celebrated the Old South, the Lost Cause, and whiteness. To these ends, white southerners spread images of faithful slaves and emphasized the harmonious relationships of masters and slaves in an imagined and romanticized past. Despite these circumstances, Black musicians in New Orleans threatened to put a stop to the entire reunion unless they had the right to play in it. The city's white musicians, furthermore, stood by their side and refused to prioritize sentimentalism for the veterans over their modern-day labor interests, which relied on cooperation with their Black colleagues.

In the debates over the reunion music, Black and white southerners revealed key insights into what it meant for African Americans to have a presence at seemingly white-only spectacles. Both Black and white southerners relied on the control of historical memory to realize their contemporary political and economic goals. Confederate veterans simultaneously refused Black musicians the right to play and denied the political significance of their presence at their reunion, yet they characterized Black music as a vestige of the Old South, where enslaved people willingly made music for their white masters. Black musicians, however, fought for professional recognition in the present, which threatened the stereotype of the naturally gifted, feckless Black performer. Although white southerners romanticized the enslaved Black musician, who made music willingly for the master, they balked at the new generation of professional talent, who insisted on setting terms of employment and compensation. Unlike their enslaved ancestors, this generation of Black musicians had the power to choose when, where, and for whom to play. When Black performers showed up at the spectacles staged on behalf of the major political parties, third parties, and reform movements, Black and white spectators interpreted the spectacle through the same lens. As disfranchisement became the law of the land in the former Confederate states, African Americans manipulated southern nostalgia for Old South performers to access political spaces.

CHAPTER 3

"FURIOUS MUSIC"

African Americans, Political Spectacles, and Street Theater in the Post-Disfranchisement South, 1909–32

JOSEPH C. WYSOR, A DEMOCRAT FROM PULASKI COUNTY, SPENT A CONSIDERable part of his career working to disfranchise Black Virginians. Wysor's regional rival, Republican A. P. Gillespie from Tazewell County, also supported the elimination of the Black vote. In May 1900, Virginians narrowly approved a referendum calling for election reform, and Wysor and Gillespie both served on the committee challenged with devising the new laws. Among many proposals, Wysor suggested a plan using the literacy test and poll tax to disfranchise voters. To register, voters would have to read a selection from the Constitution, write their own names, and pay a $1.50 poll tax. The committee debated and negotiated for years.

By March 1904, the Democrats, including Wysor, found common ground on a plan including an understanding clause. The Republicans, led by Gillespie, objected to it because they believed Democrats would manipulate the understanding clause for fraudulent purposes. Despite these objections from Republicans, the committee finally approved a combination of poll taxes, residency requirements, and literacy tests. As a result, Virginians passed the most regressive voting reform in the country.[1] The laws did not, however, completely deny African Americans their political voice.

On the morning of August 22, 1904, Republicans staged a campaign rally for their candidates to represent Virginia's Ninth District in Congress. They started their meeting at 11:30 a.m. and, according to the local Republican press, attracted one of the "largest and most representative gatherings of the stalwart citizens of Tazewell" ever assembled in the county. For two hours, they listened to Republicans discuss the campaign's major issues. The Republicans hired a Black band from the nearby town of Pocahontas.[2] In Richmond's the *Times-Dispatch*, a Democratic newspaper, a Tazewell correspondent commented that a "notable feature of the Republican speaking was the absence of the ladies and a large attendance of negroes."[3] With this statement, the Democrat hoped to link the Republicans with African Americans and position his own party as the preferred party of white women.

After the Republican meeting in Tazewell, the Democrats took control of the courthouse for their own campaign rally featuring Wysor and other Democrats. According to a reporter to Richmond's the *Times Dispatch*, the Democrats "had possibly the largest crowd that ever attended a public speaking in Tazewell." In the press, the Democrats contrasted their meeting with the Republican event by portraying their massive audience as consisting of "the leading ladies and gentlemen" of the county.

Although the Republican meeting had concluded, the Black musicians remained in attendance in a demonstration of rough music. During the Democrats' meeting, the musicians "acted in a most disrespectful manner" and rendered "the air with discords" to prevent people from hearing the speeches.[4] At some point during Wysor's speech, the Black musicians had made their point and exited the courthouse. As he greeted a crowd of white women entering the courthouse, he remarked, "As the negro band goes out, let the ladies come forward." With these comments directed toward the Black musicians, he recognized the band's political power because it had successfully disrupted his speech, but he also segregated the courthouse and political sphere. He hoped to divide the political parties based on race and gender. Republicans did not let Democrats off the hook for these race-based tactics.

Republicans defended the participation of African Americans and criticized Democrats for constantly focusing on racial issues. In response to Wysor's comments directed toward the Black musicians, Tazewell's Republicans launched attacks on the Democratic candidate. The editors of the *Tazewell Republican* pointed out that the Democrats, specifically Wysor, had employed the exact same band for his gathering in the town of Pocahontas. The Republican editors remarked that "but for their music," he "would not have secured the small audience he did get." They deplored the hypocrisy and characterized him as a "cheap demagogue" who used "the negro for both offensive and defensive purposes" and would certainly "try to hold a 'nigger' between him and the fire" upon reaching the "Democratic hades." They criticized his statesmanship as "negrophobia" and characterized his racial tactics as "old, stale and played out."[5] By 1904 Democrats had used these race-based methods and disfranchisement laws to dominate politics in the South, including Virginia.

DISFRANCHISEMENT AND VOTER TURNOUT IN THE EARLY TWENTIETH CENTURY

In both the North and the South, many political leaders advocated changes in political style meant to keep the masses, regardless of race, away from the polls. In the 1870s, middle-class liberal reformers commenced a campaign against spectacular politics because they favored an elitist, educated political style that condemned universal manhood suffrage, unwavering party loyalties, and impassioned spectacular politics, but the movement took a long time to bear fruit because Americans continued voting in record numbers until the end of the century.

Reformers hoped to eradicate real and perceived corruption, so they attacked the principle that every man should have the right to vote. In the North, reformers adopted subtle methods to restrict the right to vote, such as immigration restrictions, secret ballots, and tighter registration requirements. They hoped to eliminate machine politics and vote-buying, which had been hallmarks of democracy for more than a century. In the South, reformers took the direct approach of disfranchising Black citizens with poll taxes, literacy tests, and other methods.[6]

After the end of Reconstruction in 1877, white southerners, who had already started to retake control of many southern state legislatures, completed the process they referred to as "Redemption" by returning to power in all of the former Confederate states. They chose the term because to them it portrayed Reconstruction as the true political evil, not the war or slavery. With the Civil War a recent memory, Democrats had regained power over the South, but they did not view their work as complete until they overturned the entire political order that emerged with emancipation and Confederate defeat. They could only truly return to an antebellum status quo by eliminating the right to vote for the people freed by the war.[7]

After Black men gained the right to vote, white southerners immediately went about manipulating Black voters through intimidation and fraud. They intimidated them at the polls to prevent them from voting, like in South Carolina, where a paramilitary organization known as the Red Shirts intended to help Democratic candidates, notably Wade Hampton III, by violent means if necessary. In Mississippi, white gun clubs drilled in the streets before election day to threaten Black and white Republican voters. Across the South, similar scenes played out in the days up to and including election day. In addition to these violent methods, white southern Democrats used fraudulent means. At the voting booths, election officials destroyed ballots cast by Black men, or they simply counted the vote for someone else. Democrats regained control of the South by invalidating Black votes, but they still had not eliminated Black men's right to vote.

By the end of the nineteenth century, six southern states had passed laws or constitutional amendments, such as poll taxes and literacy tests, to eliminate the right to vote for Black men. In 1888 Republican Benjamin Harrison won election to the presidency and took office with a Republican majority in both houses of Congress. Fearing the ascending power of Republicans on the national level, Democrats looked to consolidate control in the South. In the mid-1880s, Florida provided for a poll tax at their constitutional convention, but it did not go into effect until 1889, when the Florida state legislature finally passed election laws to enact it. In 1889 and 1890, Tennessee disfranchised Black men with poll taxes. In 1890 and 1892, Mississippi and Arkansas joined them with the passage of constitutional amendments. By the end of the 1890s, South Carolina and Louisiana had also taken steps to eliminate Black voting rights. In 1898 the United States Supreme Court permitted poll taxes and literacy tests, thus sanctioning the new political order.

By 1908 the remaining former Confederate states had passed similar laws or amendments. The Populists' insurgency in the last part of the century had stirred even reluctant Democrats to action on Black voting rights. From 1900 to 1902, North Carolina, Alabama, Texas, and Virginia passed disfranchisement measures, which left only Georgia of the former Confederate states. By 1908 Georgia had passed a constitutional amendment to further disfranchise Black voters.

Disfranchisement represented just one part, albeit an extremely powerful part, of the movement to restrict voting to the so-called better classes of people. Reformers also argued that responsible citizens did not have absolute party loyalties but sought information to reach independent conclusions. Americans no longer felt inspired to express themselves through popular demonstrations because of the emphasis on enlightened politics and disillusionment with partisanship. Without spectacles and guidance from the partisan press, which had started to give way to the independent press, less-educated voters did not invest their time or interest into issue-based political campaigns. People lost the enthusiasm for local politics. Through the independent press, journalists separated less educated people from politics with their fact-based, unbiased reporting. These journalists reported sensational news and features but relegated political news to smaller coverage. Democrats and Republicans had forsaken political spectacle in favor of intellectual methods, such as the dissemination of pamphlets and other educational materials. Partisan spirit and high voter turnout lingered but eventually faded.[8]

By the turn of the century northerners had become apathetic toward popular politics, which deviated from an overall trend toward spectacular displays in other aspects of life. During the 1890s, politicians could not compete with new forms of entertainment made possible by mass consumerism and new technology. In urban areas, Americans attended theatrical performances, viewed movies at the cinema, visited amusements parks such as Coney Island, and cheered on hometown teams at sporting venues.[9]

Americans incorporated these spectacles into their daily lives, but they turned their everyday realities into spectacles, too. Across the country, Americans dramatized race relations for mass consumption through stage productions, musical performances, and even lynching.[10] Spectacles became intertwined with many elements of urban twentieth-century life.[11]

Despite the movements to disfranchise Black voters and eliminate the role of popular spectacle in politics, African Americans continued to use the political spectacle, which remained prevalent in the South, as an opportunity to make a political statement. They continued to vote in municipal elections, which gave them more opportunity as white politicians courted and helped register blocs of Black voters while condemning one another for these methods. In the solidly Democratic South, African Americans creatively expressed their political views, and they played Democratic politicians against one another to find small measures of freedom and opportunity. With the entry of the United States into World War I, African Americans migrated out of the South, and they took their methods with them, thus keeping political spectacle alive in the North at time when it seemed a remnant of the past. Across the country, African Americans took advantage of opportunities created by the war to express their patriotism through spectacle.

THE PROHIBITION MOVEMENT, DISFRANCHISEMENT, AND POLITICAL SPECTACLE

In the nineteenth century, African Americans had played a major role in the South's prohibition referenda; both sides courted their votes, but prohibitionists eventually blamed African Americans for the inability to pass the measures. For two decades after emancipation, prohibition's supporters and opponents suspended centuries-old stereotypes linking African Americans, intemperance, and insurrection because they each wanted Black votes for their cause. When they did portray African Americans as intemperate, they emphasized the need for reform and hoped to bring Black supporters to the cause of temperance. By the dawn of the twentieth century, prohibitionists had brought back these stereotypes and pinpointed Black voters as the main reason for the failure of local-option campaigns.

Prohibitionists and anti-prohibitionists agreed that African Americans should not hold the outcome of these contests in their hands. Prohibitionists argued that African Americans had a biological inclination to drunkenness and that prohibition would save African Americans from animalistic behavior and help both races avoid racial conflict. Saloonkeepers, however, had enormous power in electoral affairs because they could mobilize voters, especially Black voters, through urban political machines. Anti-prohibitionists did not come to the defense of Black voters. By excluding Black voters, white southerners could safely split on issues, like prohibition, without fearing Black political power.[12]

Prohibitionists targeted African Americans as their greatest obstacle to success. "One of the chief causes of this great temperance movement is, as you might have guessed—the negro," stated a *New York Times* reporter in a feature article on reform in the South. Ferdinand Cowle Iglehart, who traveled the country speaking on behalf of temperance, argued: "There are reasons why the south should take the lead in this prohibition movement. It was necessary to remove the saloon from the negro to save southern industry and civilization."[13] According to a *New York Times* reporter, "It is when these [African Americans] drink of the vile, cheap whiskies that they are most liable to commit the crimes which the Southern white man avenges so swiftly and so terribly." Gilbert D. Raine, who edited the *Memphis News Scimitar*, characterized African Americans "as children in intellectual and moral development" and concluded that "easy access to intoxicants is dangerous to them and to their white neighbors." Alabama author Alfred B. Williams added, "The Blacks are great consumers of liquors of the cheaper grade, and, therefore, of the kind which does the greatest harm," and stated that "the negroes drink beyond their limit of the cheap, vile whiskies, and are then in the mood to commit the crimes for which they afterward suffer." Prohibitionists provided other reasons. According to one author, "The negro vote, outside of the preachers and teachers and a few others, could always be controlled by the saloon forces." Another author argued that "liquor tends to demoralize negro labor."[14] Although these racist condemnations rarely appear in the prohibition contests of the nineteenth century, they became prevalent in the early twentieth century, which coincided with disfranchisement laws and amendments.

As the prohibition movement stalled, prohibitionists became leading advocates for disfranchisement. In the late 1890s, Alabama prohibitionists supported disfranchisement for African Americans in their state because they could not pass any local-option prohibition laws. In 1901 white Alabamians disfranchised African Americans at their state constitutional convention. Afterward, Alabama's prohibitionists supported legislation to keep African Americans from consuming alcohol. During the 1905 gubernatorial election in Georgia, candidate Hoke Smith supported disfranchisement. According to Smith, Georgia's white residents suffered from Black voting and the power of the state's liquor interests. He explained that the liquor interests purchased Black votes with liquor. By eliminating both, he argued, Georgia's white population would prosper. In Tennessee, prohibitionists had also supported disfranchisement, and they successfully accomplished their prohibition goals after having previously eliminated the Black vote.[15] Across the South, prohibitionists had made it clear: they did not want African Americans to have any power to derail their movement.

In the early twentieth century, white southerners hindered, but did not eliminate, Black participation in some of the most important prohibition contests; white women continued to make an impact on these elections. Due to the connections between African Americans, disfranchisement, and prohibition, it became difficult for African Americans to participate in these spectacles.

In 1901 Alabamians held a spectacular statewide campaign to decide the prohibition question, which energized white male and female Alabamians but left out African Americans.[16] During the campaign, "the entire machinery of the Protestant churches, the women and children, and the strict moral argument were thrown into the fight on the pro-amendment side." In preparation, women and children rehearsed their prayers and hymns for the election-day spectacle.[17] On November 27, Calhoun County residents concluded "the most memorable campaign in the history of Alabama" with an all-day speaking program and free barbecue meal provided by the anti-prohibitionists. At the event, about twenty thousand county residents gathered "to voice their protest against placing in the power of an unwise legislature the right to invade their homes." The event included "ladies from the best families in the state," who tended to support prohibition but here participated on behalf of anti-prohibition. They had a reserved spot in the audience, where they listened to the speeches for three hours "without evidence of weariness."[18] On November 29, Montgomery residents flocked to a rally on behalf of prohibition. Before the program commenced, women and children marched through the city carrying banners and singing songs, and many men testified that they "could not vote against the amendment in the face of such a display."[19] By participating in these spectacles, women and children gained notoriety for their political strength and work and seemed to have a bit of influence. In Alabama, political spectacle remained an important feature of the campaign. Unlike previous prohibition campaigns, African Americans seemed absent in this election.

On election day, white Alabamians celebrated their unilateral control over politics and debated the utility of these popular demonstrations. "There was a time when elections in the south were farcical," explained the *Birmingham Age-Herald* editors, because "hordes of negroes were entitled to vote without any legal restriction." The editors celebrated, "Today we have practically only a white electorate." In fact, one reporter lamented that more fascinating campaigns had occurred during Reconstruction because "the newly enfranchised negro held the balance of power in politics." In addition to these electoral reforms, officials passed a series of measures to reduce spectacle. They restricted access to the polling stations by keeping people thirty feet away, permitting only ten people in the booth at a time, and forced people to leave after five minutes. They mandated that voters may only speak to election officials while near the booths.[20]

Despite these laws, white Alabamians continued to make politics into a spectacle, and these spectacles entailed frequent participation on behalf of disfranchised groups. Women and children, who got the day off from school, went to many of the polling places in the state and remained there all day. They performed many of the typical rituals, such as serving coffee and sandwiches, singing hymns, praying, and pinning ribbons onto voters' lapels. Like previous campaigns, brass bands arrived on the scene to support the anti-prohibitionists. The reporter did not identify these musicians as Black, which had been a notable feature of previous spectacles, in which Black men and white women fought each other over the future of alcohol. These musicians engaged the female singers in a competition, which became "heated and interesting" as the musicians played ragtime songs. According to one reporter, the musicians had an impact. The reporter explained that anti-prohibitionists rallied around the song "Home, Sweet Home" because the amendment threatened to eliminate home-storage and personal consumption of liquor.[21]

When the amendment failed, white Alabamians celebrated the outcome and their complete control of politics. After the polls closed, immense crowds gathered at the offices of the *Birmingham Age-Herald* and *Mobile Register* to await the results. When it became clear that voters had defeated the amendment, Mobile residents "cheered and cheered and cheered" and "threw off the safety valve of their feelings and gave vent to their joy and delight."[22] After disfranchisement, the spectacle did not change much in form and substance, except that African Americans had, at least in Alabama, lost their role in the public spectacle.

Although African Americans did not participate in some of the major prohibition campaigns of the era, they did not completely disappear on the issue. In 1908 the residents of Sedalia, Missouri, debated the prohibition question. During the campaign, the "temperance workers seemed to have all the best of it in the way of displays, streets parades and crowds at the public meetings." On election day, female prohibitionists followed key leaders of the saloon interests to catch any hint of electoral fraud but did not find anything because the saloon interests did not buy votes and "made it a point to see that there was no liquor to be obtained." Instead of providing alcohol, liquor advocates provided ice cream to their supporters and workers, which included African Americans. For the most part, the election "was without serious incident, free from all the squabbles at the polling places." The prohibitionists had won in the streets with their spectacles, but they failed to cast enough ballots to pass the local option and, according to early reports, graciously conceded.[23]

When it became known that African Americans worked on behalf of the anti-prohibitionists on election day, the prohibitionists became furious. According to Missouri Anti-Saloon League Superintendent Rev. U. G. Robinson, the liquor interests employed one hundred Black workers for the election. He explained that the liquor interests intended to pay the Black workers one rate if successful and another if they did not prevail. He admitted, "These men were not paid for their votes, but for their work in winning votes against local option."[24] Missourians had not passed disfranchisement laws, and African Americans milled around the polling places, taking their rightful spot in the contest.

When African Americans did participate, they sometimes encountered resistance from white women. On March 11, 1907, Knoxville, Tennessee, residents experienced an election that they "never saw and never dreamed of and doubtless will never see again" as residents went to the polling places to cast their ballots on the prohibition issue. Unlike Missouri, Tennesseans had passed disfranchisement laws, which specifically targeted the Black populations of the state's largest, and Blackest, cities. Throughout the day, prohibitionists and anti-prohibitionists engaged in typical spectacles, such as parades and marches. In the Black sections of the city, "whites and Blacks of all ages and both sexes fought the livelong day." At one saloon, women and children arrived and "blocked the stairway and commenced a prayer service that continued for hours and kept the negroes, thought to have been bought for the saloons, blocked for hours."[25] Like the prohibition spectacles of the previous century, Tennessee's prohibition contest played out in the streets in militaristic style. The Knoxville journalist reporting on the incident described the events as if they had unfolded on the battlefield with Black men and white women engaged in combat against one another. By using this type of language, Americans continued to interpret the polls as a masculine space with acceptable, even appreciated, participation by disfranchised groups.

In 1914 prohibitionists in Norfolk, Virginia, gathered to hear a program of speakers, including African Americans, on behalf of their cause. Virginians disfranchised Black voters at their 1902 state constitutional convention in Richmond but that did not stop Black participation in this prohibition campaign dominated by white Virginians.[26] Throughout the campaign, Virginia temperance reformers held open-air revival-like meetings. The members of the WCTU staged elaborate displays and organized massive parades. At these events, the female prohibitionists sang songs, such as "We're Out for Prohibition" set to the tune of "Dixie." The anti-prohibitionists adopted a cynical attitude toward these spectacles and characterized them as an attempt to win votes they could not win by reason.[27] At one prohibition meeting, Black minister Charles E. Morris, who served as the pastor of the "largest colored church in Norfolk," spoke before the white audience. He explained that prohibition had prevailed in the white districts of the city, but he lamented that saloons had found refuge in the Black sections, where they affected the community. He argued, "You have taken the ballot away from us, yet we are outraged by having this scourge forced upon us, and we appeal to your chivalry to relieve us from being debauched and pauperized any longer." He encouraged the white voters to help defeat the saloon interest. He said, "I ask this league to use its power and influence to aid us in keeping fifty saloons from breathing the breath of hell into our nostrils when we stop from our homes or walk to our work."[28] Despite lacking the right to vote, Morris had a place in the political debate at the revival-like meetings of the prohibition movement.

Although Texans had disfranchised African Americans with a poll tax amendment in 1902, African Americans participated in the 1915 statewide campaign to decide the prohibition issue in the state.[29] On July 25, 1915, prohibitionists gathered for numerous local rallies as part of the statewide movement. At these meetings they sang songs, listened to speakers, and signed pledges to support the cause by any means necessary. In Lamar, Texas, residents gathered at the Lamar Air Dome, which was "packed to capacity." In a speech, Rev. A. L. Andrews made African Americans one of his key talking points. He laughed at the anti-prohibitionists' attempt to persuade voters through reasoning. He referred to their arguments as "jokes" and explained, "Nobody believes it, not even the antis themselves." He argued, "They know they can't bring you out on the issue, so they are using the vaudeville, the pictures, and the negro band" to persuade voters to oppose the prohibition amendment. By 1915 politicians portrayed the employment of African Americans on behalf of an opposing campaign as a condemnable offense and sign of desperation.[30]

Outside of the South, African Americans participated in the various spectacles associated with prohibition campaigns. On October 25, 1916, Baltimore's Black anti-prohibitionists gathered for a meeting at Merryman's Hall. When prohibitionists learned that the city's Black residents had gathered for this meeting, they hired the Towson Colored Band to disrupt and break up the meeting. They believed that the Black musicians "would coax the negroes from the hall." The music had "the desired effect," and the audience filed out of the building.[31] This type of reporting helped portray African Americans as unsuitable for politics. Although they had gathered for a political purpose, according to the reporter, the African Americans could not resist the temptation of the music coming from outside.

On July 4, 1921, anti-prohibitionists gathered in New York City for a rally to oppose national prohibition. On the day of the parade, 200,000 sweaty marchers "braved a broiling sun" to protest the Volstead Act and Eighteenth Amendment. The protesters emphasized the desire for personal liberty and even marshalled religious arguments on their behalf. For the most part, the parade consisted of Italians and Germans plus working-class labor activists. They carried banners and signs along the route. The parade "furnished a novel spectacle" because most marchers carried American flags and flags of their home nations. On one float, "a pretty girl in thin and scantily garments" stood near a mammoth bunch of grapes while other women surrounded her "dressed in the costumes of the nations." At the end of the parade, a "contingent of negroes" made their way down the route led by a "cakewalking negro drum major."[32]

Although disfranchisement curtailed some Black expression at the political spectacles surrounding the prohibition movement, they did not completely disappear. Black participation in twentieth-century prohibition contests seems to have been limited by racist stereotyping and effective disfranchisement, but African American found better opportunities in other movements.

THE SPECTACLES OF THE LABOR MOVEMENT

During the 1870s and 1880s African Americans actively participated in labor organizations, specifically labor unions; but white southerners alienated the Black working class after the onset of an economic depression. In 1893 a depression hit the country and made biracialism within the labor movement less likely, but African Americans still formed their own unions and participated at biracial labor spectacles. From 1922 to 1928, African Americans formed citywide labor organizations affiliated with the American Federation of Labor in major southern cities. In 1928 the National Urban League lamented that the majority of Black workers in unionized industries could not join their respective unions, but they did calculate that 81,658 Black workers belonged to American trade unions with another 4,453 Black workers in local trade and federal labor unions.[33]

In the twentieth-century South, African Americans faced many obstacles to their continued access to political power. Economic depression jeopardized Black labor rights. Yet politics entailed more than voters and their ballots, and the labor movement did not simply rely on dues-paying members to thrive. Instead, the labor movement relied on parades, rallies, barbecues, flag-raising ceremonies, and similar spectacular events.

In the twentieth century, African Americans continued to have a noteworthy presence at Labor Day events across the South. In 1901 Atlanta's labor leaders organized a Labor Day celebration and parade, which featured numerous bands including the Dixie Colored Band of Atlanta. The leaders of the city's many unions and companies provided floats for the parade. In addition to the Black band, the female members of the Atlanta Typographical Union planned to arrive for Labor Day with "gay but not gaudy" uniforms that they promised would "be a sight well worth seeing."[34] In 1905 Norfolk's Black laborers staged "the best and the largest parade ever held here by the negroes." They formed a procession of a thousand men that extended for one-half mile and employed three Black bands.[35] In Atlanta's 1907 Labor Day parade, a "negro band marked the advent of the negro adjunct to unionism and fully 400 expert bricklayers and kalsominers [sic] followed this musical organization and negro marshal."[36] In the 1918 Labor Day parade in Brunswick, Georgia, Black musicians and Black laborers marched among four to five thousand other laborers in the "biggest Labor day celebration . . . ever known to this city." After the parade, the laborers celebrated with dancing, barbecue, baseball, and speeches.[37]

African Americans seemed to have participated in Labor Day spectacles without much opposition, but white men did balk at ceding positions of honor to them. Each year, Cincinnati's union leaders drew from a hat to determine their place in line. In 1911 the Black union of hod carriers won the honor of leading the parade, and they intended to assume this position with Black musicians at their lead. Many white laborers withdrew from the city's Labor Day parade because they refused to follow a Black band and Black union laborers.[38]

In addition to Labor Day celebrations, African Americans employed musicians to harass southern leaders on behalf of labor rights. In February 1900 Black servants journeyed to northern cities for better work, facilitated by employment agencies that helped clients find the best jobs. Due to the work of the agencies, many servants left, which, according to a Lynchburg, Virginia, reporter, gave local housekeepers "quite a serious problem in the matter of securing servants." Lynchburg's civic leaders took steps to curtail the work of the employment agencies and keep Black labor closer to home, such as imposing a tax on these agencies. In support of the servants and their own enterprise, an employment agency hired a Black band to parade the city's streets with "a number of colored boys bearing banners on which good jobs and high wages in Northern cities were advertised."[39] For African Americans, street theater, like the scene the played out in Lynchburg or in the Labor Day festivities of the South, remained an acceptable venue of political expression, in part because power at the ballot box had been limited.

AFRICAN AMERICANS AND POLITICAL SPECTACLE IN THE SOLID SOUTH

By the end of the nineteenth century, African Americans had started looking beyond the Republican Party for allies. Most African Americans remained loyal, especially in national elections, to the party of Abraham Lincoln and emancipation, but many Black southerners had become frustrated with the lack of progress toward racial equality, which had stalled after Reconstruction ended.

After disfranchisement, African Americans continued to perform at spectacles in many of the same ways they had before the lost the vote. They set the tone for events with music, paraded through the streets, humiliated white supremacist politicians, manipulated memory of the Civil War and Confederate defeat, and tied the Republican Party to victory and emancipation. With the South solidly Democratic, however, African Americans often had to choose which Democrat to support in an attempt to play candidates against one another and gain small concessions.

When African Americans helped set the tone for Democratic events, but they could not always overcome a speaker's deficiencies. In July 1902, a former governor of South Carolina, Democrat John Gary Evans, spoke at a campaign meeting in Walterboro, South Carolina. Before he spoke, a Black band struck up the famous tune "There Will Be a Hot Time in the Old Town Tonight." "It was wondered if this tune was prophetic," commented a reporter, who lamented, "but it was not" because of a worn-out voice from a previous engagement.[40] By choosing certain music, Black musicians could alter the atmosphere and set expectations for a campaign event.

Democrats employed Black musicians for campaign purposes yet harshly attacked African Americans in their speeches at the same events. In the 1906 gubernatorial race in Georgia, Democrat Clark Howell, who served as editor of the *Atlanta Constitution* alongside Henry Grady, campaigned against Democrat Michael Hoke Smith, who had edited the *Atlanta Journal* and had Populist leanings.[41] On April 16, Howell rallied voters in Swainsboro, Georgia, and the local managers employed a Black band from Savannah for the occasion. When he arrived at the train depot, hundreds of supporters gathered to greet him, and the brass band added "some lively music" to the "already overflowing enthusiasm."[42] Eventually, Howell made his way to the courthouse, which swelled with people. In addition to the packed building, hundreds of people gathered outside to hear him. For two hours, Howell spoke to "the largest crowd of people who ever assembled at a political gathering." In Swainsboro, he spoke mostly on the disfranchisement question.[43] Despite his passionate position on disfranchisement, his campaign managers deemed it appropriate to acquire Black music for his campaign rallies.

Upon learning of the presence of a Black band at Howell's address in Swainsboro, Smith's former employer, the *Atlanta Journal*, condemned Howell for not employing white musicians for the campaign event. The editors of the *Journal* criticized the event organizers for choosing a Black band, which they identified as Middleton's Cornet Band, for the occasion when "it is known that there is a white band in Savannah trying hard to get a foothold and is looking for just such engagements as this to help them get along." In their criticism of Howell, the editors recognized the economic importance of these engagements. They admitted that the Black band "attracted a good deal of attention" for the rally. Then they praised Smith for hiring the white musicians from Savannah for his rally in Statesboro.[44] From the perspective of white editors, the employment of a Black band did not seemingly have any political meaning, but it did entail economic opportunity, and they believed that white musicians should get the first shot at these gigs.

In response to this attack, a Howell supporter defended the use of Black musicians and criticized the *Atlanta Journal* for creating racial tension. In a letter to the *Americus Times-Recorder* reprinted in Howell's *Atlanta Constitution*, a writer condemned Smith's *Atlanta Journal* for reaching the "very limit

Clark Howell had Black musicians at his rallies during his 1906 campaign for Georgia governor. Library of Congress, Prints & Photographs Division, LC-DIG-ggbain-15413.

of disgusting demagoguery" in its report of the Swainsboro rally. The author criticized the editors of the *Atlanta Journal* for their attempt "to drag the color line into the affairs as if it were a heinous crime for white citizens to listen to the music of a negro band." He argued that *Atlanta Journal* editors "gladly seized upon the opportunity to engender race hatred." He characterized their "recent exudation of claptrap" as just an opportunity for them to "make a little cheap thunder" for another Democratic candidate, Hoke Smith.[45] In an era of disfranchisement and segregation, white Democrats tended to reserve their condemnation for Black voters, whereas Black performers often escaped unscathed and, on occasion, even earned white defenders.

In some cases, the presence of Black musicians made such a strong and obvious political statement that Democrats rejected them. On July 31, 1907, Governor James K. Vardaman staged a rally in Jackson, Mississippi, and he needed music for the procession. He hoped to win a seat in the United States Senate, and the evening's parade and subsequent rally provided him one last chance to convince voters to send him to Washington, DC. Congressman John Sharpe Williams, who opposed him, staged a rally on the

Hoke Smith's supporters condemned Clark Howell for his engagement with Black musicians. Library of Congress, Prints & Photographs Division, LC-USZ62-66573.

same night, and he had already contracted all of the local musicians for his event. To acquire musical talent, Vardaman's campaign sent for musicians from Vicksburg. "By mistake," explained a reporter commenting from the perspective of the Vardaman campaign, "the people at the Vicksburg end sent a crowd of tooters as Black as the ace of spades." While dining at the Mississippi State House, Vardaman looked out the window and saw twenty-two "darky musicians lined up in front of the Governor's mansion tuning up their instruments in preparation for the Vardaman parade." Upon seeing the Black musicians, Vardaman exclaimed, "A nigger band!" and almost "fell from his dinner chair in a faint." Immediately, he sent an aide to inform the brass band that they must return to Vicksburg "by the first train."[46] After sending away the musicians, Vardaman carried out his final rally. Like Williams's campaign event, the Vardaman's rally consisted of street parades and fireworks.[47] Despite his popularity in Mississippi, Vardaman did not win in the 1907 senatorial election, but he did become a US senator in 1911 and served one term.[48]

In 1907, James K. Vardaman exclaimed in horror at the sight of a Black band arriving in town for his campaign rally, but W. C. Handy recalled playing for him on a different occasion. Library of Congress, Prints & Photographs Division, LC-USZ62-38764.

Given Vardaman's reputation, he undoubtedly felt humiliated at the prospect of marching behind Black musicians, so it seems plausible that organizers in Vicksburg sent him a Black band on purpose to embarrass him; or, the Black musicians embraced the opportunity for economic or political reasons. During Vardaman's political career, he developed a reputation for his use of racial tactics, which alienated many moderates, especially in the northern states. Nonetheless, he was massively popular with white Mississippians. He condoned mob law and lacked respect for white people who refused to lynch insubordinate African Americans. He supported lynching and condemned President Theodore Roosevelt for hosting Booker T. Washington at the White House.[49] He even earned the nickname "White Chief" because of his "espousal of white superiority theories."[50] In an era featuring prominent many white supremacists marching behind Black bands or using their music to publicize events, Vardaman's extremism prevented him from using this tactic. He seems to have considered the possibility that someone had intentionally sent him Black musicians to humiliate him. According to a reporter, Vardaman remained angry about the mix-up and "undecided whether a joke has been played on him or whether he is a victim of a famine in white musicians in Mississippi." He asked one of his aides to investigate in order "to ascertain whether a joke was played on him."[51]

W. C. Handy had participated in this campaign on both sides, but he fondly remembered his time working with Williams and regretted his performances for Vardaman.[52] Given Handy's comments on the two politicians, it seems possible that Williams had support in Mississippi's Black communities, so a Black band may have taken the opportunity to humiliate Vardaman, especially given his reputation for racial tactics. For the most part, white politicians welcomed Black musicians because their performances helped reinforce an image of the Old South. In rare circumstances, white politicians, like Vardaman, had espoused such hateful racial rhetoric that they resented the appearance of Black musicians at campaign events, which would have made them susceptible to a stunt like this one. Vardaman's campaign, however, had employed Handy's band on at least one occasion. For Vardaman, there was a difference choosing to employ a Black band and having one show up in surprise.

With the Democratic Party firmly in control, African Americans sometimes had no other option but to humiliate the candidate or officeholder, not necessarily to anyone's benefit except for their own brief feeling of satisfaction. In November 1905, Black musicians from Company A of the Capital City Guards from Montgomery, Alabama, caused quite a stir when they mocked the former Confederacy. At the time, they were the only Black soldiers in the Alabama National Guard. As they marched to their barracks, the Black musicians leading the company played "Hang Jeff Davis on the Sour Apple Tree," which condemned the Confederacy's first and only president.[53] As the fifth stanza of the abolitionist anthem "John Brown's Body," the Jefferson Davis verse, especially in the context of the entire song, expressed a desire for revenge against slaveholders. It was immensely popular during the Civil War, especially among soldiers, who considered it a fine marching companion. The tune, which has its origins in the South, served the basis for many songs, including "John Brown's Body" and Julia Ward Howe's "Battle Hymn of the Republic."[54] The reporters did not indicate that the Black marchers sang the words to the song or only played the tune. If the marchers only played the tune, the reporters inferred that the Black musicians had intended to play the Davis verse. When questioned, the Black musicians smartly denied playing this particular song. Despite these denials, white officers created a petition to encourage the Governor William D. Jelks, a Democrat, to muster the soldiers out of camp. Governor Jelks did, in fact, muster the soldiers out, but he claimed to know nothing of the incident and sent them out because they "could not be called upon in the emergencies for which troops are now used in Alabama, which are to suppress riots or to disperse a mob."[55] If Jelks had acknowledged the political implications of the band's musical selection, he would have recognized the political awareness and aptitude of the Black musicians. By remaining silent, he hoped to keep the Black band invisible. The Black musicians made headlines with this performance, which spread their own contemporary view on the past and present.

In most performances, Black performers played their roles as scripted because of the economic opportunity. Employed by white Democrats, Black musicians often played southern tunes, which generated sectional spirit for the Democratic Party. On August 30, 1909, thousands of Louisville, Kentucky residents "lined the downtown streets" to witness the Jeffersonian barbecue parade, which reporters characterized as "the greatest political spectacle in years." The parade featured twelve bands, drum corps, and thousands of people on foot and horseback. The marchers carried American flags, banners, and torches of red or green. "As the parade weaved its course through the downtown streets," observed a reporter, "the Democratic hosts were greeted with practically unceasing cheering" by enthusiastic crowds of spectators. In the parade, a Black band led the marching clubs representing the white-majority tenth ward. According to a reporter, the Black band "put greater spirit into the crowds as it passed" than any other. Behind them, the marchers of the eleventh and twelfth wards made their way through the city streets alongside "great numbers of attractive floats" and "pretty girls and women." As the marchers paraded through the streets, event organizers launched fireworks, which "lit up the tall buildings in reds and greens and yellows." Throughout the event, there "was no stoppage of music and the glare of vari-colored lights was continuous." The musicians played "Dixie" and "My Old Kentucky Home." Although Kentucky had been a slave state, the state did not secede from the Union, but many Kentuckians fought on both sides of the Civil War. The Stephen Foster song "My Old Kentucky Home," which happened to be a favorite of formerly enslaved abolitionist Frederick Douglass, evoked sympathy for enslaved people, so it may have seemed out of place at a Democratic rally, but the crowd did not seem to mind because they greeted the songs "wild and lusty cheering." When the festivities ended, it took the local railroads hours to empty the city streets of all the participants. Reflecting on the event, a reporter argued that it "was evident that patriotism and the old-fashioned Democratic spirit" prevailed in Louisville.[56]

During the 1920s, the Ku Klux Klan served as the militant arm of the Lost Cause and the Democratic Party, but African Americans attended events alongside the hooded Klansmen, which sometimes earned them scorn from their race. In 1925 the Ku Klux Klan arranged to have a picnic in Council Bluffs, Iowa. They reached out to the largest Black band in Omaha, Nebraska, to provide the music. The Black leader of the band, Dan Desdunes, claimed to have accepted the contract, but he withdrew the offer after "an avalanche of public opinion" caused him to cancel.[57] On November 11, 1925, an Armistice Day parade in St. Petersburg, Florida, featured the KKK. Although the KKK had a well-known white supremacist and Protestant Christian ideology, Jews and African Americans participated. At the back of the parade, Black schoolchildren and Black military veterans marched.[58] Rather than staying away from the Klan, the Black and Jewish marchers prioritized the opportunity to demonstrate their loyalty to the country and claim their place in the parade. For some performers, the economic opportunity offered by events like campaign rallies or picnics compelled African Americans to make difficult choices.

On at least one occasion, African Americans took advantage of their proximity to the Klan to make a statement. On November 14, 1927, Black musicians participated alongside white people in an Armistice Day parade in Ft. Worth, Texas. During the parade, the Black musicians marched behind the Ku Klux Klan. As they marched behind the white-hooded Klansmen, the Black musicians played "The Old Gray Mare Ain't What She Used to Be." By selecting this music, the musicians hoped to portray the Klan members as outdated, useless remnants of the past.

As the Democratic Party tightened its hold on the South, African Americans had fewer opportunities to trumpet the Republican Party. Often, state and local elections came down to Democrats competing against one another, and, in these contests, African Americans sometimes picked a candidate willing to offer some concessions. If they could choose only a Democrat, some African Americans decided to use the opportunity to mock the candidates, the Lost Cause, and white supremacy. In the Solid South, the third parties and the ballot referenda provided better opportunities for African Americans. These issues divided white southern Democrats, so the opposite sides often courted Black votes to gain an edge. They helped African Americans register and protected their path to the polls to vote.

THIRD PARTIES AND SPECTACLES IN THE SOUTH

Like they had done for the People's Party, African Americans welcomed an alternative to the Democratic Party in the South. Although none of the third parties that emerged in the twentieth century had as much success as the People's Party, they still drew support from Black southerners, who did not have many other options in the post-disfranchisement South.

During Roosevelt's 1912 tour of the South on behalf of the Progressive Party, which Roosevelt affectionately referred to as the Bull Moose Party, crowds of Black and white supporters greeted the former president at every stop. When he arrived in Cheraw, Alabama, a "straggling crowd of white men and a few negroes" met Roosevelt and Booker T. Washington of the nearby Tuskegee Institute. In fact, the "white residents hung back in a rather embarrassed fashion" at this particular stop on the tour until Roosevelt personally requested that they come forward.[59] At political rallies, African Americans had access to leading politicians even when they did not have access to the voting booth. This scene repeated itself across the South during Roosevelt's failed campaign for the presidency.

On September 28, 1912, Roosevelt spoke in Atlanta. Before the speaking began, an "imposing procession" led Roosevelt from the train station to the auditorium, which included automobiles headed by a band. The speaking engagement, which one reporter characterized as "one of the most remarkable political meetings ever held in the southland," had the character of a "crusade rather than a campaign meeting." African Americans and women attended the event. Many spectators wore red bandanna handkerchiefs emblazoned with the picture of Roosevelt or of a moose. In the auditorium, the event organizers reserved a section of two hundred seats for female spectators and a small section in the top gallery for Black spectators.[60]

On August 9, 1912, Baltimore's Black and white supporters of the Bull Moose Party met and staged a parade and meeting in the city. Throughout the day, "the members of this new political movement bubbled over with enthusiasm, lustily cheered each mention of Roosevelt's name and applauded the Marylanders who participated in the convention." At the Camden railroad station, five hundred men gathered to welcome Maryland's delegates to the Bull Moose Party convention, including Black delegate Louis H. Davenport.[61] Led by the Fifth Regiment Band, they started to move through the city with "the suffragists bringing up the rear in automobiles." The marchers made their way and "lighted red torches and wore around their necks bandanna kerchiefs and the Roosevelt emblems." Baltimore residents gathered along the sidewalks to cheer on the procession. Although the Bull Moose Party refused to seat some of the Black delegates to the convention, "color lines were not drawn in the parade," and African Americans "marched beside whites." Upon reaching Rennert Hotel on Saratoga Street, a series of speakers commenced a program of speeches, which included Joseph P. Evans, a Black man.[62] The convention, which had an explicitly political purpose, refused to seat the Black delegates, but the parade represented a public event and welcomed Black participation.

In the 1930s, many Black southerners turned to the Communist Party of America and visibly participated in the party's rallies and meetings despite hostility to the party and Black political action. Based out of Birmingham, the Communists looked to gain support in the Deep South and Tennessee, and they found quite a bit of success with African Americans in Alabama's Black Belt. In the South, African Americans made up about 80 to 90 percent of the Communist Party's membership and visibly agitated on behalf of the working class. They held rallies in outdoor parks, especially at Birmingham's Capitol Park.

On May 22, 1930, a Black crowd gathered for a mass meeting of the Communist Party, in which speakers Tom Johnson, Frank Burns, and Walter Lewis advocated for self-determination for Alabama's Black population and desegregation in restaurants and public transportation. Later that month, communists staged a rally of about seven hundred Black people and one hundred white people in Capitol Park, where they rallied to demand aid for unemployed workers and protested the arrest of communists. When Birmingham's city officials responded with laws denouncing the Communist Party, 250 Black workers returned to Capitol Park to support the party against hostility. At a September 1930 rally, the Black communists remained in Capitol Park until police forced them to leave. During the winter of 1930, Black communists participated in a series of rallies on behalf of the unemployed.[63]

In 1932 socialists gathered in Richmond, Virginia, to hear six-time presidential candidate Norman Thomas speak. According to a reporter, socialists in northern states "throw their arms around Negroes and call them 'comrades.'" In southern states, explained the reporter, "the party members resort to the same old customs of the white folks down here of segregating." At the speaking engagement, African Americans had to sit in the gallery "from which vantage point the speakers could be very well seen but not heard" because the building manager restricted access to the first floor to white spectators. Party organizers "were powerless to do anything about it."[64]

In the twentieth century, African Americans could not express themselves with the vote, but they could show their support in public at rallies and parades. They claimed membership in political parties with their presence and their performances. World War I opened up new opportunities to claim citizenship rights by fighting in the military but also at home, where African Americans could demonstrate their loyalty to the nation even as that nation conspired to take away their rights.

WORLD WAR I, PATRIOTISM, AND SPECTACLE

During World War I, African Americans frequently participated in patriotic rallies, albeit in segregated ways. Patriotic rallies still entailed partisan elements, and African Americans laid claim to membership in the nation and political parties with their participation at these events. Despite the dire circumstances of world war, African Americans could only lend patriotic support if it accommodated segregation and white mainstream cultural norms. They could march and perform in parades and fundraisers, but they could not always attend these events as spectators because of segregation laws.

Amid the rhetoric of democracy and freedom of World War I, African Americans, including those in military uniform, encountered danger within the United States. In 1917 Black soldiers stationed in Houston engaged with the Houston Police Department, and the ensuing deadly violence resulted in courts-martial, executions, and life imprisonment for many Black soldiers. During the Red Summer of 1919, several race riots occurred, including major events in Chicago, East St. Louis, and Knoxville, among others. With racial tensions at a fever pitch, African Americans could not always know how white Americans would react to their presence, but they found ways to express their patriotism through public spectacle.

During World War I, President Woodrow Wilson reviewed hundreds of American soldiers, including Black soldiers and Black musicians, parading through Baltimore's streets. On April 6, 1918, Wilson arrived in Baltimore as part of a Liberty Loan drive. Before a crowd of 15,000 people, the "negroes marched well and their band was classed as the best of several in the parade."[65] During the performance, the six-foot-five-inch tall drum major of the 368th Infantry band, Sergeant Landin, who had skin "almost as Black as the ace of spades" cakewalked "with a grin that forced thoughts of pickaninnies and watermelons into the heads of those who saw him."[66] With this performance, Sergeant Landin became regionally famous and Americans, especially white Americans, clamored to have his band participate in their fundraisers. Like so many Black performers before him, Landin earned by portraying the feckless Black character that white audiences desired to see. By manipulating negative stereotypes, African Americans could infiltrate the public sphere and gain economic opportunity.

Later that month, the white residents of Baltimore organized two fundraising campaigns. On April 18, Colonel W. Bladen Lowndes organized a fundraiser for the War Savings Stamp Campaign at the Garden Theater. The event featured speeches from Maryland's former governor, Phillips Lee Goldsborough, and Albert G. Towers, who served as chairman of the Public

Service Commission. It also featured the Black musicians of the 368th Infantry Band and, of course, Sergeant Landin. These musicians provided "excellent playing of classical, patriotic and ragtime music," and the "deportment of the drum major" put the audience "in a fine humor."[67] To attend, residents simply had to purchase one or more Thrift Stamps to help the war effort.

African Americans had a particularly high interest in attending the event because they wanted to see this Black band, "one of the many that is to cheer the colored boys on while they try to get the Kaiser." When they could not enter the Garden Theater, "some of the colored people made utterances that would be regarded as seditious." They assumed that they could not enter the fundraiser because of the venue's segregation policy, and the fundraiser's organizers confirmed these suspicions. After the debacle, the Maryland Council of Defense arranged for a separate fundraiser for Baltimore's Black residents, who refused the offer. In response to the situation, a spokesperson for the fundraiser explained, "I am sorry that any of our colored people went to the theater and thereby were insulted by being refused." He did not apologize for refusing them. He did admit, however, that "in these perilous times such treatment to the race has a tendency to dampen the patriotic ardor of the colored people." He explained, furthermore, that the war effort required "those who would aid in every way to crush Germany should see that petty race prejudices in this country are forgotten" to win the war.[68] On stage, the musicians became separate from the rest of the crowd. They played a role familiar to white Americans: the performer and entertainer. African Americans could not, however, mingle with white society on the dance floor and in the audience, even to the benefit of the war effort.

The Black bands of colored regiments often participated at these types of fundraisers. On April 28, 1918, in Baltimore, the 251st Field Artillery Band, including bandmaster and graduate of the New York Institute of Art Dorsey Rhodes, "sailed through a most difficult program" and "surpassed every expectation of the crowd." After the performance, the "crowd clamored for more before the serious work of selling stamps got under way."[69] This event occurred at the Garden Theater in Baltimore, which meant that African Americans could not attend and mingle with white society, but they could entertain whites.

When African Americans received military honors, they still encountered racial stereotypes. In July 1918, the Black soldiers in the 517th Engineer Reserve Corps stationed in Atlanta received their national and battalion banners. They gathered at the camp's parade grounds for the ceremony, which featured a series of speeches and prayers wishing them well. After the speeches, an officer presented the Black soldiers with "no less than a thousand big slices of real Georgia watermelon." The Black soldiers picked up their slices "of the reddest watermelon" and returned to their place in line. For some time thereafter, it "was simply the old situation of 'the Georgia nigger and the watermelon.'" He observed that "there was smacking of lips and rolling of eyes, and above all, a cessation of conversation that lasted with the supply of watermelon." After eating, a Black band from Augusta "burst into several popular airs." With these words, the newspaper reporter suggested that when eating watermelon, Black men ceased in their role as respectable soldiers.[70] With the design of the spectacle, white officers could reinforce negative stereotypes of African Americans and insult them even under the pretext of honor and praise. They could diminish the political significance of Black men in military uniform, which had caused so much tension among white Americans, by reducing them to an animalistic caricature.

During the war, Americans, including Black southerners, used spectacular demonstrations to register citizens for military service. In September 1918, amid "the strains of martial music played by military and civilian bands," thirty thousand Atlanta residents registered for military service. In order to attract all men of military age and fitness, officers organized a massive parade, which started at the state capitol on Washington Street and weaved through many of the city's principal streets, including Mitchell Street and Peachtree Street near the opera house. At the very end of the procession, a Black band from Camp Gordon marched, as well. After the parade, the musicians broke off from the main body and set up at each registration site to attract potential enlistees. The military designated some of the registration sites as "colored only," and it seems likely that Black musicians manned these particular sites.[71] Like their white neighbors, Black Atlantans contributed to the war effort with their participation at spectacles. Although biracial, the military segregated the spectacle and the registration drive by putting the Black musicians at the back of the parade. Given the prevalence of segregation, disfranchisement, and lynching, Black civil rights leaders debated as to whether Black men should or would enlist in the armed forces. Although some Black leaders believed that the war provided Black men the chance to demonstrate their patriotism and masculinity in an attempt to claim political rights, many Black leaders, specifically A. Philip Randolph and Chandler Owen of the *Messenger*, argued that Black men would not and should not enlist as a form of protest.[72] Given the uncertainty as to whether or not African Americans would join the military, military leaders hoped to use spectacular means to generate enthusiasm for the war and gain volunteers from the Black community, but they tailored their methods to accommodate segregation and discrimination.

James Reese Europe's band played throughout Europe during World War I, such as this performance in London. Upon returning home, they created a sensation playing for American audiences. Library of Congress, Prints & Photographs Division, LC-DIG-anrc-00856.

After the war, African Americans received a hero's welcome in Black-dominated northern cities, including Harlem, but they did not always earn recognition for their military service. On February 17, 1919, Lieutenant James Reese Europe, known to many by the nickname Jim Europe, led his band and the Black soldiers of the 15th New York National Guard Regiment, also known as the 369th Infantry or Harlem's Hellfighters, on a parade through Harlem. His band had "'jazzed' all over France and Belgium to cheer up wounded and unwounded soldiers" during the war. For the performance, Lieutenant Europe procured new instruments because their old instruments revealed "signs of strenuous use" after more than 100,000 miles of travel in the war. In the report, the newspaper reporter focused on the musicians' effort "entertaining soldiers" despite the fact that the majority of the regiment participated in the actual fighting and even earned France's highest military honor, the Croix de Guerre. While the military service went unnoticed in white newspaper reports, this Black band traveled all over the country as part of victory celebrations.[73]

Europe traveled from his boyhood home in Mobile, Alabama, to Harlem, where he achieved fame and eventually joined the military. He arrived in Harlem in 1910 "with a strong pair of lungs" for playing the trombone and "some ideas about syncopation that other musicians refused to accept."

James Reese Europe led his band in a concert at a Paris hospital, which was just one of many performances across Europe during World War I. Library of Congress, Prints & Photographs Division, LC-DIG-ds-09800.

When the United States entered the war, New York organized the 15th National Guard Regiment. Colonel William Hayward asked Europe to lead the regiment's band. During the war, they became "so popular among the soldiers that they were kept traveling all the time." They also played for French president Henri Poincaré and American General John J. Pershing. Upon returning to the United States, Europe and his band played all over the country in victory celebrations, which earned them even more fame and economic opportunity. On May 9, 1919, Europe and his band played at Mechanic's Hall in Boston. When he told a drummer to pick up the pace, the drummer confronted Europe and slashed his throat, killing the famous bandleader.[74] During the war, the fighting men of the 15th National Guard Regiment achieved quite a bit of success, but their band received the most notice and applause upon its return home.

When African Americans returned from the war to the United States, they participated alongside white soldiers in celebratory parades. In March 1919,

Nashville residents organized a parade to welcome back the city's Black and white soldiers. In the planning process, the organizers did not immediately plan to honor the Black soldiers until a committee of Black civic leaders protested. After consulting with the committee, the organizers arranged for four to five hundred Black soldiers to march in the parade and for a forty-five-piece Black band to provide music, as well. In addition to the parade, the event's organizers wanted to provide the soldiers with a meal. They provided the "same food and same amount per capita" for the Black soldiers, but they fed them at the city's Black chapters of the Young Men's Christian Association.[75] At celebration spectacles, African Americans earned recognition of their martial contributions to the war, but organizers designed the spectacles to remind them of their inferior status.

THE 1920S AND THE GREAT MIGRATION

After the war, African Americans continued to participate in partisan spectacles on behalf of both political parties, but often in segregated events and increasingly in northern locales. In the early twentieth century, African Americans migrated northward in pursuit of economic opportunity, especially during World War I, and political rights. They also found a stronger Republican Party in terms of membership and electoral success, and the Republican Party remained their preferred choice, with some reservation, until President Franklin D. Roosevelt and President Harry Truman started to position the Democratic Party as the party of civil rights. In the North, the electoral contests remained vibrant because it had two, and sometimes more, legitimate parties. As African Americans concentrated in northern and border states, they appeared more often at campaign events.

In fact, Black civic leaders considered Black musicians a vital piece of the political process, and they expected African Americans to participate in campaign spectacles. In 1912 the editors of the *Chicago Defender* remarked, "All the candidates seemed to have ignored the colored bands this season as well as our colored musicians." The editors lamented that the candidates continued to use Black churches for rallies. The editors argued that "the people should rise as one and demand that if the colored bands are not good enough to use for political use, then their houses of worship should not be." In conclusion, he called upon Black women to safeguard the sanctity of the church and for the Black community to "demand of the man who would want your vote to give you work."[76] With these comments, the Black editors of the *Chicago Defender* connected economic opportunity with political power. They expected economic opportunity and, in return, would deliver Black votes to the candidates that played along.

As Democrats started to attract more Black votes in the 1920s and 1930s, Republicans worked hard to keep Black votes. In 1923 a Black Republican, Henry Lincoln Johnson, spoke to a Baltimore audience of eight or nine hundred people, which served "as a test of Republican negro solidarity." In addition to the speech by Johnson, two white civic leaders came to speak to the Black audience after giving addresses at a meeting and torchlight parade of white Republicans.[77]

In local and state elections held in northern and border states, African Americans contributed to campaigns. In 1922 Youngstown, Missouri, mayor George Lawrence Oles credited a young evangelist and musicians for his campaign success. He explained, "I hired American, Italian, and negro bands. I gave 'em horns and red fire. It took people by storm. Nothing like that had been tried since the old 'cutthroat' campaign days." Although Oles suggests that spectacle had diminished, his comments imply that the people would still willingly come out for spectacular events if the candidates would use the method.

African Americans participated frequently in campaign events held on behalf of Democratic presidential candidate Al Smith, especially in northern and border states. During the 1928 election, Smith stopped in Topeka, Kansas. "A noisy throng surrounded the rear of his train at the Topeka terminal," observed a reporter, who added that "the music of several bands" contributed to a festive atmosphere. Among them, a Black band struck up the vaudeville tune "The Sidewalks of New York" to welcome the New Yorker to the prairie.[78] Smith used the song as his campaign song throughout his tour of the country.[79] A month later, a Black band along with a crowd of "enthusiastic Democrats" welcomed Smith back to Albany after sixteen days on the campaign trail.[80]

In 1932 Lieutenant Governor E. H. Winter of Missouri, a Republican, ran for governor. On September 16, he officially kicked off his campaign with a rally and parade in Warrenton. In the evening, Warrenton's Republicans "turned out en masse to celebrate the formal opening of his drive for votes in the November election." They carried banners and torches through the town's streets led by musicians, including a Black band. As the Black band led the parade, another local band from Central Wesleyan College played at the courthouse lawn, where Winter gave his speech to an enthusiastic audience.[81] As they had done before World War I, African Americans were among the first members of the public sphere to greet candidates to the community. They also helped set the tone for the event with their enthusiastic playing.

African Americans took initiative and used spectacles to intimidate unfavorable candidates by putting them in humiliating circumstances. In 1928 Senator James Watson of Indiana traveled to Chicago to address a Black audience at a local armory. The event's organizers arranged for him to speak between two "colored spellbinders." After the first speaker, Watson stood up to speak but did not say a word. Then, the program continued. According to Black civic leaders, the audience detested Watson because of his ties to the Ku Klux Klan. According to one observer, "Well, he better not talk here if he knows the time, the place, and the girl. We'll burn him up. He's K. K. K."[82] If he had been intimidated by the program and presence of Black speakers, he did not concede that point, instead explaining that he had a bad throat and could not speak.

During the late 1920s and early 1930s, African Americans had a visible and audible presence at political events for both Hoover and Roosevelt. At President Herbert Hoover's inaugural parade in 1929, a Black civic leader led the delegation from Mississippi. On March 3, S. D. Redmond, who served as the chairman of the Mississippi Republican State Executive Committee and the only Black person to lead a state executive committee, dined with fellow Republicans at the Mayflower Hotel. On March 4, he led Mississippi's Republicans in the inaugural parade. As of 1929, African Americans still tended to support Republicans, whether they reflected these allegiances at political spectacles or not.

By 1932 African Americans would become central features of spectacles staged on behalf of Franklin D. Roosevelt. In an event in Indianapolis, Black bands and Black marchers paraded through the streets in advance of the Democratic candidate and his wife.[83] African Americans had not yet completely left the Republican Party, especially in the South. In July 1932, Republicans staged a rally in Little Rock, Arkansas, to celebrate Hoover's candidacy for a second term. The Republicans recognized that African Americans had become disillusioned with the Republican Party, so they urged African Americans to attend and made special appeals to the Black community by focusing on how Reconstruction had helped Black businesses.[84]

African Americans expected a place in the public sphere. They participated in campaign rallies, inauguration ceremonies, and impromptu gatherings on behalf of both major political parties. By participating they generated enthusiasm, drove voters to the polls, and helped Republicans and Democrats spread a sectional interpretation of the Civil War. They even made unlikely alliances with Democrats and Confederates for the sake of economic opportunity and advantageous political alliances. When denied access to politics, they had various methods to make themselves visible participants in politics, such as street theater and rough music. They used these means to harass politicians and demand recognition of their political aptitude. In an era of disfranchisement, white politicians sought out Black performers to rally and persuade not only white voters, but in some locales, Black voters, too.

CHAPTER 4

"TO DO OUR BIT FOR GOOD GOVERNMENT"

W. C. Handy, E. H. Crump, and the 1909 Memphis Mayoral Election

IN 1909 THREE WHITE POLITICIANS—EDWARD H. CRUMP, JOHN J. WILLIAMS, and Walter W. Talbert—vied to become the next mayor of Memphis. Each of the candidates utilized traditional campaign tactics, such as speeches, rallies, advertisements, and posters, to win the office. In a familiar move played by southern office-seekers, these mayoral candidates also employed Black musicians to campaign on their behalf.

African American musician and bandleader W. C. Handy, who eventually became known as the Father of the Blues, recognized that white southern politicians used this tactic elsewhere. He explained, "in Memphis as in Clarksdale it was known to politicians that the best notes made the most votes, and there came a time when we were called upon to do our bit for good government." The Crump campaign hired Handy's band because, as Handy reasoned, "Beale Street was expected to cast a lot of votes, and it was squarely up to us to get them."[1] Crump needed Black support to win the election. Given the opportunity to play for the campaign, Handy used his music to influence Memphis politics and to help a white politician gain power, but he also seized the opportunity to gain power for himself and his race.

During the 1909 mayoral campaign, Black musicians participated in the electoral process by informally campaigning on behalf of all the major candidates. They attracted African Americans to registration sites in Beale Street taverns. In the streets, they generated enthusiasm for their respective candidates by competing with other bands to attract the largest audiences. In 1909 Crump and Handy took advantage of the racial dynamics and political culture of Memphis to launch their famous careers.

BLACK POLITICAL MOBILIZATION IN MEMPHIS

After the Civil War, Memphis became the site of racial discord and race-based violence as freed people moved into the city previously dominated by Irish and German immigrants. The influx of soldiers, government officials, missionaries, and freed people substantially increased the city's population despite a decline in the white population of the city. By 1865 Memphis had a Black population of 11,000.[2] In 1866 the Memphis police, most of whom were Irish immigrants, collided with Black soldiers in the city streets. From May 1 to May 3, white rioters destroyed Black property and businesses, raped Black women, and killed forty-six African Americans without punishment from the federal government despite a congressional investigation.[3] Although the Memphis riot seemed like an ominous start to freedom for the Black community, the city quickly became a site of Black entrepreneurship and political activism.

Upon arrival in Memphis, many African Americans started their own businesses, especially on and near Beale Avenue, later known as Beale Street. At the corner of Beale Avenue and Gayoso Street, Robert R. Church Sr. established the city's first Black-owned saloon. His wife, Louisa, owned a hair salon. During the 1866 riot, Church had been a target because of his success and suffered a grievous gunshot wound to the head, which left him occasionally incapacitated and often suicidal for the rest of his life. Despite the injury, Church became a business and political leader in the city. He invested in Beale Avenue, where he owned several saloons, a hotel, and a restaurant. On the same street, he leased property to many Black business owners. Through these efforts, Beale Avenue became a bustling Black business center and Church became the first Black southern millionaire. Outside of Beale Avenue, Church owned hundreds of residences and acres of land. He launched a political and philanthropic career and became connected to Black civic leaders around the country, notably W. E. B. Du Bois.[4]

In addition to the work of Church and Black business owners, Black Memphians organized on the grassroots level by establishing their own churches, and these churches became the foundations for community organizations, such as schools and mutual-aid societies.[5] Mostly through the efforts of Black churches, Black Memphians established numerous schools in the city without financial help from the Freedmen's Bureau. In Memphis, the Black community insisted on hiring and promoting Black teachers in their own schools, which made them significantly different from schools sponsored by the Freedmen's Bureau and white northern missionaries. Although the schools suffered from financial problems and white apathy and retaliation, Memphis's Black community maintained the schools. In 1867 Black Memphians created the Education Association of Memphis to facilitate the creation and maintenance of schools. For the benefit of the entire Black community in Memphis, they insisted on providing tuition-free education. In Memphis, these institutions became central to Black political activism.[6]

In the first decade after emancipation, Black Memphians organized politically and lent their support to the Republican Party. After the war, Black Memphians gained citizenship and voting rights protected by the Republican-controlled state legislature. African Americans established political clubs and fraternal organizations. Through these institutions, they reached out to white neighbors to form powerful coalitions. At every level of government, African Americans had power in the city. They supported political outsiders, specifically northern-born Republicans, in their bids to fill a power vacuum in Memphis politics left by the war and Reconstruction. In addition to their support of white candidates, they held office, served on grand juries, and worked for the city's police force.[7]

After Tennessee Democrats regained control of the state in 1870, African Americans became disillusioned with the Republican Party and looked for alternatives. As schools in Memphis deteriorated, Black Memphians came to resent the paternalism of northern Republicans, who did not produce any lasting change in Black life yet continued to expect Black support. After the passage of the Civil Rights Act of 1875, Memphians debated whether to integrate the city's schools. Many white Memphians refused to pay taxes to support integrated schools, which further disillusioned the city's Black residents with the Republican Party. They blamed the party for failing to pass any meaningful land or economic reform, which would have enabled the Black community to more adequately fund their own public schools on par with the white schools. In the same year, white principal J. H. Barnum and Black schoolteacher S. H. Thompson, who had feuded with one another for years, each went to the school board and demanded their counterpart's removal. In the conflict, Memphis's antebellum elites, who had formed numerous urban reform organizations and supported the Democratic Party's bid for redemption, sided with the Black schoolteacher Thompson. Unlike the southern-born white supporters of Thompson, northern-born white Memphians supported the white principal Barnum.

Rather than loyally following the party of emancipation, African Americans would now negotiate their own political allegiances to secure tangible gains. Democrats took advantage of Black dissatisfaction with the Republican Party and reached out to the Black community in an attempt to reassert their party's dominance in local affairs. They wanted to portray themselves as friends of Black southerners, so they donated money to Black schools and churches. Nathan Bedford Forrest, who had served in the Confederate military and founded the Ku Klux Klan, donated funds to help rebuild a Black church in the city. Within the Black community, prosperous landholders tended to side with the city's Democrats. In contrast, Black laborers continued to support the Republican Party. In Memphis, racial identity did not seem to make a reliable indicator of party allegiance.[8]

In the mid- to late 1870s, the shifting loyalties of African Americans affected the outcome of municipal elections. In 1875 African Americans and Democrats opposed the Republican-controlled school board. They cooperated to elect a Black principal to manage the city's Black schools. On July 4, 1875, Black mutual-aid societies held their annual celebration of the nation's independence. At the event, notable ex-Confederates, including Forrest, spoke to the crowd of thousands of Black Memphians. Later that year, more than half of the city's Black voters cast their ballots for Democrat John Fillipin for mayor, who beat the Republican John Loague by a massive majority. For a decade, African Americans would affect the outcome of Memphis's municipal elections because of their willingness to vote for Democrats, but the alliance proved short-lived and shortsighted when Democrats led the crusade to reform voting practices in Tennessee and the South.[9]

In 1888 Democrats convincingly won in the Tennessee statehouse; their victory paved the way for voting restrictions. After years of healthy party competition, Democrats hoped to use their considerable advantage to eliminate Republican opposition led by former Unionists in East Tennessee and African Americans in the cities. In April 1889, the state legislature passed a law enacting the secret ballot. Notably, the law only applied to four counties, Shelby, Davidson, Knox, and Hamilton, in order to target its application on the Black populations in Memphis, Nashville, Knoxville, and Chattanooga. In addition to the secret ballot, the Tennessee legislature passed new registration requirements to eliminate repeat voters and an influx of Black voters from Mississippi and Arkansas on election day. When the state legislature passed these laws, the editors of the *Memphis Appeal* rejoiced in the simultaneous demise of Black voting and the Republican Party in the state.[10] In 1890 Tennessee legislators finally passed the poll tax provided for in the state's 1870 state constitution.[11]

The voting restrictions had an immediate effect on Tennessee's politics. Memphis newspapers reported that political spectacle seemed to have disappeared. In the 1890 midterm elections, *Memphis Avalanche* reporters indicated that "everything was quiet as the grave" at the city's polling stations. They reported that the election had occurred with "no excitement, no loud talk, few ward workers, few spectators" and that it "was not like an election at all." Specifically, they emphasized the absence of Black voters, thus demonstrating the success of the voting restrictions.[12] Likewise, *Memphis Appeal* reporters praised the new measures for restricting the ballot to "intelligent, taxpaying, school supporting classes" and providing a solution to the "race problem" because the measures eliminated "the ignorant Negro."[13] Although Memphis's Democratic newspapers seemed satisfied with the effects of voting requirements, political machines in the city continued to rely on African Americans for support. If Black voters and spectacles indeed disappeared, these features of Memphis electoral politics did not stay away for long.

Despite voting restrictions many Black Memphians continued to vote and wield power, albeit in different ways. According to Black civic leader George W. Lee, African Americans played an "important part in the primaries and general elections of both Democratic and Republican parties." During the nineteenth century, according to Lee, African Americans "were in the ascendency at the city hall of Memphis, where they were identified with every department of the government." After the Republican Party lost control of the city, however, "the estrangement of the two races in politics" increased until every Black officeholder had "been dropped from positions of trust." From this point forward, "white ward bosses" controlled "large numbers of Negro votes" and patronage appointments.[14]

Although the circumstances had changed, African Americans continued to vote in large numbers. In the first decade of the twentieth century, at 52,000 they made up about half of the city's population, which made them a powerful demographic in municipal politics. Political bosses won the often-decisive support of Black voters in Memphis with paternalistic gestures of appreciation, such as parks and improvements in services. They helped Black voters pass literacy tests and paid their poll taxes in exchange for support. Black women, who most definitely did not have the right to vote, held suffrage meetings and encouraged Black men to pay their poll taxes and vote in the best interests of their families.[15]

In the late nineteenth and early twentieth centuries, Black Memphians had a powerful voice in local, regional, and national politics. In 1889 Ida B. Wells, from Holly Springs, Mississippi, became a co-owner and editor of the Black newspaper *Free Speech and Headlight*. Based in Memphis, she worked alongside Reverend Taylor Nightingale of Beale Street Baptist Church. She published articles about racial injustice in the city and the country. In response to the lynching of three Black men in 1889, Wells undertook an investigation of lynching, which resulted in the publication of her book *Southern Horrors: Lynch Law in All Its Phases*. In the book, she argued that there "is

Robert Church, W. C. Handy, and George W. Lee played an important role in the politics of Beale Street in turn-of-the-century Memphis. Image courtesy of Memphis and Shelby County Room, Memphis Public Library & Information Center.

little difference between the Antebellum South and the New South." Due to the lack of racial progress, she concluded, "a growing disregard of human life" had spread throughout the country. She called upon African Americans to leave the South unless lynching and segregation ended. She characterized Black labor as "the backbone of the South" and that the region would suffer without it.[16] She became a leading advocate of federal anti-lynching laws.

In addition to Wells, African Americans had a voice in Memphis politics through the church and voluntary organizations. In response to a derogatory 1903 editorial in the *Memphis Commercial-Appeal* on the biological inferiority of African Americans, Reverend John H. Grant and Reverend T. J. Searcy met with the editors, who agreed to publish their written response to the racist editorial. In their response, the ministers boasted Black achievements since emancipation and called for greater friendship between the races.[17] In 1908 Black bank clerk Bert Roddy hosted a picnic for the Black community in Memphis. Roddy and his peers anticipated white violence if they tried to use any of the city's existing parks for their gathering, so they petitioned park commission chairman Robert Galloway for the privilege. After Galloway denied the request, the chairman implied to Roddy that African Americans should have their own public spaces in the city. Roddy organized the Colored Citizens Association for the purposes of acquiring a park for Black use. Through this organization, Roddy mobilized Black voters. He referred to Black voters as "a sleeping political power" in the city. He wanted his organization to vote as a bloc for the candidates that had the most to offer the Black community. Specifically, he wanted officeholders that would deliver on a promise of a new park for Black Memphians. His organization would eventually become a key contributor to the Crump machine.[18]

HANDY AND CRUMP ARRIVE IN MEMPHIS

Born in 1873 in Florence, Alabama, William Christopher Handy became an accomplished musician despite the wishes of his conservative parents, who made him return his first guitar and forbade him from playing popular music.[19] In 1892 he left work at a factory in Birmingham, Alabama, joined a quartet, and went to Chicago. There he hoped to find work for his band because the city hosted the World's Fair, but economic depression made work difficult to find, so they quickly disbanded. Although the rest of the band returned to Alabama, Handy continued to travel and work throughout the Midwest.

In 1896 he joined his first successful orchestra, Mahara's Colored Minstrels, managed and promoted by white Chicagoans. Although they performed belittling songs in blackface, Mahara's Minstrels and other Black musicians stood to benefit economically from massive white audiences. By playing for white audiences, blackface minstrels integrated their music into the national mainstream and gained recognition of their professional talents. Before Handy's arrival, Mahara's Minstrels had already become one of the most famous and successful minstrel acts in the country.[20] Handy only stayed with the group for a year and returned to Alabama.

In 1897 Handy returned to Alabama and taught music at the Agricultural and Mechanical College in Huntsville, where he started to work as a composer, and where he remained until 1902. He traveled around the region for a few years studying and playing music. During these travels, he encountered the kind of music in the Mississippi Delta that inspired him to compose and play the blues.[21]

When Handy arrived in Memphis in 1905, he had a humble start. He organized his own band, but they did not immediately dazzle Memphis, where residents continued to give preference to the orchestras of Charlie Bynum and R. K. Eckford.[22] The 1909 Memphis mayoral election provided him and his band their opportunity for a big break.

Born in 1874 in Holly Springs, Mississippi, Edward Hull Crump came from a wealthy family. His father owned a cotton plantation and had served as an officer in the Confederate army. In 1878 Crump's father died of yellow fever, and his mother had a difficult time keeping the family solvent. In 1894 Crump arrived in Memphis to pursue economic opportunities, but he quickly became enmeshed in Memphis politics.

Although Crump initially had a difficult time finding work in Memphis, he quickly ascended the social and political ladder. In 1896 he became a bookkeeper for the Woods Carriage Company, which soon merged with a saddle company. In 1900 Crump became the secretary and treasurer of the newly formed Woods-Chickasaw Manufacturing Company. He eventually purchased and owned the company. In 1902 Crump married Bessie Byrd McLean, the daughter of a wealthy Memphis businessman.

By 1904 Crump had become the director of the Memphis Business Men's Club. He won election with the help of Frank D. Rice, who would become Crump's perennial campaign manager. Together they would eventually take control of Memphis and, to a large extent, the state of Tennessee.

In 1906 Crump became a member of the Board of Public Works Supervisors and locally famous among middle-class Memphians as a reformer, which irritated Memphis's traditional elite. After a year, he resigned and announced his candidacy for a spot on the Board of Fire and Police Commissioners. Upon claiming the office, he busted saloons and gambling houses, which earned him solid support from Memphis's middle class. He became a leading advocate of commission government in an attempt to more efficiently reform the city. In 1909 he decided to run for mayor.[23]

THE 1909 MEMPHIS MAYORAL ELECTION

On August 9, 1909, Memphis opened voter registration for municipal elections in November, and the registration followed strict rules and had oversight from the candidates, judges, and other public officials. On the opening day, the editors of the *Memphis Commercial-Appeal* anticipated that these registration books would be the "most accurate and representative ever compiled." The first registration period lasted ten days, and the candidates subjected the registration books to intense scrutiny.[24] During registration, Democrat John J. Williams sent "a personal representative" to most of the city's precincts. These representatives copied each name from the registration books into a personal book. Each night, Williams's supporters cross-referenced each voter's address with their actual residence. Crump and Democrat Walter W. Talbert expressed satisfaction in the fairness of the registration process and did not take these extreme steps.[25]

In an attempt to limit registration, the election commission did not help voters locate their local registration sites. The locations of the registration books changed, and the hours in which registration sites opened varied. Except for the courthouse, the registrars chose registration sites different from those used in the past, so voters had "to study the city map to locate the registration books of their ward." The registrars had instructions to prominently display banners to indicate a business as a registration site. On the first day of the registration period, many registrars failed to display the banners. *Memphis Commercial-Appeal* editors indicated, "It is the only guide that voters have, and there is a great deal of confusion growing out of the fact that the usual places of registration in many instances have been changed."[26] Despite the confusion and the best attempts of the city to minimize voter turnout, Memphians registered in unprecedented numbers.

For the most part, the *Memphis Commercial-Appeal* editors praised the registration sites selected by the election commission. From their perspective, the commissioners "exercised more than the usual prudence in selecting these places." Specifically, the editors rejoiced in the fact that the commissioners avoided saloons "as nearly as possible," yet they lamented that saloons had "not entirely been avoided."[27] Although many in Memphis hoped the election would eliminate the power of tavern keepers and African Americans, inner-city saloons nevertheless played a major role in the registration, especially for the Black community.

During the registration period, Black musicians helped register Black voters in the city's saloons along Beale Avenue. Although Crump and his chief opponent, Williams, had not yet entered the race, they had wealthy supporters willing to register voters, especially Black voters in the Fifth, Sixth, and Seventh wards. In Memphis, a mayoral candidate needed an estimated six thousand votes to win a majority, so the two thousand Black voters living on or around Beale Avenue played a significant role in deciding the election.

Crump and his supporters knew he could win plenty of votes in Memphis's white neighborhoods, but they predicted that these votes would not be enough to win the election. Although Crump did not make any personal

According to some in Memphis, Handy first played the blues at the P. Wee Saloon on Beale Street. Handy recalls playing his famous tune "Mr. Crump" on the streets during the day. The Beale Street saloons played an important role in the voter turnout of African Americans. Image courtesy of Memphis and Shelby County Room, Memphis Public Library & Information Center.

attempts to reach Black voters in this particular campaign, his supporters certainly did.[28] The other candidates had supporters willing to do the same. According to Handy, "three leading Negro bands were sent out by the managers of each candidate to whoop it up and bring home the bacon."[29] Jim Mulcahy, an Irish political boss in Memphis who supported Crump, employed Handy and his band to play in the Black taverns on Beale Avenue, such as the P. Wee Saloon or Hammitt Ashford's saloon at the corner of Fourth Street, which Lee called "the most ancient and superb of all the saloons." Handy's band played music to attract African Americans into the taverns. There, the Crump's representatives purchased a few rounds of drink, paid the balance on any outstanding poll taxes for these voters, and gave the newly registered voters their poll tax receipts and ballots marked for the candidate.[30] In this way, Handy influenced the 1909 mayoral election but also gained notoriety for himself.

For the 1909 campaign, Crump's opponents hired Handy's more accomplished rivals, Bynum's Superb Orchestra and the Eckford and Higgins Imperial Orchestra, to attract Black voters into taverns.[31] Handy explained, "Bynum's with their flashy cornetist, Frank McDonald, hoped to win Beale Street for one candidate."[32] Charlie Bynum, from Huntsville, Alabama, organized his band out of Midway Café on the corner of Beale Avenue and Fourth Street and achieved quite a bit of success in Memphis. In fact, he may have been the first to play blues music in Memphis, but he never composed the songs nor sold them commercially. Bynum worked alongside Jim Turner, who had traveled with Handy in Mahara's Minstrels and later joined Handy's band in Memphis.[33] Meanwhile, R. K. Eckford's band "tried to blow another man into office with the help of Teddy Adams, the speed demon clarinetist."[34] Like Bynum's, Eckford's band had established itself as a major act on Beale Avenue.[35] These three bands played for the three major candidates, Crump, Walter W. Talbert, and John J. Williams, over the course of the registration period.

For a long time, Black musicians had played their music on the streets of Memphis. In 1864 the Third US Colored Heavy Artillery played in the city's parks and squares and gained a favorable reputation, at least among the city's Republicans. A few days before the 1866 Memphis Riot, the Memphis newspapers reacted with disgust at the sight of these same Black military musicians playing in a city square. More than fifty years later, Black musicians continued to ply their trades on public streets, parks, and squares, but they now showcased their talents and helped register and mobilize Black voters. By employing these Black musicians, white politicians, or at least their managers, admitted that Black musicians played an acceptable, even desirable, part of the political process.[36]

During registration, Memphians turned out in immense numbers and broke records, thus signaling the start to a competitive campaign. In the early days of registration, the candidates made every effort "to bring out the full registered vote of the city."[37] The *Memphis Commercial-Appeal* editors pleaded with citizens to register to vote because "a superior set of officers must be elected" to make the transition to commission-style government on January 1, 1910. They encouraged "good men" to register "to take an active part in public affairs" and "cast a vote when good citizenship and good government demand it." They wanted to counter the effects of machine politics by encouraging all eligible Memphians to register.[38]

By the time registration ended on August 19, more than 11,000 Memphians had registered, which represented a substantial increase over the 1907 election. The *Memphis Commercial-Appeal* editors had not anticipated such heavy registration given the unseasonably hot weather. Nonetheless, people turned out because of "keen interest" in the campaign.[39] Memphians would have another opportunity to register when the books opened for a few days in October.

When registration ended, only Talbert had officially announced his intention to run for the mayor's office, but newspapers predicted that Crump, Williams, and a socialist candidate would soon enter the fray. Talbert announced his candidacy months before anyone else and quickly distributed copies of his platform to Memphis voters. He aggressively pursued victory.[40] He drew his support from the suburbs, so his campaign threatened to take away votes from Crump and send Williams into office.[41]

Throughout the campaign Talbert frequently went on the attack. In fact, he earned a reputation for negativity. According to the *Memphis Commercial-Appeal*, Talbert "developed a decided talent for letter writing, and almost every week indulges in caustic criticism of one or the other of his opponents through the pages of the daily papers."[42]

For the most part, Talbert portrayed himself as an outsider and friend of the business class. In a speech at Memphis's Peabody Hotel, Talbert jostled his audience. He explained that the "people of Memphis ought to wake up to several matters" because they "have simply gone to sleep over several of our opportunities." In the speech, Talbert, who drilled as a member of the Chickasaw Guards, specifically argued for the construction of an armory to supply the local militia. He proposed that the building would provide space for massive meetings and conventions as well. He insisted that the armory would make Memphis a premier destination for business conventions and political delegations, so the building would pay for itself.[43] By making this appeal, Talbert hoped to win support of Memphis's business class, who seemed likely to play a major role in this election because Memphis had expanded its borders and recently annexed some of the surrounding suburbs.[44]

On August 22, 1909, Crump announced his intention to run with the purpose of bringing commission-style government and efficient reform to the people of Memphis. He became popular with Memphis's white suburban progressives. He advocated for efficient "business government." Crump preferred commission government because he believed, like most Progressives, that it would help eliminate corruption and waste. The commission would have executive and legislative powers. In many ways, it would operate like a company board of directors with the mayor in charge of the city's several departments. Crump appealed to Progressives because of his reputation for reform. Among Crump's many reforms, he argued for the public ownership of utilities and tougher law enforcement, especially with regard to the city's saloons. By taking a stand against gambling and drinking as a member of the Board of Police and Fire Commissioners, he had earned support from progressives and humiliated Mayor James H. Malone, who had enjoyed the support of the saloon and gambling interests.[45]

Crump ran his campaign in an efficient style that mirrored his politics. He once again appointed Rice to manage the campaign.[46] Crump and Rice hired more than a dozen campaign speakers to do most of the public appearances. Among them, Charles M. Bryan, a lawyer and poet, became one of Crump's leading advocates and made most of the campaign's public appearances. Crump adopted a different approach to reach voters. He preferred "a method of campaigning successful in the past."[47] While Bryan and two other young men, William J. Bacon and Leo Goodman, did most of the orations, Crump focused on personal connections.[48] He visited the various wards to make a "personal and hand to hand canvass," which he used to great success to "upset the old order of things a few years ago."[49] He had gained a reputation in Memphis for his kindness and honesty. In a *News Scimitar* profile of Crump, cartoonist E. A. Bushnell indicated that "Mr. Crump has the stamp of good fellowship all over him." He characterized him as "having a very peculiar and extraordinary personality" and as "very approachable, cordial, considerate and obliging."[50] Although Crump had assembled a crack team of political campaigners, he had an uphill battle to win the election.

On August 27, Williams, a Democrat, joined the race and provided Crump a seasoned adversary, and many Memphis political insiders predicted that Williams would win the office. In 1894 Williams made his first bid to win the mayor's office by reinvigorating a once-powerful coalition of working-class Irish and African Americans, which had been replaced in 1879 by an all-white ruling elite. During the 1894 campaign, Williams earned endorsements from Memphis's labor unions, but he lost the election to incumbent W. Lucas Clapp because of the massive support Clapp received from Memphis's white suburbanites.

In 1898 Williams prevailed in the mayoral race after building up his biracial coalition. By this time, he had gained the support of Memphis's criminal interests, as well, notably George Honan and Mike Shanley. Honan controlled gambling in Memphis. Shanley had murdered a rival gang leader. In 1904 Honan and Shanley became involved in a gunfight with the sheriff's department, which resulted in the death of two deputies, one of whom was a Black man. Honan faced trial in the deaths, but he avoided conviction because his defense attorney successfully portrayed the Black deputy as disrespectful toward white people. Although none of Williams's political allies served a prison sentence, the city's white suburbanites became increasingly concerned about the power wielded by Memphis's gamblers and gangs. In response, Williams reached out to white suburbanites and seemingly alienated his criminal supporters. During his administration Memphis annexed the suburbs, and suburban residents enjoyed lower tax rates than city dwellers. Williams commissioned the construction of two new parks, and had many of the city's roads paved. He promised tougher enforcement of gambling and drinking laws in the city. In 1905 mayoral candidate James H. Malone, an independent, lured the support of Memphis's criminal class, who harassed voters and obstructed voting on election day. Malone prevailed and took office.[51] Although Williams lost, he did not disappear and became the favorite to retake the office in the 1909 campaign.

In September and early October, the race picked up the pace as the three candidates, especially Talbert, educated voters in the city's newspapers with open letters, platform declarations, and critical advertisements. In the newspapers, Talbert penned a series of open letters to his opponents. In one open letter, Talbert called out Crump's past record as a city official. He condemned Crump for "cold feet" with regard to the public ownership of an electric plant. He also referenced two ballot-stuffers who served jail time for election fraud on Crump's behalf. Talbert admitted that Crump earned praise for raiding gambling dens, but he condemned Crump failing to keep up the fight. He suggested that Crump counted on the support of "the most noted keepers of gambling places in the city." He argued that Crump, who still served on the Board of Police and Fire Commissioners, threatened "city employees into the belief that their jobs depend upon the support that they give to you in your race for mayor."[52] In a later letter, Talbert characterized Crump as an "unseasoned, erratic young person" with "a record for public service that is in effect null and void."[53] Like Talbert, the other candidates used the newspapers to articulate their ideas and criticize their opponents.

Williams, who released his official platform in the *Memphis Commercial-Appeal*, intended to improve the city's infrastructure and services and took special notice of the needs of the poor. When he announced his candidacy, he promised to "urge the establishment in a gradual way a system of public baths for the poor of both races."[54] He also focused on the city's sanitation system, which he characterized as "the all important consideration in any city."[55] He also intended to improve the extend the city's street system and viaducts. He aimed to manage the city government in a "high state of efficiency."[56] The three major candidates all focused on similar reforms and emphasized efficiency in their policy declarations.

In addition to the educational campaign waged in the city's newspapers, Williams and Talbert employed spectacular methods to energize voters. On

August 30, both Williams and Talbert held campaign events for the public. Williams hosted an event in the Postal Telegraph Company building, which served as his campaign headquarters. They congregated at 8:00 p.m. "with the purpose in view of mapping out future action to promote his interests." To the same ends, Tablet's campaign staged an event in the Royal Building.[57] Throughout the campaign, these two candidates held nightly meetings at their campaign headquarters attended by ward clubs.[58] Of the candidates, Talbert gained the most notoriety for his stump speeches. In October the *Memphis Commercial-Appeal* credited Talbert with "making a lively campaign" with "several surprises in store for his opponents."[59]

On September 26, Crump officially commenced his campaign. Unlike Talbert and Williams, Crump waited until late September to open a campaign headquarters because he preferred "short, sharp campaigns."[60] He established his campaign headquarters in the Security Bank building on Madison Avenue, in close proximity to his opponents' headquarters.[61] In a letter to the *Memphis Commercial-Appeal*, he announced that he intended to run for mayor because of his "profound interest in the success of the commission form of government" taking hold in Memphis as of January 1, 1910. From his previous experience in Memphis government, he understood the "wasteful, cumbersome, inefficient and unbusinesslike manner in which the large affairs of this city have been administered." He concluded that the current system "made anything like prompt and systematic business methods impossible." He emphasized his intention to "obtain the most for the people for the least money" and "to run this city as thoroughly in all of its departments as I would any large business corporation."[62] Like the other candidates, Crump expressed the need for efficiency in government, but he had the business background to back up his promises.

During the last three weeks of the campaign the candidates became increasingly visible, with nightly public appearances to reach out to male voters and female supporters. In late October, the three candidates staged public rallies and reached out to women in their advertisements. During the Progressive Era, women became increasingly entangled in party machinery, especially because of the era's emphasis on reform. They used their domesticity to influence politics by taking up matters such as child labor policy and prohibition. The political parties hoped to attract women to their ranks for numerous reasons. In the rough world of electoral politics, candidates reached out to women because their support would serve as a sign of candidates' virtue. They also hoped that women would persuade their husbands or fellow politicians to pass reforms. In Memphis, women took an interest in the mayoral campaign and participated in rallies. Notably,

Crump and Williams hoped to improve the city's sanitation, which had been of major interest to female reformers in American cities.[63] On October 21, Talbert hosted a rally on Madison Avenue open to men and women.[64] On October 29, Crump's campaign team hosted a rally on Madison Avenue for the clubs representing the recently annexed suburbs of Lenox and Mt. Arlington. Although Crump did not speak on his own behalf, his team of orators, including Bryan and Goodman, did speak. They extended an invite to the women of these suburbs.[65]

Throughout the campaign, the candidates charged their opponents with nefarious practices and relying on Black voters to win the election, and these charges picked up in the last few weeks of the race. Talbert levied the most critical charges on the other candidates for their pursuance of Black votes. He praised the enactment of the secret ballot because it "meant almost the elimination of the negro from politics." He encouraged the voters of Memphis, "Go back to the reconstruction days! Think of what our people of the South suffered to rid our country of the domination of the negro!"[66] Crump boldly criticized Williams and African Americans when he placed an advertisement in the *News Scimitar* featuring a fist brandishing a whip. The wielder of the whip had a tag around his wrist with the words: "'Nigger' Divekeepers for Williams." At the violent end of the whip, numerous Black figures marched together into a polling booth. In the advertisement, he charged that because "the white voters of Memphis are overwhelmingly in favor of E. H. Crump, Joe Williams has resorted to the scheme of thrusting himself into office by the negro dive vote." He condemned Williams for registering "great hordes of the most degraded negroes in the First precinct of the Fifth ward."[67] Williams, who received the most criticism for pursuing Black voters, made his own charges against the candidates, especially against Crump. He claimed that Crump "never submitted his races to the Democratic primaries, for the very obvious reason that he could not then buy up, corral and drive in the negro votes, yet endeavor, at the same time, to divert the public's eye by maliciously charging such nefarious campaign methods to his opponents."[68] In the educational campaign waged in the newspapers, the candidates blamed African Americans for fraudulent voting and condemned each other for pursuing Black votes. In the spectacular campaigns, however, the candidates turned to Black musicians to rally Black voters.

Despite the eagerness of the candidates to eliminate African Americans from politics, all three of them employed Black musicians for their campaigns. In Memphis, Black musicians set up on the city streets to play music to mobilize Black voters. The same musicians that worked during the registration drive now set up in taverns and the city streets to help energize the

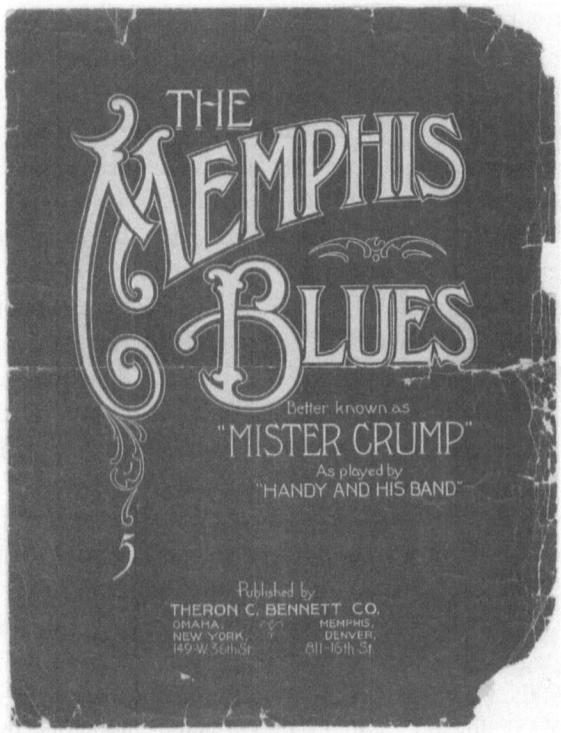

After the campaign concluded, Handy rebranded his song as "The Memphis Blues" and published it. Image courtesy of Memphis and Shelby County Room, Memphis Public Library & Information Center.

electorate for their respective candidates. Specifically, they worked to cultivate name recognition and personality for the candidates.

Handy embraced his role as a musician for the Crump campaign and wanted to find a melody to capture Crump's policies. He tried out various melodies and songs, some of which "might have expressed the mood and temper of Mr. Crump's platform" but "would certainly not have pulled any votes for him." Handy recognized, "Hot-cha music was the stuff we needed, and it had to be mellow."[69] After trial and error, Handy discovered the right tune. Handy's creation, a blues song named "Mr. Crump," featured notable characteristics of Black music in regard to form and melody that he had encountered in his travels through the Mississippi Delta. The blues derived from previous African forms of music common to the antebellum South, such as the field holler and call and response. In the field holler, a solo singer expressed himself through strong rhythm, melody, and delivery.[70] The song implemented a three-chord basic structure, which according to Handy, "was that already used by Negro roustabouts, honky tonk piano players, wanderers, and others of their underprivileged class." In addition to the chord structure, Handy wanted to use notes in the melody that suggested "the typical slurs of the Negro voice" such as flat thirds and seventh notes.[71] Black musicians integrated these African elements into European-style folk ballads, which utilized a three-line form with alternating rhymed couplets.[72] In Black culture, musicians employed all of these tactics to "express his personal feelings in a sort of musical soliloquy."[73] Handy created the melody and the rhythms by listening to other Black musicians throughout his travels in the American South, but he developed the lyrics to the song after listening to the comments of Black citizens of Memphis.

Handy had written the tune to "Mr. Crump" and played it successfully to enthusiastic audiences before he wrote the lyrics. Many African Americans resented Crump's reform platform, which Handy described "as palatable to Beale Street voters as castor oil." While playing the song, Handy "heard various comments from the crowds" and from the members of his band who expressed "their own feelings about reform." According to Handy, "most of these comments had been sung, impromptu, to my music." African Americans used Handy's music to express their own views on Crump's campaign. Handy captured these comments and put them into his own lyrics for the song:

> Mr. Crump won't 'low no easy riders here
> Mr. Crump won't 'low no easy riders here
> We don't care what Mr. Crump don't 'low
> We gon' to bar'l-house anyhow—
> Mr. Crump can go and catch hisself some air!

Despite the unflattering lyrics, Handy did not think the song did any harm to the Crump campaign, and Crump likely never heard these lyrics in the streets. If anything, these lyrics may have helped voters remember Crump's name.[74] Handy had a humorous disposition and, like many African Americans in Memphis, doubted Crump could or would eliminate taverns within the city and reform Memphis's nightlife.[75] Having finished the song complete with lyrics, Handy set out on the city of Memphis to showcase his talents to eager and attentive white audiences.

Handy's band played the new composition on the streets of downtown Memphis to energize Black and white voters for Crump. "Thoroughly rehearsed and intoxicated by the new melody," Handy explained, "my musicians arrived at Main and Madison riding in a band wagon and got set to play the blues to the general public for the first time in America." After the band had set up its equipment, he "flashed the sign and the boys gave. Feet

During the campaign, Handy played all of Memphis's most important nightspots. Image courtesy of Memphis and Shelby County Room, Memphis Public Library & Information Center.

commenced to pat. A moment later there was dancing on the sidewalks below. Hands went into the air, bodies swayed like the reeds on the banks of the Congo." The people on the streets begged for more while in "the office buildings about, the white folks pricked up their ears. Stenographers danced with their bosses. Everybody shouted for more." Handy said the band "heard them on all sides demanding that we play the song again. One bystander came directly in front of us and insisted on knowing the name of the tune." Guitarist George Higgins told the inquiring person, "That's 'Mr. Crump,'" and continued playing the song for the enthusiastic audience.[76]

The band performed the song in theaters and concert halls across Memphis throughout campaign season. "From that day our band was swamped with calls," recalled Handy. His band divided "into three groups, each carrying violin, clarinet, cornet, trombone, guitar, and bass." The band sent out a call across the South for musicians to bolster the size and prevalence of the group. According to Handy, all "of the parks and dance halls employed us. When the demand reached its height, we were using sixty-seven musicians."[77] On these occasions, Handy played the song for mostly white audiences to the benefit of his own career, which supported Crump's mayoral campaign as well.

By November the candidates and the musicians had both completed an exhausting three-week run of public appearances. The three leading candidates had presented "hundreds of speeches" and had held meetings "in every ward of the city and in the new annexed territory." The public appearances gave voters an opportunity to "hear the merits of their favorite candidate excited and the demerits of such candidate's opponents held up to the light." According to the *Memphis Commercial-Appeal*, the "enthusiasm of many of the voters" had been "aroused to such a pitch as to indicate that an election was close at hand."[78] In the final days, the candidates made their last appeals, in the newspapers but especially in the city streets.

On November 2, Talbert staged his final campaign rally before election day. In the highly contentious Nineteenth Ward, Talbert hosted a meeting at the Jefferson Theater on the corner of Decatur Street and Lane Street attended by a "large crowd." As usual, Talbert spoke on his own behalf.[79] Simultaneously, Crump supporters gathered in the Eighth, Ninth, Tenth, and Eleventh Wards, and Williams's forces held rallies at Gaston Park in the coveted Thirteenth Ward.

On November 3, Crump and Williams staged their final rallies and events to energize voters for the upcoming battle. During the afternoon, William Wallace Saxby Jr., director of Memphis's Christian Brothers High School Band, the Memphis Philharmonic Orchestra Association, and the Memphis Municipal Park Band, led one of these elite groups in a parade of the city streets in support of Williams.[80] From 7:00 to 8:00 p.m., one of Saxby's bands performed a concert at Court Square in the city's center. Afterward, Williams staged his final rally at the same location, where he spoke to "one of the largest crowds of the campaign." In his speech, he emphasized his record as mayor and a public official. On Williams's behalf, Shelby County Sheriff Frank L. Monteverde spoke to the massive audience.[81]

Meanwhile, Crump held a mass open-air meeting at Gaston Park in the "much-fought-over" Thirteenth Ward. Once again, Crump did not speak at his own event. Instead, he counted on "a dozen or more" of his campaign's best speakers to energize an audience of seven hundred to a thousand people.[82] At these events the candidates and their supporters launched "rockets and red fire," and the "two rival campaigns will be closed in a burst of oratory and fireworks in the good, old-fashioned style." After concluding the rallies, the candidates finally had the opportunity "to take a few hours' rest before the work of election day begins on Thursday morning."[83] After months of campaigning, the candidates made a final push on election day.

ELECTION DAY IN MEMPHIS

On November 4, Memphians enjoyed a beautiful autumn day, went to the polls to cast their ballots, and hit the streets to participate in the election-day spectacle. Memphis police monitored each of the city's election sites, and Chief of Police W. C. Davis toured every precinct by automobile.[84] In the morning, Mayor Malone changed the assignments for the police officers, which led to some confusion and worried election officials. Based on these developments and the anticipation of heavy voting, the *News Scimitar* editors predicted that "today's election gives every promise of being as hot as anyone could desire."[85] Memphians did not disappoint these predictions.

In the morning, Memphians went to the polls, but they also paraded and drove through the city streets to demonstrate their allegiance to their candidates. First, Crump and his supporters paraded. The procession featured the same Saxby's band that had played at Williams's final rally held the previous evening. In twelve carriages and fifteen automobiles, Crump's supporters followed him and the band on the parade route "all carrying huge Crump banners." In addition to these parades, Williams and Talbert supporters appeared on the streets, "but they did not attempt a parade" and "went at once to the different polling places." Instead, Williams's supporters gathered for "a lively scene in and around" their headquarters. Here, his lieutenants assembled to receive final instructions and campaign literature, which they distributed at the polling precincts. The Williams supporters demonstrated the "same spirit of confidence in final victory" as at the other headquarters. Williams did not show up at his headquarters to greet his supporters. Instead, he waited in his office all day for the election results.[86] The election-day spectacle had a hot start, but it would only grow livelier throughout the day.

At 11:30 a.m., Crump assaulted a Black voter in the first precinct of the Fifth Ward because he suspected election fraud. According to the *Memphis Commercial-Appeal*, the "mix-up in the Fifth was a sensational one." Robert Houston, a Black man, entered the polling station at 425 Beale Avenue. When he exited the building, he left with an official, unmarked ballot "for the purpose of marking it for an ignorant voter." Crump noticed the illegal behavior and confronted Houston. Will Parsons, who owned a nearby saloon, spoke up on behalf of Houston. At some point, Crump "handed the negro a right swing to the point of the jaw." Memphis police officers arrested Houston and Parsons for election fraud. Later, a local judge issued a warrant charging Crump with assault and battery.[87]

Despite Crump's open hostility toward Black voters, he tallied significant votes from Black voters on Beale Avenue. Although Handy admitted, "I am sure he would he would have been easily elected without me," his song "Mr. Crump" may have helped Crump with Black voters.[88] In general, Memphians predicted that Williams would carry the downtown wards and Crump would win in the suburbs. Although Williams won the Fifth Ward and the Black vote generally, Crump earned ninety-four votes at the Beale Avenue precinct where he assaulted Houston. Notably, Crump carried the only other precinct located on Beale Avenue. In the Seventh Ward, voters cast ballots at the indoor swimming pool on the corner of Beale Avenue and Orleans St. At this precinct, Crump received 252 votes to Williams's 135 votes.[89] With these small victories, Crump cut into Williams's base and threatened to win the election. To win, Crump would have to succeed in the hotly contested Thirteenth Ward.

In the Thirteenth Ward, Memphians buzzed around the polling precincts with the greatest activity. Throughout the campaign, the candidates battled over this ward's 1,800 registered voters. Located near the railroad shops and the city's manufacturing district, this ward consisted mostly of railroad workers and union laborers. At Robinson's Drug Store on the corner of McLemore Street and Rayburn Street, more than 100 campaign workers assembled to make their last impressions on undecided voters. When voters entered the polling booths, these workers cried out and the entire area "sounded like a circus." The campaign workers used "rough tactics" at this polling precinct throughout the day, "but every person seemed to be in a holiday mood and no trouble occurred." At each of the three precincts of the Thirteenth Ward, Crump triumphed, especially at Robinson's Drug Store, where he collected 354 votes, his largest total of any polling place.[90]

Amid the election-day fervor, twelve jurors collectively made their way to the polling place near the courthouse. the *News Scimitar* explained, "If you see a crowd of twelve men march two by two to a polling place today, don't think it is a detachment of militia or a political marching club." At the time of the election, Bonny Burchett faced murder charges in the death of Mercedes Donovan. During murder trials, jury members could not separate themselves from the other jurors nor have any outside contact. To vote, they had to march together to the polling places to cast their ballots under the supervision of sheriff's deputies, which they did in the afternoon.[91] On election day, spectators went outside to observe spectacles like this one as just one part of the entire day's experience. By reporting on it, newspapers helped cultivate the image of the spectacular election by informing readers of the happenings they may have missed.

Across the city, election officials called on citizens to visit and remain at the precincts to deter illegal behavior. In the late afternoon, John H. Crain issued a statement to Memphis voters warning them about illegal behavior. As the secretary of the Shelby County Election Commission, he had been made aware of attempts to raid ballot boxes. Crain declared that the "presence of law-abiding citizens in force will prevent" illegal behavior. He requested "all good citizens who want to see a fair election and honest count" to return to their polling places at 5:00 p.m. and remain there until the polls closed at 7:00 p.m.[92] Despite all of the rules designed to prevent voter fraud, Memphis officials considered large crowds at the polls a safeguard of the democratic process.

After the polls closed, Memphians earnestly speculated about the outcome of the contest and gathered with one another to await official results. Outside the *Memphis Commercial-Appeal*'s offices, a crowd of five to eight thousand people awaited live updates of "the first and most accurate" election returns in the city. The crowd started building before the polls closed, and many thousands thronged the streets by 8:00 p.m. There, they watched the returns flashed up on a screen as soon as editors got word from the courthouse. It seems that the crowd consisted mostly of men, but women had plenty of interest in the outcome. In addition to the massive crowd outside of the building, newspaper employees fielded thousands of inquiries via telephone from curious Memphians. After the polls closed, three telephone lines at the *Memphis Commercial-Appeal* remained in constant use from 7:00 p.m. until midnight. During the night, the newspaper's three telephone operators answered more than ten thousand calls. With regard to the phone calls, an editor remarked, "One of the most surprising features was that more than half of the calls were from women." The editor suggested that women called the newspaper offices because "the men folks" went to view the results on the bulletin board.[93] In these segregated ways, Memphians participated in the events of election night with one another.

In the largest and closest vote in Memphis history, Crump prevailed by a mere seventy-nine votes out of more than twelve thousand cast. The *Memphis Commercial-Appeal* first announced the results to the thousands of spectators outside of its offices. Crump's supporters applauded and cheered the results together in Court Square.[94]

On Crump's victory, the *Memphis Commercial-Appeal* editors expressed cautious optimism regarding Crump's abilities and the city's impending experiment with commission-style government. They claimed that Crump had a "great responsibility" to satisfy the people's demands for a "divorcement of politics from the machinery of city government." They explained that the commission government depended greatly "upon the character of work the commissioners themselves do." In conclusion, they hoped that "this election marks the passing from an era of politics to business in our city government."⁹⁵

The *News Scimitar* joyously received the news of Crump's election. In the wake of his victory, the editors declared, "Mr. Crump seems to have excellent material in him." They characterized his victory as a sign that the people want a "more compact and more responsible form of government and prefer a man fully in sympathy with the experiment." They expected Crump to "give the city a clean businesslike administration and reduce waste to a minimum."⁹⁶ Memphians had high expectations and hopes for Crump, but the voter turnout gave them reasons to have even higher hopes in the future of the city.

During an era of disfranchisement, Memphians expressed satisfaction at the high voter-turnouts because it testified to their city's civic awareness and growth. According to the *News Scimitar*, "citizens in general were much gratified at the big vote rolled up, which would have been some hundreds larger had not poll tax books given out." With regard to the voter turnout, the editors remarked, "It is gratifying because it shows people are aroused to an interest in city affairs." They expressed satisfaction in the fact that the "big bulk of this registered vote is white" with fewer than "2,000 negroes being on the books." the *News Scimitar* explained, without too much harsh judgment, that African Americans "voted heavier than they have for many years" and "dictated the result in some precincts" because of their presence. Unlike the response Maconites had to Black voters in their city in 1898, Memphis editors did not call for any election reform nor condemn any candidates for pursuing Black voters.

CRUMP AND BLACK MEMPHIANS

Immediately after Crump took office, Black Memphians wrote to him and requested the creation of a park for the Black community. By April 1910, Robert Galloway, who served on the parks commission, reasoned that the "better classes" of African Americans in the city should have "some place of amusement" of their own to "go and spend a day."⁹⁷ At the time, the parks commission had not yet selected a site and would not make a decision for several years, so African Americans kept up the activism. The Colored Citizens of Memphis requested the rights to a piece of land they called Douglass Park. They considered this location ideal because of its proximity to the Louisville & Nashville Railroad, which the Black community had used "for at least thirty years in going to this locality with our picnics." In the meantime, they

Robert Church Jr. had a lasting and impactful relationship with Mayor E. H. Crump. Image courtesy of Memphis and Shelby County Room, Memphis Public Library & Information Center.

asked the mayor for continued rights to use this land for church picnics.98 In 1913 the city bought the land known as Douglass Park "for the exclusive use of negro citizens." In 1914, J. H. Cannon wrote to Crump requesting a space for him and his family to visit "after our toils" for the purposes of "rest or recreation." In advance, he thanked Crump "for anything you award us." Crump assured Cannon that they had purchased the park and had asked the parks commission to "begin at the earliest possible date" to put the "park in first-class condition."99 He would have contact with members of the Black community on many other issues.

During his tenure Crump had constant dialogue with Black Memphians; they sent him requests for new services and other concessions, which he greeted with respect and consideration. By the time Crump took office, Robert Church Jr. had taken over for his father as a major player in Memphis politics, and he continued his father's work on behalf of the Black community. He made visits to Crump's office to parlay.100

In addition to Church Jr.'s work, Black Memphians continued to organize into fraternal organizations and voluntary societies, such as the Colored

Men's Civil League. These organizations appealed to Crump for assistance and favors.[101] In July 1910, African Americans reached out to him on behalf of "the many negro boys and girls of this great city who are wards of the state" to establish a home for the city's neglected and delinquent children. They offered to supply the land for the building but only needed the city's help with the construction.[102] To this request, Crump promised his "most careful consideration."[103] By 1912 he had started working with local doctors and dentists to provide care for the Black schoolchildren of the city and to employ a Black physician at the hospital.[104] In 1912 T. O. Fuller of the Howe Institute asked Crump to exempt his institution from licensing because its funds "go to the development of the school and not for individual profit." The institution trained Black children "to make them good citizens" by instructing them in cooking, sewing, carpentry, and printing.[105] In 1914 he wrote to the Southern Baptist Convention about the site of a theological seminary for training Black ministers. He argued that "Memphis is the logical location for the proposed institution" because of its large "honest, hard-working" Black community, who "would doubtless give enthusiastic support to a school of this kind."[106] In the same year, Crump banned the showing of Thomas Dixon's *The Leopard's Spots* because he received complaints from the Black community about its portrayal of Black people.[107] By taking an interest in the needs of the Black community, Crump strengthened his political machine. He understood their importance in Memphis politics, and he received Black support throughout his career. His campaign manager, Rice, worked to register Black voters. In the next election, these voters helped Crump defeat Williams by seven thousand votes. With Black and white support, Crump's machine lasted deep into the twentieth century.[108]

THE CRUMP MACHINE

Crump dominated Memphis politics from 1909 until 1948, and he remained an important political figure until his death in 1954.[109] During his tenure as mayor, he pursued a variety of reform programs; he advocated a city-owned electric company to keep rates low for businesses, government, and citizens. His government regulated child labor, enacted measures to improve sanitary conditions in the city, created a Board of Charity to provide for the city's poor, and instituted a Board of Censors to review movies and plays for potentially harmful conduct. In 1916 Crump lost his position as mayor because he failed to uphold Tennessee's prohibition law, but he continued to rule Memphis from behind the scenes. From 1916 until 1924, he served as Shelby County

For decades after winning the 1909 mayoral election, Boss Crump controlled politics in Memphis. Image courtesy of Memphis and Shelby County Room, Memphis Public Library & Information Center.

Trustee. In 1930 he won election to the United States House of Representatives where he served until 1935. Until 1948 his political machine dominated Memphis and Tennessee politics.

By 1948 African Americans changed their tactics. Black voters became more independent at the encouragement of their civic leaders. Unable to mobilize Black voters, Crump's machine alienated them in favor of more predictable and loyal voters. From 1909 until 1948, however, the Crump machine had put its weight behind successful candidates for city, county, state, and national offices. Over the course of his career, he controlled Memphis and forever altered the nature of the Democratic Party in the South, specifically in Tennessee and the Mississippi Delta.[110]

W. C. HANDY: FATHER OF THE BLUES

With the song "Mr. Crump," Handy not only helped its namesake win the election; he became a famous musician and eventually a music publisher.

Although Handy was not the first person to play the blues in Memphis, Handy became known as the Father of the Blues because he published the music and made it accessible to white audiences. George W. Lee poses with a poster celebrating Handy's famous Beale Street compositions. Image courtesy of Memphis and Shelby County Room, Memphis Public Library & Information Center.

He and his band had become the leading Black band in Memphis in the early twentieth century, and they played all of the most important gigs in the city.[111] They played a concert at the Alaskan Roof Garden, which Handy characterized as the "leading uptown dance spot of white Memphis," thus providing "white society an opportunity to hear our wonderful xylophonist and drummer Jasper Taylor."[112] The popularity of the song encouraged Handy to publish it. In 1910 Handy met with Crump; he showed the mayor the lyrics, which he had written on brown wrapping paper. Handy asked Crump for permission to name the song after him and Crump agreed.[113] Eventually, Handy changed the name and lyrics, in addition to making a few changes to the structure and melody, before trying to sell it. The new song, "The Memphis Blues," became a major hit but not to the immediate benefit of its composer. Handy lost the copyright privileges to "Memphis Blues," but undeterred, he composed numerous popular songs over the course of his

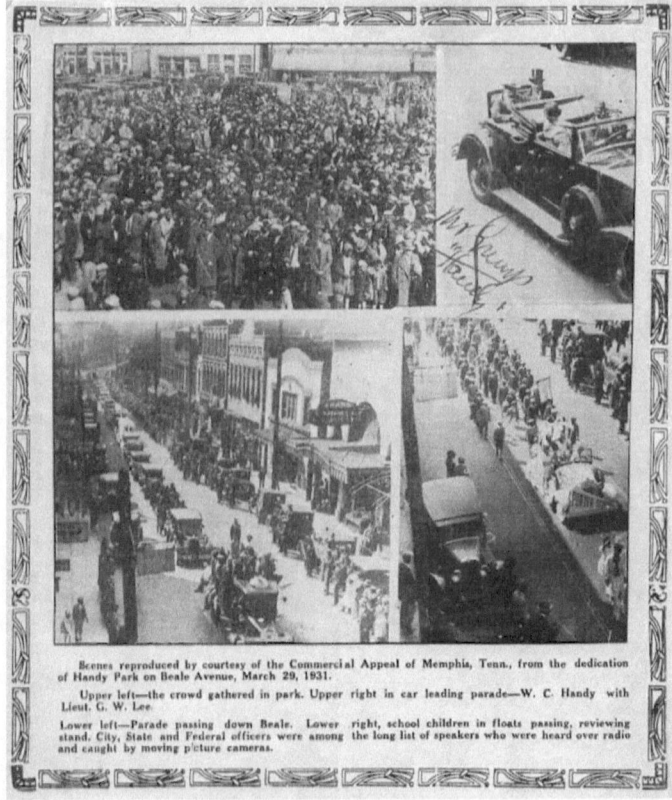

In 1931, Handy rode with Lee to the dedication of Handy Park in Memphis. Image courtesy of Memphis and Shelby County Room, Memphis Public Library & Information Center.

career, such as "St. Louis Blues," "Yellow Dog Blues," and "Beale Street Blues." He started his own music company, which published Black musicians.[114] By playing for the Crump campaign, Handy had launched his career.

The two men's legacies remained forever linked. Many years later, people generously and retroactively gave Handy credit for persuading "Memphis that Crump was a man in a thousand." According to *New York Times* columnist Lewis Nichols, Handy's band gained fame and "attracted attention" because "it paid its candidate compliments in a rhythm that was at the same time strange and haunting." Casting the ballots, Nichols explained, "the electorate signified its hopeful desires. When the returns came in, Crump was the new Mayor—and the blues had arrived."[115] According to another author, "politics started the 'blues'" because "Handy wrote a campaign song for Edward H. Crump that helped the 'Boss' to become Mayor of Memphis."[116] Given the fame Handy eventually achieved, people appreciated and shared a narrative

Handy Park now celebrates Handy with a statue of the Father of the Blues. Image courtesy of Memphis and Shelby County Room, Memphis Public Library & Information Center.

tying Handy's big break to the Crump campaign. In that close election, Handy may have helped the candidate on Beale Street in a minor way, but in accounts of the election and Handy far removed from the contest, they put the focus on the ascendant Father of the Blues.[117]

The 1909 Memphis mayoral election serves as one of many examples of African Americans actively participating in campaign events on behalf of white southern candidates during Jim Crow, yet this example features prominent and renowned political and musical figures at the beginning of their careers. Handy, a Black musician, and Crump, a southern Democrat, have a highly unlikely and perhaps perplexing relationship considering the racial politics of the early twentieth South. Although Crump and his opponents condemned Black voting and Reconstruction, their political machines employed Black musicians to rally Black voters on their behalf. The Black musicians seized the opportunity for their own purposes. Handy and his band worked on behalf of the Crump campaign because it provided them economic opportunity, access to white audiences, and political influence.

EPILOGUE

"I DIDN'T REALLY KNOW HOW TO SHOW MY OPPOSITION"

Street Theater in the Twenty-first Century

IN LATE JULY 2015, KU KLUX KLAN AND NATIONAL SOCIALIST MOVEMENT Party members marched to the statehouse in Columbia, South Carolina, to protest the removal of the Confederate flag from statehouse grounds in the aftermath of the mass murder at Emanuel African Methodist Episcopal Church. Local sousaphonist Matt Buck, a white man, joined the marchers with the intent of humiliating them. Along the parade route, Buck played Richard Wagner's "Ride of the Valkyries" and another tune with a bass line similar to "The Elephant March" from Disney's *The Jungle Book*. Buck, who knew the latter tune from a scene in television show *Family Guy*, explained, "I didn't really know how to show my opposition, so that was my way of doing it." He added, "My goal was to embarrass them, and I think I did a little bit." After Buck's serenade, YouTube user Diana Martin uploaded a video of the encounter to the internet, where it went viral. Across the globe, newspaper reporters and internet bloggers picked up on the story of how Buck resisted the white supremacists marching through South Carolina's capital. When asked about his methods, Buck responded, "I wanted to embarrass the KKK, rather than curse, harass, or become violent like some other protesters."[1]

In reaction to this story, many observers have reflected on Buck's white privilege and suggested that a Black performer could not have pulled off the same protest without repercussions.

From 1877 to 1932, African Americans had used similar means to articulate their views on politicians and reformers, causes and platforms. They expressed themselves with performance at all types of political and cultural spectacles. Like Buck, they used performance because they lacked other options. In an era of disfranchisement, segregation, lynching, and limited economic opportunity, African Americans adopted subtle yet nonetheless public and successful forms of resistance. With these performances, they pursued upward mobility and political influence.

After Reconstruction ended, white southerners embarked on a mission to make African Americans invisible in the political sphere. They used intimidation and legislation to cut off Black and poor white voters' access to the ballot box. Across the South, disfranchisement had an immediate impact on voter turnout. It had its most devastating effects on the Black vote.[2]

The lack of voting rights did not necessarily entail the complete loss of political power. In the late nineteenth and early twentieth centuries, women could not vote, but they nonetheless agitated on behalf of political parties and reform movements. They attended rallies and orations, marched in parades, gathered for bonfires and flag-raising ceremonies. They persuaded men to vote on their behalf. Through these forms of participation, they counted themselves as members of the public sphere.[3] In spite of disfranchisement, African Americans similarly made themselves a visible member of the public sphere without inciting trouble.

In twenty-first-century South Carolina, Matt Buck did not experience any meaningful backlash for his performance. He explained, "A few people had a few things to say, but nobody really confronted me or anything."[4] In public, nineteenth-century African Americans performed some dangerous behavior, but they rarely suffered any backlash for confronting white women or humiliating white politicians, which would seem exactly like the kind of behavior that would have resulted in lynching. They successfully adorned the character of the feckless Black performer, which satisfied white desires for minstrel performances. By assuming these roles, Black southerners escaped trouble yet voiced political views.

With the performance in South Carolina, Buck demonstrates that the behavior analyzed in this study does not have chronological or geographical boundaries. It existed before Reconstruction ended in 1877. It continued after the election of President Roosevelt in 1932.

It was not and has not solely been used by Black southerners, either. Buck, a white man, used these methods. In October 2016, the mostly Latino members of the Nevada's Culinary Workers Union set up a wall of taco trucks outside of a property owned by then-presidential candidate Donald J. Trump. The protest mocked Trump's threats to build a wall between the United States and Mexico and manipulated comments made by Marco Gutierrez, who founded Latinos for Trump and claimed that immigration at the current rate would lead to "taco trucks on every corner" of the country.[5] Latino culinary workers took these words and policies and used them to structure their protest.

Although many people from diverse backgrounds in different times and places have used these methods to carve out a small political space, this book focuses on the American South from 1877 to 1932 because it seemed the least likely time and place to find public Black political behavior.

During a period of disfranchisement and lynching, African Americans accessed the political sphere by adorning the character of the humble, loyal servant and the feckless Black performer, which helped them escape the harsh repercussions reserved for African Americans who stepped out of their prescribed role in southern society. Behind these characters, African Americans sometimes exhibited dangerous behavior before white audiences in the quest for political and economic power.

As a result, African Americans exercised a spectrum of political behavior. They attacked white supremacy in the courts and in the legislatures. They built up their own communities. Based on the findings of this study, they also accessed otherwise unavailable spaces, such as campaign rallies and parades, and made themselves seen and heard. They did not always accomplish much with their efforts. At times, they earned some brief fame, a bit of cash, or a laugh at their oppressor's expense. At other times, they reached massive audiences, earned fame and fortune, or humiliated politicians. By participating in political spectacles in a variety of ways, African Americans struck back against white supremacy, just like their ancestors in Reconstruction and their successors in the civil rights movement.

NOTES

INTRODUCTION

1. W. C. Handy, *Father of the Blues: An Autobiography* (New York: Da Capo Press, 1941), 79–82; Adam Gussow, "'Make My Getaway': The Blues Lives of Black Minstrels in W. C. Handy's *Father of the Blues*," *African-American Review* 35 (Spring 2001): 5–28; Adam Gussow, "Racial Violence, 'Primitive' Music, and the Blues Entrepreneur: W. C. Handy's Mississippi Problem," *Southern Cultures* 8 (Fall 2002): 56–77.

2. Handy, *Father of the Blues*, 79–82; Gussow, "'Make My Getaway,'" 5–28; Gussow, "Racial Violence," 56–77.

3. Handy, *Father of the Blues*, 79–82; Gussow, "'Make My Getaway,'" 5–28; Gussow, "Racial Violence," 56–77.

4. Handy, *Father of the Blues*, 79–82; Gussow, "'Make My Getaway,'" 5–28; Gussow, "Racial Violence," 56–77.

5. Handy, *Father of the Blues*, 79–82; Gussow, "'Make My Getaway,'" 5–28; Gussow, "Racial Violence," 56–77.

6. Robert Higgs, "Race and Economy in the South, 1890–1950," in *The Age of Segregation: Race Relations in the South, 1890–1945*, ed. Robert Haws (Jackson: University Press of Mississippi, 1978), 89–90; Joel Williamson, *The Crucible of Race: Black-White Relations in the American South Since Emancipation* (New York: Oxford University Press, 1984), 251.

7. C. Vann Woodward, *The Strange Career of Jim Crow: A Commemorative Edition* (New York: Oxford University Press, 2001), 3–8, 11–18, 67–72; Dan Carter, "Southern Political Style," in *The Age of Segregation: Race Relations in the South, 1890–1945*, ed. Robert Haws (Jackson: University Press of Mississippi, 1978), 50–66.

8. Woodward, *The Strange Career of Jim Crow*, 3–8, 11–18, 67–72; Edward L. Ayers, *The Promise of the New South: Life after Reconstruction* (New York: Oxford University Press, 2007), 136–46; Glenda Elizabeth Gilmore, *Gender and Jim Crow: Women and the Politics of White Supremacy in North Carolina, 1896–1920* (Chapel Hill: University of North Carolina Press, 1996); Jane Dailey, Glenda Elizabeth Gilmore, and Bryant Simon, *Jumpin' Jim Crow: Southern Politics from Civil War to Civil Rights* (Princeton, NJ: Princeton University Press, 2000); Ida B. Wells-Barnett, *Southern Horrors: Lynch Law in All Its Phases* (New York: New York Age Print, 1892), http://www.gutenberg.org/files/14975/14975-h/14975-h.htm; Grace Elizabeth Hale, *Making Whiteness: The Culture of Segregation in the South, 1890–1940* (New York: Pantheon, 1998); Lisa Lindquist Dorr, *White Women, Rape, and the Power of Race in Virginia, 1900–1960* (Chapel Hill: University of North Carolina Press, 2004); Amy Louise

Wood, *Lynching and Spectacle: Witnessing Racial Violence in America, 1890–1940* (Chapel Hill: University of North Carolina Press, 2009); Paul Ortiz, *Emancipation Betrayed: The Hidden History of Black Organizing and White Violence in Florida from Reconstruction to the Bloody Election of 1920* (Berkeley: University of California Press, 2005); Leon F. Litwack, *Trouble in Mind: Black Southerners in the Age of Jim Crow* (New York: Alfred A. Knopf, 1998), 404–22.

9. Donald E. Devore, *Defying Jim Crow: African American Community Development and the Struggle for Racial Equality in New Orleans, 1900–1960* (Baton Rouge: Louisiana State University Press, 2015), viii–ix.

10. Leslie Brown, *Upbuilding Black Durham: Gender, Class, and Black Community Development in the Jim Crow South* (Chapel Hill: University of North Carolina Press, 2008); Devore, *Defying Jim Crow*, 122–45, 151–54; R. Volney Riser, *Defying Disfranchisement: Black Voting Rights Activism in the Jim Crow South, 1890–1908* (Baton Rouge: Louisiana State University Press, 2010); Gary M. Lavergne, *Before Brown: Heman Marion Sweatt, Thurgood Marshall, and the Long Road to Justice* (Austin: University of Texas Press, 2011).

11. Historian R. A. Lawson, in his book *Jim Crow's Counterculture: The Blues and Black Southerners* (Baton Rouge: Louisiana State University Press, 2010), likens this dynamic to the cabin culture of enslaved people, who removed from the master, had a measure of freedom to express themselves; also see Adam Gussow, *Seems Like Murder Here: Southern Violence and the Blues Tradition* (Chicago: University of Chicago Press, 2002), 2–4, 22–58, 68–75.

12. Court Carney, *Cuttin' Up: How Early Jazz Got America's Ear* (Lawrence: University Press of Kansas, 2009); Bejamine Filene, *Romancing the Folk: Public Memory and American Roots Music* (Chapel Hill: University of North Carolina Press, 2000).

13. Eric T. Lott, *Love and Theft: Blackface Minstrelsy and the American Working Class*, 20th Anniversary ed. (New York: Oxford University Press, 2013), 3–8.

14. David Krasner, "The Real Thing," in *Beyond Blackface: African Americans and the Creation of American Popular Culture, 1890–1930*, ed. W. Fitzhugh Brundage (Chapel Hill: University of North Carolina Press, 2011), 99–123; Karen Sotiropoulos, *Staging Race: Black Performers in Turn of the Century America* (Cambridge, MA: Harvard University Press, 2006), 42–162; Gussow, *Seems Like Murder Here*, 2–4, 22–58, 68–75; Lawson, *Jim Crow's Counterculture*.

15. Marvin McAllister, *Whiting Up: Whiteface Minstrels and Stage Europeans in African American Performance* (Chapel Hill: University of North Carolina Press, 2011); Regina Bendix, *In Search of Authenticity: The Formation of Folklore Studies* (Madison: University of Wisconsin Press, 1997), 3–7.

16. Gussow, *Seems Like Murder Here*, 2–4, 22–58, 68–75.

17. Lawson, *Jim Crow's Counterculture*; 31–32, 47–57, 170–95; Sotiropoulos, *Staging Race*, 163–96.

18. Violet Alford, "Rough Music or Charivari," *Folklore* 70 (December 1959): 505–18.

19. Alford, "Rough Music or Charivari"; E. P. Thompson, "Rough Music Reconsidered," *Folklore* 103 (1992): 3–10; Mark McKnight, "Charivaris, Cowbellions, and Sheet Iron Bands: Nineteenth-Century Rough Music in New Orleans," *American Music* 23 (Winter 2005): 407–14.

20. Guy DeBord, *Society of the Spectacle* (Detroit: Black and Red, 1967); Nathan Markovitz, *Racial Spectacles: Explorations in Media, Race, and Justice* (New York: Routledge, 2011), 4–5; Douglas Kellner, "Media Culture and the Triumph of the Spectacle," in *The Spectacle of the*

Real: From Hollywood to Reality TV and Beyond, ed. Geoff King (Bristol, UK: Intellect Press, 2005); Douglas Kellner, *Media Spectacle* (New York: Routledge, 2003).

21. David Waldstreicher, *In the Midst of Perpetual Fetes: The Making of American Nationalism, 1776–1820* (Chapel Hill: University of North Carolina Press, 1997), 3, 7–13, 18–24; Jason Schaffer, *Performing Patriotism: National Identity in the Colonial and Revolutionary American Theater* (Philadelphia: University of Pennsylvania Press, 2007), 7–9.

22. Susan G. Davis, *Parades and Power: Street Theatre in Nineteenth-Century Philadelphia* (Philadelphia: Temple University Press, 1986), 2–7, 9, 12–13; Michael E. McGerr, *The Decline of Popular Politics: The American North, 1865–1928* (New York: Oxford University Press, 1986), 5–6, 3–41; Sean Wilentz, "Artisan Republican Festivals and the Rise of Class Conflict in New York City, 1788–1837," in *Working-Class America: Essays on Labor, Community, and American Society*, ed. Michael H. Frisch and Daniel J. Walkowitz (Urbana: University of Illinois Press, 1983), 37–77; Michael E. McGerr, "Political Style and Women's Power, 1830–1930," *Journal of American History* 77 (December 1990): 865–68; Davis, *Parades and Power*, 2–4, 46–47, 119, 149, 161–65; Robert F. Moss, *Barbecue: The History of an American Institution* (Tuscaloosa: University of Alabama Press, 2010), 54–55, 64–65; also see Daniel Walker Howe, *What Hath God Wrought: The Transformation of America, 1815–1848* (New York: Oxford University Press, 2007).

23. Mark W. Summers, "The Press Gang: Corruption and the Independent Press in the Grant Era," *Congress & the Presidency* 17 (Spring 1990): 29–44; McGerr, *The Decline of Popular Politics*, 6–7, 14–38; Hannah Rosen, *Terror in the Heart of Freedom: Citizenship, Sexual Violence, and the Meaning of Race in the Postemancipation South* (Chapel Hill: University of North Carolina Press, 2009), 44, 48, 61–64, 273; Jack D. Foner, *Blacks and the Military in American History: A New Perspective* (New York: Praeger, 1974).

24. Summers, "The Press Gang," 29–44; McGerr, *The Decline of Popular Politics*, 6–7, 14–38; Rebecca Edwards, *Angels in the Machinery: Gender in the American Party Politics from the Civil War to the Progressive Era* (New York: Oxford University Press, 1997), 25–28, 35, 53–54, 65, 81–83, 100–106, 128.

25. Edwards, *Angels in the Machinery*, 66–68; James Corbett David, "The Politics of Emasculation: The Caning of Charles Sumner and Elite Ideologies of Manhood in the Mid-Nineteenth-Century United States," *Gender & History* 19 (August 2007): 324–45; Craig Thompson Friend, *Southern Masculinity: Perspectives on Manhood in the South since Reconstruction* (Athens: University of Georgia Press, 2009).

26. McGerr, *The Decline of Popular Politics*, 186–215.

27. McGerr, *The Decline of Popular Politics*, 186–215.

28. Wood, *Lynching and Spectacle*, 1–15; also see Hale, *Making Whiteness*.

29. I have reason to believe that spectacle continued in the North, as well. In this book I only examine the South but have come across instances of spectacular demonstration in the North. I have even included a few of them in these pages. I believe that future work should examine spectacle across sectional lines.

30. James C. Scott, *Weapons of the Weak: Everyday Forms of Peasant Resistance* (New Haven, CT: Yale University Press, 1985), xv–xvi.

31. Perman, *Struggle for Mastery*; McGerr, *The Decline of Popular Politics*.

32. Portions of chapter 4 were previously published in *Louisiana History* 56 (Summer 2015): 315–43, copyright Louisiana Historical Association.

33. Portions of chapter 6 were previously published in *Southern Cultures* 20 (Summer 2014): 52–68, copyright Center for the Study of the American South.

CHAPTER 1: "OUT IN FULL FORCE": BLACK PARTICIPATION IN SPECTACULAR POLITICS BEFORE DISFRANCHISEMENT, 1877–99

1. "Buried in Effigy at Clinton," *Watauga Democrat*, November 17, 1892, 1.
2. James L. Hunt, *Marion Butler and American Populism* (Chapel Hill: University of North Carolina Press, 2003), 33–37, 40–41, 47–49, 52–57.
3. "Buried in Effigy at Clinton."
4. Hunt, *Marion Butler*, 64–67.
5. "A Populist Meeting at Monroe Broken Up by a Shower of Pepper," *The Landmark* (Statesville, NC), November 11, 1893; "From Our Raleigh Correspondent," *Charlotte Democrat*, November 17, 1893; "A Populist Meeting at Monroe Broken Up by a Shower of Pepper," *Watauga Democrat*, November 23, 1893; "More Pepper at Monroe," *Daily Charlotte Observer*, November 11, 1893, 1.
6. For examples, see coverage of Virginia's Republican convention here: "Revolt Against Mahone," *New York Times*, May 18, 1888, 1.
7. "Speech by Hon. W. P. Gillenwaters," *Daily Chronicle* (Knoxville, TN), September 25, 1880, 4.
8. "Radical Congressional Convention," *The Enquirer* (Yorkville, SC), October 7, 1880, 1.
9. "The Critic Abroad," *The Critic* (Washington, DC), March 25, 1891, 3.
10. "The Critic Abroad," 3.
11. John F. Marszalek, *A Black Congressman in the Age of Jim Crow: South Carolina's George Washington Murray* (Gainesville: University Press of Florida, 2006); Charles W. Calhoun, *Conceiving a New Republic: The Republican Party and the Southern Question, 1869–1900* (Lawrence: University Press of Kansas, 2006); Harris M. Bailey Jr., "The Only Game in Town: The South Carolina Republican Party in the Post-Reconstruction Era," *Proceedings of the South Carolina Historical Association* (Columbia: University of South Carolina Press, 1992); J. Morgan Kousser, *The Shaping of Southern Politics: Suffrage Restriction and the Establishment of the One-Party South* (New Haven CT: Yale University Press, 1974); Stanley Hirshson, *Farewell to the Bloody Shirt: Northern Republicans and the Southern Negro, 1877–1893* (Bloomington: Indiana University Press, 1962).
12. "Political Meetings: Republican Meeting on Saturday," *The Enquirer* (Yorkville, SC), October 7, 1880, 2.
13. "The Canvass: Political Meetings," *Staunton Spectator* (Staunton, VA), October 16, 1889, 3.
14. "Republican Rally," *The Intelligencer* (Anderson Court House, SC), November 14, 1889, 3.
15. "Wild Republican Talk," *Daily Citizen* (Asheville, NC), October 17, 1892, 1.
16. "Radical Rally," *Memphis Appeal*, June 30, 1880, 1.
17. "Woodstock Ablaze! The Republicans Celebrate—A Large Crowd in Town—Five Hundred People in Line," *Shenandoah Herald* (Woodstock, VA), November 23, 1888, 3.

18. "Another Serenade to Judge Hawkins," *Daily Chronicle* (Knoxville, TN), July 24, 1880, 4.

19. Editorial, *Pulaski Citizen* (Pulaski, TN), August 26, 1880, 2; "Again: Republicans Everywhere Victorious," *Daily Chronicle* (Knoxville, TN), November 5, 1880, 1.

20. *Maryville Times* (Maryville, TN), March 17, 1886, 5; "Lindsay for Attorney General," *Maryville Times* (Maryville, TN), January 27, 1886, 1; *Maryville Times* (Maryville, TN), April 7, 1886, 3.

21. "Congressman Brumm: Discussion of the Tariff Before a Negro Audience," *Richmond Dispatch*, October 19, 1889, 1.

22. Edwin Tribble, "Marching Through Georgia," *Georgia Review* 21 (Winter 1967): 423–29.

23. "From Washington," *Alexandria Gazette and Virginia Advertiser*, March 4, 1887; Errol G. Hill and James V. Hatch, *A History of African American Theatre* (Cambridge: Cambridge University Press, 2003), 141–42; "Minstrel Songs and Negro Melodies from the Sunny South: New Coon in Town," Johns Hopkins University, Levy Sheet Music Collection, Box 138, Item 008, http://jhir.library.jhu.edu/handle/ 1774.2/15300; "James Monroe Trotter," Getting Word: African American Oral History Project, accessed August 31, 2020, https://www.monticello.org/getting-word/people/james-monroe-trotter; Also, see Lott, *Love and Theft*.

24. "From Washington," *Alexandria Gazette and Virginia Advertiser*, March 4, 1887; Lott, *Love and Theft*.

25. "Race Trouble in Kentucky," *Staunton Spectator* (Staunton, VA), November 21, 1894, 4.

26. "Speech of S. Brown Allen," *Staunton Spectator* (Staunton, VA), August 29, 1882, 3.

27. "Local News," *Alexandria Gazette and Virginia Advertiser*, November 11, 1887, 3.

28. "Local News," 3.

29. "Buchanan's Reception," *Daily Tobacco Leaf-Chronicle* (Clarksville, TN), October 18, 1892, 1; "Blacks Guy Buchanan," *Memphis Appeal-Avalanche*, October 18, 1892, 1.

30. "Blacks Guy Buchanan," 1. According to the *Oxford English Dictionary*, late-nineteenth-century English speakers in Great Britain and the United States used the word "guy" to refer to the action of representing someone in effigy. They derived the term from Guy Fawkes, who intended to blow up Parliament. On Guy Fawkes Day, Britons carried effigies of Guy Fawkes through the streets. Americans used the term to refer to the same type of activity.

31. "She Is Sleeping in the Valley," *Daily Tobacco Leaf-Chronicle* (Clarksville, TN), October 17, 1892, 1.

32. "Excitement at Sumter," *Yorkville Enquirer* (Yorkville, SC), October 17, 1878, 2.

33. "Correspondence of the Yorkville Enquirer: Letter from Chester," *Yorkville Enquirer* (Yorkville, SC), October 17, 1878, 2.

34. George C. Rable, *But There Was No Peace: The Role of Violence in the Politics of Reconstruction* (Athens: University of Georgia Press, 1984), 132; Nicholas Lemann, *Redemption: The Last Battle of the Civil War* (New York: Farrar, Straus & Giroux, 2007), 74–80.

35. "Letter from Chester," *Yorkville Enquirer* (Yorkville, SC), October 9, 1884, 2.

36. "Shelby Democrats," *Courier-Journal* (Louisville, KY), July 10, 1888, 1.

37. For more information on pole-raising ceremonies, see McGerr, *The Decline of Popular Politics*, 27–33. According to McGerr, these ceremonies declined by the turn of the century in the North.

38. "Our Federal Union," *Daily Globe* (St. Paul, MN), March 18, 1892, 1.

39. "Marching from Georgia," *St. Louis Post-Dispatch*, March 20, 1892, 6.

40. "Marching from Georgia," 6.

41. "Third Ward Complications," *The Gazette* (Fort Worth, TX), March 23, 1895, 6.

42. "Mr. Stevenson's Letter," *New York Times*, October 31, 1892, 1; Jean H. Baker, *The Stevensons: A Biography of an American Family* (New York: W. W. Norton, 1997), 148–50.

43. "Adoration for Adlai," *Memphis Appeal-Avalanche*, October 20, 1892, 1.

44. Editorial, *Hamilton Times* (Hamilton, AL), November 24, 1892, 2.

45. "The State Canvass," *Pulaski Citizen* (Pulaski, TN), August 24, 1882, 2.

46. R. Penstock, "The Inaugural Ball," *Progressive Farmer* (Winston, NC), January 25, 1893, 3.

47. "Letter from Chatham: Mr. Self, a Member of the Last House, Hits Some Blows at His Political Enemies," *Progressive Farmer* (Winston, NC), June 6, 1893, 8.

48. "Put at Light Work: A Reply to the Vienna Correspondent of the Western Sentinel," *Progressive Farmer* (Winston, NC), May 16, 1894, 4.

49. "The Norwood Serenade," *Atlanta Constitution*, August 31, 1880, 1; Lewis Nicholas Wynne, *The Continuity of Cotton: Planter Politics in Georgia, 1865–1892* (Macon, GA: Mercer University Press, 1986), 121–23.

50. "Republican Bulldozing Tactics," *St. Louis Post-Dispatch*, October 19, 1888, 2.

51. "Brookhaven's Great Barbecue," *Memphis Appeal-Avalanche*, October 19, 1892, 1.

52. "All Negroes Barred Out," *Washington Post*, November 6, 1899, 9.

53. McGerr, *The Decline of Popular Politics*, 214–15.

54. James W. Endersby, "Prohibition and Repeal: Voting on Statewide Liquor Referenda in Texas," *Social Science Journal* 49 (2012): 505; George Cantrell, "'Dark Tactics': Black Politics in the 1887 Texas Prohibition Campaign," *Journal of American Studies* 25:1 (April 1991): 85–86; Stephen A. West, "'A Hot Municipal Contest,' Prohibition and Black Politics in Greenville, South Carolina, after Reconstruction," *Journal of the Gilded Age and Progressive Era* 11 (October 2012): 519–24.

55. James W. Endersby, "Prohibition and Repeal: Voting on Statewide Liquor Referenda in Texas," *Social Science Journal* 49 (2012): 505; Cantrell, "'Dark Tactics,'" 85–86; Stephen A. West, "'A Hot Municipal Contest': Prohibition and Black Politics in Greenville, South Carolina, after Reconstruction," *Journal of the Gilded Age and Progressive Era* 11 (October 2012): 519–24.

56. Hanes Walton Jr. and James E. Taylor, "Blacks and the Southern Prohibition Movement," *Phylon* 32:3 (1971): 250–58.

57. West, "'A Hot Municipal Contest,'" 519–51.

58. James W. Endersby, "Prohibition and Repeal: Voting on Statewide Liquor Referenda in Texas," *Social Science Journal* 49 (2012): 505; Cantrell, "'Dark Tactics,'" 85–86; West, "'A Hot Municipal Contest.'"

59. Brendan J. Payne, "Defending Black Suffrage: Poll Taxes, Preachers, and Anti-Prohibition in Texas, 1887–1916," *Journal of Southern History* 83:4 (November 2017): 815–52.

60. Cantrell, "'Dark Tactics,'" 85–93.

61. "A Big Demonstration: The Greatest Anti-Prohibition Rally Texas Ever Saw," *New York Times*, July 27, 1887, 1.

62. "Women in Politics: The Prohibition Battle Fought in Texas Yesterday," *St. Louis Post-Dispatch*, August 5, 1887, 5; H. Paul Thompson Jr., *A Most Stirring and Significant Episode: Religion and the Rise and Fall of Prohibition in Black Atlanta, 1865–1887* (DeKalb: Northern

Illinois University Press, 2013), 215–16; Endersby, "Prohibition and Repeal," 505; Cantrell, "'Dark Tactics,'" 85–86.

63. "Women in Politics: The Prohibition Battle Fought In Texas Yesterday," 5; Thompson, *A Most Stirring and Significant Episode*, 215–16; Endersby, "Prohibition and Repeal," 505; Cantrell, "'Dark Tactics,'" 85–86.

64. "Women in Politics: The Prohibition Battle Fought In Texas Yesterday," 5; Thompson, *A Most Stirring and Significant Episode*, 215–16; Endersby, "Prohibition and Repeal," 505; Cantrell, "'Dark Tactics,'" 85–86.

65. Eric Russell Lacy, "Tennessee Teetotalism: Social Forces and the Politics of Progressivism," *Tennessee Historical Quarterly* 24:3 (Fall 1965): 219–40; Grace Leab, "Tennessee Temperance Activities, 1870–1899," *East Tennessee Historical Society's Publications* 21 (1949): 52–68.

66. "At Loggerheads," *Daily American* (Nashville, TN), September 15, 1887, 1.

67. "Real Oratory: A Splendid Oration in Favor of Prohibition," *Daily American* (Nashville, TN), September 25, 1887, 7; Walton and Taylor, "Blacks and the Southern Prohibition Movement," 256.

68. "Rum Rules in Tennessee," *New York Times*, September 30, 1887, 1.

69. "Rum Rules in Tennessee," 1.

70. "A Local-Option Contest: Lynchburg Greatly Stirred Up—Brass Bands and Oratory," *The Sun* (Baltimore, MD), January 10, 1890, 3.

71. Untitled News Brief, *Morning Oregonian* (Portland, OR), August 25, 1888, 4.

72. Ayers, *The Promise of the New South*, 136–42; Williamson, *The Crucible of Race*, 251–56; Dorr, *White Women*, 15–28.

73. Rachel F. Moran, *Interracial Intimacy: The Regulation of Race and Romance* (Chicago: University of Chicago Press, 2001).

74. Dorr, *White Women*, 15–28; Diane Miller Somerville, *Rape and Race in the Nineteenth-Century South* (Chapel Hill: University of North Carolina Press, 2004), 200–202.

75. Untitled News Brief, *Morning Oregonian* (Portland, OR), August 25, 1888, 4.

76. Steven Hahn, *A Nation under Our Feet: Black Political Struggles in the Rural South from Slavery to the Great Migration* (Cambridge, MA: Belknap Press of Harvard University Press, 2003), 373–77; Jane Dailey, *Before Jim Crow: The Politics of Race in Postemancipation Virginia* (Chapel Hill: University of North Carolina Press, 2000), 53.

77. Dailey, *Before Jim Crow*.

78. Dailey, *Before Jim Crow*, 15–47, 48–76; Hahn, *A Nation under Our Feet*, 373–79.

79. Dailey, *Before Jim Crow*, 15–47, 48–76; Hahn, *A Nation under Our Feet*, 373–79.

80. McGerr, *The Decline of Popular Politics*, 12, 22–27.

81. Hahn, *A Nation under Our Feet*, 375–80; Dr. William H. Henning to William Mahone, July 14, 1881, William Mahone Papers, box 187; County Canvassers, Lunenburg County, 1881, WMP, box 187; County Canvassers, Buckingham County, 1881, WMP, box 187; Local Readjuster Organization and Expenses, Louisa County, n.d., WMP, box 188; Readjuster Organization, King and Queen County, n.d., WMP, box 189; Readjuster Organization, Southampton County, n.d., WMP, box 189.

82. "Election Day," *Petersburg Index Appeal* (Petersburg, VA), November 8, 1881, 2.

83. "Your Duty, Virginians!" *Petersburg Index Appeal* (Petersburg, VA), 2.

84. "Republicans of Petersburg," *Petersburg Index Appeal* (Petersburg, VA), November 8, 1881, 1.

85. "The Returns: Giving the Results of Yesterday's Elections in Virginia and Other States," *Daily Dispatch* (Richmond, VA), November 9, 1881, 1.

86. "The Republican Victory," *Daily Dispatch* (Richmond, VA), November 11, 1881, 1.

87. Leon Fink, *Workingmen's Democracy: The Knights of Labor and American Politics* (Urbana: University of Illinois Press, 1985), xii–xiv, 1–5, 149–77; Matthew Hild, *Greenbackers, Knights of Labor, and Populists: Farmer-Labor Insurgency in the Late-Nineteenth-Century South* (Athens: University of Georgia Press, 2007), 79–121; Melton Alonzo McLaurin, *The Knights of Labor in the South* (Westport: Greenwood Press, 1978); Ayers, *The Promise of the New South*, 216–17, 234–35; Hahn, *A Nation under Our Feet*, 41–42. With regard to Black participation in the Knights of Labor, Steven Hahn explains, "This is not, in short, a picture of stasis, insularity, or social retreat; it is one of movement, interaction, and assertion."

88. "The Knights of Labor: The Big Demonstration To-Day at Richmond," *St. Louis Post-Dispatch*, October 11, 1886, 2; "The General Assembly: Proceedings of the Knights of Labor Yesterday," *Atlanta Constitution*, October 12, 1886, 1.

89. "The Knights of Labor at Richmond," *The Independent: Devoted to the Consideration of Politics, Social and Economic Tendencies, History, Literature, and the Arts*, October 28, 1886, 5.

90. "The Knights and the Negro," *Daily Courant* (Hartford, CT), October 23, 1886, 2.

91. "The Knights," *Daily Courant*, 2.

92. Michael Kazin and Steven J. Ross, "America's Labor Day: The Dilemma of Workers' Celebration," *Journal of American History* 78 (March 1992): 1294–1307.

93. Kazin and Ross, "America's Labor Day," 1294–1307.

94. Kazin and Ross, "America's Labor Day," 1294–1307.

95. Kazin and Ross, "America's Labor Day," 1294–1307.

96. "Labor's Day: Wage-Worker's Holiday Celebrated by Thousands," *Daily American* (Nashville, TN), September 8, 1891, 1; "Great Turnout: Local Industrialists Excel Previous Efforts," *Daily American* (Nashville, TN), September 4, 1894, 1.

97. "How Labor Day Was Celebrated," *St. Louis Post-Dispatch*, September 7, 1896, 8.

98. Charles Postel, *The Populist Vision* (New York: Oxford University Press, 2007), 4–5; Ayers, *The Promise of the New South*, 264–96.

99. "Populist Camp Meeting," *Galveston Daily News* (Galveston, TX), July 13, 1896, 3.

100. Omar H. Ali, *In the Lion's Mouth: Black Populism in the New South, 1886–1900* (Jackson: University Press of Mississippi, 2010), 3–6; Postel, *The Populist Vision*, 4–5, 12–19, 173–78; Ayers, *The Promise of the New South*, 264–96; Deborah Beckel, *Radical Reform: Interracial Politics in Post-Emancipation North Carolina* (Charlottesville: University of Virginia Press, 2011), 160–70; Helen G. Edmonds, *The Negro and Fusion Politics in North Carolina, 1894–1901* (Chapel Hill: University of North Carolina Press, 1951), 1–5, 10, 14–29; 34–66.

101. Ali, *In the Lion's Mouth*, 8–10, 78–112.

102. Beckel, *Radical Reform*, 160–70; Ali, *In the Lion's Mouth*, 3–6, 113–49.

103. Ayers, *The Promise of the New South*, 269–75.

104. "Hot Politics: Bloody Bowman and His Speech," *Greenville Advocate* (Greenville, AL), July 27, 1892, 1; "Hurrah for Jones and Straight Democracy," *Greenville Advocate* (Greenville, AL), August 3, 1892, 1; Ayers, *The Promise of the New South*, 270.

105. "Hot Politics: Bloody Bowman and His Speech," 1; "Hurrah for Jones and Straight Democracy," *Greenville Advocate* (Greenville, AL), August 3, 1892, 1; Ayers, *The Promise of the New South*, 270.

106. "A Disappointing Rally: Populist Leaders Speak in South Georgia to a Small Crowd," *Atlanta Constitution*, July 31, 1894, 3.

107. "Populists in Jefferson," *Atlanta Constitution*, September 6, 1894, 9.

108. "Mims at Clarksville," *The American* (Nashville, TN), October 3, 1896, 2.

109. "Col. Wilkinson at Brunswick," *Atlanta Constitution*, November 5, 1898, 7.

110. "Populists Meet: A Rally at Montezuma—Judge Hines to Speak," *Atlanta Constitution*, July 9, 1896, 9.

111. "Truths of Democracy," *The American* (Nashville, TN), July 25, 1896, 1.

112. "Populists at Stone Mountain," *Atlanta Constitution*, August 17, 1896, 2.

113. "Wright Is Heard: Populists Open Their Campaign with a Rally," *Atlanta Constitution*, August 19, 1896, 5.

114. "Pops' Campmeeting: Three Thousand Gathered at Alpharetta Yesterday," *Atlanta Constitution*, August 15, 1896, 5.

115. "Their Last Rally: Populists Hold a Meeting at the Moody Tabernacle," *Atlanta Constitution*, October 7, 1896, 5; Ayers, *The Promise of the New South*, 270.

CHAPTER 2: "A CONTEST IN MUSIC": ELECTION-DAY SPECTACLES IN THE CENTRAL GEORGIA TEMPERANCE CAMPAIGNS, 1885–99

1. P. J. Moran, "Prohibition Defeated in Bibb County by a Majority of 1,398," *Atlanta Constitution*, December 2, 1898, 1; P. H. Carder, *George F. Root, Civil War Songwriter: A Biography* (Jefferson, NC: McFarland, 2008), 118–19, 147.

2. Moran, "Prohibition Defeated in Bibb County by a Majority of 1,398," 1; Carder, *George F. Root*, 118–19, 147.

3. "A Hot Time in Macon," *The Sun* (Baltimore, MD), December 2, 1898, 2.

4. Michael E. McGerr, in his book *The Decline of Popular Politics: The American North, 1865–1928*, remarks that popular politics declined in the South because of disfranchisement. During the 1890s, interracial cooperation in the People's Party threatened conservative white power. In response, conservative white southerners successfully intimidated and disfranchised Black and poor white voters, causing voter turnout to fall from 64 percent in the elections from 1876 to 1892 to 32 percent from 1900 to 1916. By 1920 only 20 percent of voters turned out for presidential elections. He does not examine, however, whether or not these declines in voter turnout made any noticeable impact on the spectacular displays familiar to nineteenth-century Americans.

5. Megan L. Bever, *War Is a Terrible Enemy to Temperance*, PhD diss., University of Alabama, 2014, 1–7, 14–19; Thompson, *A Most Stirring and Significant Episode*, 1–9, 154–56; Gaines M. Foster, *Moral Reconstruction: Christian Lobbyists and the Federal Legislation of Morality, 1865–1920* (Chapel Hill: University of North Carolina Press, 2002), 1–8, 163–92.

6. Thompson, *A Most Stirring and Significant Episode*, 1–9, 154–56; Foster, *Moral Reconstruction*, 1–8, 163–92.

7. Michael A. Wagner, "'As Gold Is Tried in the Fire, So Hearts Must Be Tried by Pain': The Temperance Movement in Georgia and the Local Option Law of 1885," *Georgia Historical Quarterly* 93 (Spring 2009): 30–34; Thompson, *A Most Stirring and Significant Episode*, 6–10, 21, 88–90, 154–57; Ann-Marie Szymanski, "Beyond Parochialism: Southern Progressivism, Prohibition, and State-Building," *Journal of Southern History* 69 (February 2003): 109; Evelyn Brooks Higginbotham, *Righteous Discontent: The Women's Movement in the Black Baptist Church, 1880–1920* (Cambridge, MA: Harvard University Press, 1993); Brown, *Upbuilding Black Durham*, 12, 20–21, 34–35, 46–47, 82–86.

8. Wagner, "'As Gold Is Tried in the Fire, So Hearts Must Be Tried by Pain,'" 30–34, 48.

9. "The Local Option Bill Passed," *Atlanta Constitution*, September 10, 1885, 4; "Whisky or No Whisky: The Atlanta Prohibitionists Preparing for the Fight," *Atlanta Constitution*, September 20, 1885, 6G; "A Prohibition Wave: Liquor Selling in Atlanta Likely to Be Discontinued," *Daily American* (Nashville, TN), September 21, 1885, 1; Wagner, "'As Gold Is Tried in the Fire,'" 32–34, 48, 51–52; Thompson, *A Most Stirring and Significant Episode*, 9–10.

10. Wagner, "'As Gold Is Tried in the Fire,'" 30–34; Thompson, *A Most Stirring and Significant Episode*, 6–10, 21, 88–90, 154–57; Szymanski, "Beyond Parochialism," 109; Higginbotham, *Righteous Discontent*; Brown, *Upbuilding Black Durham*, 12, 20–21, 34–35, 46–47, 82–86.

11. Prohibition Scrapbook, Walter B. Hill Papers, MS 3274, Hargrett Research Library, University of Georgia, Box 2.

12. Wagner, "'As Gold Is Tried in the Fire,'" 30–54, 48, 51–52; Thompson, *A Most Stirring and Significant Episode*, 9–10.

13. Thompson, *A Most Stirring and Significant Episode*, 44–137.

14. Wagner, "'As Gold Is Tried in the Fire,'" 30–54, 48, 51–52; Thompson, *A Most Stirring and Significant Episode*, 34.

15. "Whisky or No Whisky," 6G; "Wet or Dry: The Impending Prohibition Issue in this County," *Atlanta Constitution*, September 27, 1885, 12.

16. "Whisky or No Whisky," 6G; "Wet or Dry," 12; "A Prohibition Wave," 1.

17. "A Prohibition Wave," 1.

18. "Prohibition in Georgia," *New York Times*, October 1, 1885, 1.

19. "Local Option," *Atlanta Constitution*, October 11, 1885, 10. The same author sent another letter to the *Atlanta Constitution*'s editors on October 25, 1885, which the editors printed on page 10. The author identifies as "S." and as a "strong temperance man," thus justifying the use of the masculine pronouns in this section.

20. "Mr. Julius L. Brown Continues: The Moderate Use and Sale of Wines and Liquors Not Morally Wrong," *Atlanta Constitution*, November 4, 1885, 3.

21. "Prohibition Points," *Atlanta Constitution*, November 5, 1885, 2.

22. "Prohibition Points," 2.

23. "Anti-Prohibition Meeting," *Atlanta Constitution*, November 4, 1885, 7.

24. Walter P. Emerson, "Sam Jones—A Study," Undated, Samuel P. Jones Papers, MSS 126, Kenan Research Center, Atlanta History Center.

25. "Prohibition Men: Sold a Big meeting at the Opera House," *Atlanta Constitution*, November 3, 1885, 11.

26. "Prohibition Men," 11.

27. "Prohibition Men," 11.

28. "Prohibition Men," 11.

29. "Taking it Straight: The Anti-Prohibition Rally at the Courthouse," *Atlanta Constitution*, November 3, 1885, 11; Herman "Skip" Mason Jr., *Politics, Civil Rights, and Law in Black Atlanta, 1870–1970* (Charleston, SC: Arcadia, 2000), 55–56.

30. Eric Foner, *Reconstruction: America's Unfinished Revolution* (New York: Perennial Classics, 2002), 314–15, 323, 423–24, 590–91; Perman, *Struggle for Mastery*, 281. For a comprehensive account of Black office-holding, see Eric Foner, *Freedom's Lawmakers: A Directory of Black Officeholders during Reconstruction* (Baton Rouge: Louisiana State University Press, 1996).

31. "Prohibition Meetings: Last Night at the Tent," *Atlanta Constitution*, November 18, 1885, 5.

32. "Awake, Awake, The Master Now Is Calling," Hymnary.Org, https://hymnary.org/text/awake_awake_the_master_now_is_calling, accessed January 31, 2018.

33. "Prohibition Meetings: Last Night at the Tent," 5.

34. Editorial correspondence, *Christian Recorder* (Philadelphia), December 3, 1885.

35. "Wet or Dry? The Question to be Settled by the Voters Today," *Atlanta Constitution*, November 25, 1885, 1.

36. "Free Lunch," *Atlanta Constitution*, November 19, 1885, 5; "Food for the Voters," *Atlanta Constitution*, November 25, 1885, 1; "Dry It Is," *Atlanta Constitution*, November 26, 1885, 1.

37. "The Procession," *Atlanta Constitution*, November 25, 1885, 1.

38. "Corralling the Voters," *New York Times*, November 25, 1885, 1.

39. "Wet or Dry? The Question to be Settled by the Voters Today," *Atlanta Constitution*, November 25, 1885, 1.

40. "Wet or Dry?," 1.

41. "The Procession," *Atlanta Constitution*, November 25, 1885, 1.

42. "Corralling the Voters," *New York Times*, November 25, 1885, 1.

43. "Corralling the Voters," 1.

44. "Corralling the Voters," 1.

45. "Wet or Dry? The Question to be Settled by the Voters Today," 1.

46. "Dry It Is," *Atlanta Constitution*, November 26, 1885, 1.

47. "Dry It Is," 1.

48. "Dry It Is," 1.

49. "Dry It Is," 1.

50. "Dry It Is," 1.

51. "Dry It Is," 1.

52. "Dry It Is," 1.

53. "A Moral Struggle," *Courier-Journal* (Louisville, KY), November 25, 1885, 2.

54. "Dry It Is," 1.

55. "Dry It Is," 1.

56. "Dry It Is," 1; Levine, *Black Culture and Black Consciousness*, 122; John W. Roberts, *From Trickster to Badman: The Black Folk Hero in Slavery and Freedom* (Philadelphia: University of Pennsylvania Press, 1989), 1; Bernard Wolfe, "Uncle Remus and the Malevolent Rabbit," in *Mother Wit from the Laughing Barrel: Readings in the Interpretation of Afro-American Folklore* (Englewood Cliffs, NJ: Prentice-Hall, 1973), 524–40; Trudier Harris, "The Trickster in African

American Literature," National Humanities Center, http://nationalhumanitiescenter.org/tserve/freedom/1865-1917/essays/trickster.htm. In 1881 Joel Chandler Harris, from Atlanta, published a compilation of Uncle Remus tales, which gave these characters from Black folklore a national audience.

57. "Dry It Is," 1.
58. "Dry It Is," 1.
59. "Atlanta Goes Dry," *Daily American* (Nashville, TN), November 26, 1885, 5.
60. "A Fight Over Prohibition," *New York Times*, November 27, 1885, 1.
61. "The Capture of Atlanta," *Daily Courant* (Hartford, CT), November 27, 1885, 2.
62. "The Triumph of Prohibition in Atlanta," *Christian Recorder* (Philadelphia), December 10, 1885.
63. "The Capture of Atlanta," 2.
64. "A Prohibition Victory," *New York Times*, November 26, 1885, 5.
65. "Atlanta Goes Dry," 5.
66. "Editorial," *Washington Post*, November 26, 1885, 2.
67. "At Home and Abroad," *Frank Leslie's Weekly*, December 12, 1885.
68. Thompson, *A Most Stirring and Significant Episode*, 196–97, 214–15, 219–20, 227–28.
69. Thompson, *A Most Stirring and Significant Episode*, 233–35.
70. "A Prohibition Defeat in Georgia," *New York Times*, August 7, 1889, 1.
71. "Means Prohibition for Rural Georgia," *Chicago Daily Tribune*, August 12, 1891, 1.
72. "Prohibition in Georgia," *Atlanta Constitution*, July 14, 1895, 9.
73. "Bush Bill Beaten," *Atlanta Constitution*, December 5, 1895, 3.
74. "The News in Macon," *Atlanta Constitution*, November 10, 1885, 2. Michael McGerr points out that this type of behavior pervaded popular politics before the 1880s but suggests that it declined along with the rest of the spectacular nature of popular politics. Often, "bettors waged money, dinners, hats, boots, or ties" but "one losing bettor had to push the winner or a pig around the town square in a wheelbarrow, shave off one side of his beard, or sit all day in a tree"; McGerr, *The Decline of Popular Politics*, 28–29; "A Prohibition Victory", 5.
75. "From Macon: The Temperance Question Agitating the Central City," *Atlanta Constitution*, January 24, 1885, 4.
76. "Why This Music from Macon," *Atlanta Constitution*, November 12, 1885, 3.
77. "Bibb Will Have a Liquor Election," *Atlanta Constitution*, September 28, 1898, 3.
78. "An Open Letter to Sam Jones," *Macon Telegraph*, November 23, 1898, 5.
79. The link between alcohol, slavery, and insurrection has deep roots. For more information, consult Patrick H. Breen, "A Prophet in His Own Land: Support for Nat Turner and His Rebellion within Southampton's Black Community," in *Nat Turner: A Slavery Rebellion in History and Memory*, ed. Kenneth S. Greenberg (New York: Oxford University Press, 2003), 115–18; Mark Edward Lender and James Kirby Martin, *Drinking in America: A History* (New York: Free Press), 26–30.
80. "About Prohibition in Georgia," *Atlanta Constitution*, September 4, 1885, 4; Thompson, *A Most Stirring and Significant Episode*, 61–63.
81. Thompson, *A Most Stirring and Significant Episode*, 63.
82. Minutes of the Sixth Annual Convention of the Women's Christian Temperance Union of Georgia, Georgia Women's Christian Temperance Union, Manuscript, Archives, and Rare Books Library, Emory University, Box 23, Folder 1, 18.

83. "Drank Too Much Whisky," *Atlanta Constitution*, February 17, 1898, 3.
84. "Stabbed at a School Meeting," *Macon Telegraph*, August 3, 1898, 3.
85. "Georgians Stand By Each Other," *Atlanta Constitution*, June 8, 1898, 3.
86. "Rioting Negroes," *Courier-Journal* (Louisville, KY), June 10, 1898, 2.
87. "The Affair at Tampa," *Atlanta Constitution*, June 12, 1898, 16.
88. Thirkfield, Wilbur P., "As to the Colored Troops," *Atlanta Constitution*, June 19, 1898, 24.
89. "A Visiting Soldier," *Macon Telegraph*, September 24, 1898, 5.
90. "Riot Imminent at Anniston," *Macon Telegraph*, November 20, 1898, 10.
91. "Negro Troops Make Trouble in Macon," *Atlanta Constitution*, November 17, 1898, 4.
92. "Soldiers Quiet in Macon Yesterday," *Atlanta Constitution*, November 21, 1898, 3.
93. Perman, *Struggle for Mastery*, 281–98; Andrew M. Manis, *Macon Black and White: An Unutterable Separation in the American Century* (Macon, GA: Mercer University Press, 2004), 16–20.
94. Frank Weldon, "The Lesson of North Carolina Applied to the Present Situation in Georgia," *Atlanta Constitution*, September 4, 1898, 5.
95. Frank Weldon, "Ladies of North Carolina Aroused to their Danger: The Terrors Negro Domination Holds for Them," *Atlanta Constitution*, September 30, 1898, 1. For more on the Wilmington Race Riot of 1898, see Cecelski and Tyson, *Democracy Betrayed*; H. Leon Prather, *We Have Taken a City: Wilmington Racial Massacre and Coup of 1898* (Rutherford, NJ: Fairleigh Dickenson University Press, 1984); Ayers, *The Promise of the New South*, 300–304.
96. Frank Weldon, "Old North State Redeemed from Negro Rule at Last," *Atlanta Constitution*, November 9, 1898, 1; "Will Keep Out," *Macon Telegraph*, November 13, 1898, 1.
97. "The Great Revolution at the South," *Macon Telegraph*, November 29, 1898, 4.
98. "Lynching the Only Law," *Macon Telegraph*, November 16, 1898, 2.
99. Cecelski and Tyson, *Democracy Betrayed*; Prather, *We Have Taken a City*; Ayers, *The Promise of the New South*, 300–304.
100. "Registration in Macon Is Heavy," *Atlanta Constitution*, November 14, 1898, 3.
101. Advertisement, *Macon Telegraph*, December 1, 1898, 7.
102. "Call It Intimidation," *Herald Dispatch* (Decatur, IL), December 2, 1898, 6.
103. "Open Letter," *Macon News*, November 28, 1898, 4.
104. Advertisement, *Macon Telegraph*, December 1, 1898, 7.
105. "The Weather Today," *Macon Telegraph*, December 1, 1898, 4; "Women at the Polls: Ladies of Macon, GA., Do Earnest Work for Prohibition's Cause," *The American* (Nashville, TN), December 2, 1898, 1; "The Antis Won," *Macon Telegraph*, December 2, 1898, 1; "The Election Today: It Will Be a Hard Fought Battle," *Macon Telegraph*, December 1, 1898, 8; "Women Pray at the Polls," *Trenton [NJ] Evening Times*, December 2, 1898, 4; "Prohibition Defeated in Bibb County by a Majority of 1,398," *Atlanta Constitution*, December 2, 1898, 1; "Woman's Work in Politics: She Can Do Heroic Work for the Cause of Good, but She Can Also Be Mighty Cute," *St. Louis Post-Dispatch*, December 2, 1898, 3.
106. "A Hot Time in Macon," 2; "Prohibition Defeated in Bibb County," 1; "Woman's Work in Politics," 3; "The Antis Won," 1.
107. Turpie, "A Voluntary War," 862–65, 876–80.
108. Joe Hayden and Theo A. Metz, "A Hot Time in the Old Town," Duke University Libraries Digital Collections, Item b0570, http://library.duke.edu/digitalcollections/hasm_b0570/#info;

Jon W. Finson, *The Voices That Are Gone: Themes in Nineteenth-Century American Popular Song* (New York: Oxford University Press, 1994), 222–23, 229, 238; C. A. Browne, *The Story of Our National Ballads* (New York: Thomas Y. Crowell, 1919), 208–9.

109. In *Jim Crow's Counterculture*, Lawson demonstrates how white Americans flocked to see blues and ragtime musicians because they seemed like authentic plantation products. Lead Belly, for example, would adorn plantation garb and exaggerate his southern vernacular for the audience's sake. For more information, consult Lott, *Love and Theft*.

110. "Prohibition Defeated in Bibb County," 1.

111. "Pray at the Polls," *Davenport Daily Leader* (Davenport, IA), December 2, 1898, 1.

112. "Prohibition Defeated in Bibb County," 1.

113. "The Antis Won," 6.

114. "The Antis Won," 6.

115. "Pray at the Polls," 1.

116. "Pray at the Polls," 1.

117. "A Hot Time in Macon," 2.

118. "Woman's Work in Politics," 3.

119. The color of the ribbons worn by prohibitionists and anti-prohibitionists vary across time and space. For more information, see J. R. Meader, *The Cyclopaedia of Temperance and Prohibition: A Reference Book of Facts, Statistics, and General Information on All Phases of the Drink Question, the Temperance Movement, and the Prohibition Agitation* (New York: Funk & Wagnalls, 1891), 57.

120. "Prohibition Defeated in Bibb County," 1.

121. "The Prohis Will Contest Election," *Macon News*, December 2, 1898, 5; "Women Took Part," *Sandusky Star* (Sandusky, OH), December 2, 1898, 1.

122. "Prohibition Defeated in Bibb County," 1.

123. "The Antis Won," 1.

124. "To Purify Politics," *Macon Telegraph*, November 27, 1898, 5.

125. "Move On Foot to Bar Negro Out of Municipal Affairs," *Augusta Chronicle*, December 8, 1898.

126. "Cause and Effect," *Macon News*, December 2, 1898, 4.

127. "The Condition of the Negroes," *Atlanta Constitution*, December 8, 1898, 4.

128. "An Orderly Election," *Macon News*, December 2, 1898, 4.

129. "A Hot Time in Macon," 2.

130. "The Antis Won," 1.

131. I have consulted minutes from the Georgia WCTU meetings from 1888, 1890, 1891, 1892, 1893, 1894, and 1900. President Sibley's speech comes from "Proceedings of the Eighth Annual Convention of the Women's Christian Temperance Union of Georgia," Georgia Women's Christian Temperance Union, Manuscript, Archives, and Rare Books Library, Emory University, Box 23, Folder 1, 19.

132. Gregory Mixon and Clifford Kuhn, "Atlanta Race Riot of 1906," *New Georgia Encyclopedia*, https://www.georgiaencyclopedia.org/articles/history-archaeology/atlanta-race-riot-1906, accessed February 13, 2018; David M. Fahey, "Temperance Movement," *New Georgia Encyclopedia*, https://www.georgiaencyclopedia.org/articles/history-archaeology/temperance-movement, accessed February 13, 2018.

133. Perman, *Struggle for Mastery*, 10–15.

BRIDGE: "A STRICTLY SOCIAL FUNCTION": THE CONTEST OF BLACK LABOR AND CONFEDERATE MEMORY AT THE 1903 UCV REUNION

1. "Big Success Will Be Reunion All Signs Point that Way: True Spirit Takes Hold of a City and a Magnificent Welcome is Promised Those Who Wore the Grey," *Sunday States* (New Orleans, LA), May 17, 1903, 11.
2. "The South's Defenders Are Gathered Here: Reunion of the United Confederate Veterans to be Opened at Noon," *Times Democrat* (New Orleans, LA), May, 19, 1903.
3. "Unions May Fight Reunion," *The Sun* (Baltimore, MD), April 13, 1903, 1.
4. "Musicians' Union: Two Interesting Questions Arise Over Reunion Music," *Daily Picayune* (New Orleans, LA), March 29, 1903, 9.
5. "No Color Line in Music: A Southern Tribute to the Melodies of the Darkies," *St. Paul Globe*, June 6, 1903, 4.
6. Norman Walker, "For Grizzled Veterans of Dixie Crescent City Gates are Ajar," *Atlanta Constitution*, May 5, 1903, B2; Janney, *Burying the Dead But Not the Past*, 146, 244n38.
7. Janney, *Burying the Dead*, 146.
8. Walker, "For Grizzled Veterans of Dixie," B2.
9. Janney, *Remembering the Civil War*, 136, 148; Ayers, *The Promise of the New South*, 334–38; David W. Blight, *Race and Reunion: The Civil War in American Memory* (Cambridge, MA: Harvard University Press, 2002); Gaines Foster, *Ghosts of the Confederacy: Defeat, the Lost Cause, and the Emergence of the New South, 1865–1913* (New York: Oxford University Press), 1987.
10. Janney, *Remembering the Civil War*, 154–59; Janney, "Written in Stone," 117–41.
11. Lydia Mattice Brandt, "Re-creating Mount Vernon: The Virginia Building at the 1893 Chicago World's Columbian Exposition," *Wintherthur Portfolio* 43 (Spring 2009): 110–11; Scott E. Casper, *Sarah Johnson's Mount Vernon: The Forgotten History of an American Shrine* (New York: Hill and Wang, 2008); "Tell of Early Days," *Chicago Daily Tribune*, May 14, 1893, 7.
12. "Confederate Veterans: Fourth Annual Reunion of the Old Soldiers," *Daily American* (Nashville, TN), April 22, 1894, 9.
13. "The Lee Statue Unveiled," *New York Times*, May 30, 1890, 1–2; Janney, *Remembering the Civil War*, 219–20.
14. "When Will They Learn Sense," *Washington Bee*, May 31, 1890, 2; editorial, *Richmond Planet*, June 14, 1890, 2; Janney, *Remembering the Civil War*, 220.
15. "The Stone Was Laid," *Richmond Dispatch*, July 3, 1896, 1; "Grand Parade of the Confederate Veterans at Richmond," *Courier-Journal* (Louisville, KY), July 3, 1896, 8.
16. "The Stone Was Laid," 1.
17. "Stephen Lee's Oration," *Richmond Dispatch* (Richmond, VA), July 3, 1896, 4.
18. "Oration of General Lee," *Southern Historical Society Papers* 24, ed. R. A. Brock (Richmond: Southern Historical Society, 1896), 370.
19. "Oration of General Lee," 374–75.
20. "July 2d, 1896," *Richmond Dispatch*, July 3, 1896, 4.
21. "The Stone Was Laid," 1; "Grand Parade of the Confederate Veterans at Richmond," *Courier-Journal* (Louisville, KY), July 3, 1896, 8.

22. "General Stuart's Servant," *Richmond Dispatch*, July 3, 1896, 3; "Grand Parade of the Confederate Veterans at Richmond," 8.

23. "A Picturesque Darkey Who Follows the Vets," *Atlanta Constitution*, May 17, 1899, 4.

24. "Augusta Yesterday," *Atlanta Constitution*, November 14, 1900, 7; Blight, *Race and Reunion*, 289; Harold Harrison Jr., "The True Story of Amos Rucker," KnowSouthernHistory .net, http://www.knowsouthernhistory.net/Articles/Minorities/ true_story_of_amos_rucker .html.

25. William A. Gordon, "Natural Home of the Negro: The South Can Safely Be Trusted with Solution of the Race Problem," *Washington Post*, May 29, 1901, 10; Elizabeth Gritter, *River of Hope: Black Politics and the Memphis Freedom Movement, 1865–1954* (Lexington: University Press of Kentucky, 2014), 16–17, 26–28.

26. Gordon, "Natural Home of the Negro," 10; Gritter, *River of Hope*, 16–17, 26–28.

27. "Willing His Estate to His Former Slaves," *St. Louis Post-Dispatch*, August 19, 1879, 3; "Remembering His Old Slaves," *Courier-Journal* (Louisville, KY), August 11, 1879, 3.

28. "After Thirty Years," *Courier-Journal* (Louisville, KY), June 15, 1891, 1.

29. Blight, *Race and Reunion*, 289.

30. "Mississippi's Pension Law," *The Sun* (Baltimore, MD), February 23, 1888, 5.

31. "Quarter's Pensions Quarter Million," *The Tennessean* (Nashville, TN), August 4, 1921, 2.

32. "Would Pension Negro Servants," *The Sun* (Baltimore, MD), January 7, 1907, 11.

33. "Old Slaves to Get Pensions in S. Carolina," *Chicago Defender*, March 17, 1923, 2.

34. Daisy Fitzhugh Ayres, "Confederate Veterans Gathering for Reunion at Capital," *Courier-Journal* (Louisville, KY), June 3, 1917, C2.

35. "Pension Raise Asked for Alabama Veterans," *The Tennessean* (Nashville, TN), December 13, 1922, 8.

36. "Confederate Negroes Hold a Reunion," *Washington Post*, September 3, 1889, 1.

37. "How He Was Wounded," *St. Louis Post-Dispatch*, June 20, 1897, C6.

38. "A Picturesque Darkey Who Follows the Vets," 4.

39. The Committee on Music consisted of John W. Carnahan, Tom Elliott, Sidney F. Lewis, L. C. Quintero, and Ed. D. Walshe.

40. "Reunion to Be Held in May," *Savannah Tribune*, January 31, 1903; "Confederate Reunion Arrangements," *Confederate Veteran* 11 (January 1903): 3; Daniel Rosenberg, *New Orleans Dockworkers: Race, Labor, and Unionism, 1892–1923* (Albany: State University of New York Press, 1988), 20–21.

41. Walker, "For Grizzled Veterans of Dixie," B2.

42. Walker, "For Grizzled Veterans of Dixie," B2.

43. Walker, "For Grizzled Veterans of Dixie," B2; E. B. Kruttschnitt, Letter to Gen. Bennett H. Young, May 14, 1903, in United Confederate Veterans Association Records, Baton Rouge LSU Special Collections, Mss. 1357, Box 22, Folder G.; E. B. Kruttschnitt, Letter to General John B. Gordon, May 14, 1903, in United Confederate Veterans Association Records, Baton Rouge LSU Special Collections, Mss. 1357, Box 22, Folder G.

44. Rosenberg, *New Orleans Dockworkers*, 1–2, 6–8, 12–18.

45. Lawrence Gushee, "Black Professional Musicians in New Orleans c1880," in *Inter-American Music Review* 11 (Spring Summer 1991): 54, 57n.

46. Musicians' Mutual Protective Union, Local no. 74, A.F.M., New Orleans, *Constitution, By-Laws and Price List* (New Orleans: W. Miller, Printer, 1903), 4, Box 28, Item 2, American Federation of Musicians Local 174–496, Hogan Jazz Archive, Tulane University, New Orleans, LA.

47. "Musicians' Union: Two Interesting Questions Arise over Reunion Music," *Daily Picayune* (New Orleans, LA), March 29, 1903, 9.

48. Sotiropoulos, *Staging Race*, 212.

49. Local no. 174, *Constitution, By-Laws and Price List*, 15.

50. Local no. 174, *Constitution, By-Laws and Price List*, 15.

51. "Musicians' Union: Two Interesting Questions Arise over Reunion Music," 9.

52. "Musicians' Union: Faces the Reunion with the Regular Kick," *Daily Picayune* (New Orleans, LA), April 1, 1903, 8.

53. "Reunion Music Will Not Be Played by the Musicians' Union," *Daily Picayune* (New Orleans, LA), April 2, 1903, 9.

54. "Musicians' Union: Faces the Reunion with the Regular Kick," 8.

55. "Reunion Music Will Not Be Played by the Musicians' Union," 9.

56. "Hotels Will All Be Filled After To-day by Veterans," *Sunday States* (New Orleans, LA), May 17, 1903, 2.

57. "Atlanta Firemen: Drum Corps Will be a Feature at Parade," *Times-Democrat* (New Orleans, LA), May 19, 1903, 3.

58. "Fine Band of Heroes," *Daily States* (New Orleans, LA), May 19, 1903, 4.

59. "The Reunion Hall Is Now Well Under Way," *Daily Picayune* (New Orleans, LA), April 2, 1903.

60. "Come Forward with Your Subscription for the Veterans," *Daily Picayune* (New Orleans, LA), April 18, 1903, 4.

61. "Musicians' Union Wants Reunion on Unfair List," *Daily Picayune* (New Orleans, LA), April 11, 1903, 2.

62. "Unions May Fight Reunion: Boycott Threatened Unless Confederates Follow Negro Bands," *The Sun* (Baltimore, MD), April 13, 1903, 1; Rosenberg, *New Orleans Dockworkers*, 20–21.

63. "No Color Line in Music: A Southern Tribute to the Melodies of the Darkies," *St. Paul Globe*, June 6, 1903, 4.

64. "No Color Line in Music," 4.

65. "No Color Line in Music," 4.

66. Blight, *Race and Reunion*, 286–89.

67. "Negro Music and Ex-Confederates," *Washington Post*, April 13, 1903, 6.

68. "To Be or Not to Be?" *The Freeman* (Indianapolis, IN), April 25, 1903, 4.

69. "No Color Line in Music," 4.

70. "To Be or Not To Be?" 4.

71. Janney, *Remembering the Civil War*, 155–56.

72. "No Color Line in Music," 4.

73. "Negro Music and Ex-Confederates," *Washington Post*, April 13, 1903, 6.

74. James C. Cobb, *Industrialization and Southern Society, 1877–1984* (Lexington: University Press of Kentucky, 1984), 1–4, 27–50.

75. Blight, *Race and Reunion*, 41, 47, 129, 211, 286.

76. George Gordon Crawford, Tennessee Coal, Iron and Railroad executive, cited in George R. Leighton, *Five Cities: The Story of Their Youth and Old Age* (New York: Ayer, 1998), qtd. in Brian Kelly, "Sentinels for New South Industry: Booker T. Washington, Industrial Accommodation and Black Workers in the Jim Crow South," *Labor History* 44 (2003): 339–41.

77. Kelly, "Sentinels for New South Industry," 339–43; Ayers, *The Promise of the New South*, 431–32.

78. Booker T. Washington, *Up from Slavery* (1901; New York: Penguin Classics, 1986), 218–25; Kelly, "Sentinels for New South Industry," 343.

79. Booker T. Washington, "The Education and Industrial Emancipation of the Negro: An Address before the Brooklyn Institute of Arts and Sciences," February 22, 1903, qtd. in Kelly, "Sentinels for New South Industry," 343.

80. Booker T. Washington, *Southern States Farm Magazine*, January 1898, qtd. in Kelly, "Sentinels for New South Industry," 34.

81. "The Alliance of White and Negro Labor," *Sunday States* (New Orleans, LA), May 17, 1903, 4.

82. "The Alliance of White and Negro Labor," 4.

83. "The Black Specter," *Daily States* (New Orleans, LA), May 19, 1903, 4.

84. "The Confederate Veterans and Their Reunion," *Daily Picayune* (New Orleans, LA), April 12, 1903, 5.

85. "Confederate Reunion Must be Made a Success," *Daily Picayune* (New Orleans, LA), April 14, 1903, 4.

86. "The Honor of the City, and Glory of the Cause," *Daily Picayune* (New Orleans, LA), April 12, 1903, 12.

87. "New Orleans as a Convention City," *Daily Picayune* (New Orleans, LA), April 12, 1903, 5.

88. "Musicians' Attack on the Confederate Reunion," *Daily Picayune* (New Orleans, LA), April 12, 1903, 14.

89. "Musicians' Attack," 14.

90. "Musicians' Attack," 14.

91. "The Musicians' Union Presents an Explanation of Its Attitude of Opposition," *Daily Picayune* (New Orleans, LA), April 9, 1903. 3.

92. "Negro Music and Ex-Confederates," *Washington Post*, April 13, 1903, 6.

93. "To Be or Not to Be?" *The Freeman* (Indianapolis, IN), April 25, 1903, 4.

94. Editorial, *Colored American* (Washington, DC), April 18, 1903, 3.

95. George De Droit, "Union Bands Are the Best," *Union Advocate* (New Orleans, LA), April 13, 1903, 1.

96. "Mr. Sporer's Statement," *Union Advocate*, April 20, 1903, 1.

97. "Mr. Sporer's Statement," 1.

98. "Mr. Sporer's Statement," 1.

99. Walker, "For Grizzled Veterans of Dixie," B2.

100. "The Musicians' Union Withdraws Attempt to Cloud the Confederate Reunion," *Daily Picayune* (New Orleans, LA), April 24, 1903, 8.

101. "The Music Committee Reports," *Urban Advocate* (New Orleans, LA), April 27, 1903, 5.

102. "Come Forward with Your Subscription for the Veterans," 4.

103. "The Honor of the City, and Glory of the Cause," 4.

104. "To the People of New Orleans," *Daily Picayune* (New Orleans, LA), April 11, 1903.
105. "Three Letters," *Daily Picayune* (New Orleans, LA), April 10, 1903.
106. "Three Letters."
107. "Big Success Will Be Reunion All Signs Point That Way," 11, in United Confederate Veterans Reunion Scrapbooks, 1903–1914, vol. 1: U.C.V Reunion: New Orleans, 1903, Louisiana and Lower Mississippi Valley Collections (Baton Rouge: Louisiana State University Libraries).
108. Walker, "For Grizzled Veterans of Dixie," B2.
109. "Big Success Will Be Reunion All Signs Point That Way," 11.
110. "Wear Buttons—Show Your Colors!" *Daily States*, May 19, 1903, 4 in United Confederate Veterans Reunion Scrapbooks, 1903–1914, vol. 1 U.C.V. Reunion: New Orleans, 1903, Louisiana and Lower Mississippi Valley Collections (Baton Rouge: Louisiana State University Libraries).
111. "The Honor of the City and the Glory of the Cause," *Daily Picayune*, April 12, 1903.
112. "A Business View of the Reunion," *Daily States* (New Orleans, LA), May 19, 1903, 4, in United Confederate Veterans Reunion Scrapbooks, 1903–1914, vol. 1: U.C.V. Reunion: New Orleans, 1903, Louisiana and Lower Mississippi Valley Collections (Baton Rouge: Louisiana State University Libraries).
113. "Confederate Veterans Meet: Their Thirteenth Annual Reunion Attracts a Large Gathering to New Orleans," *New York Times*, May 20, 1903, 2; "Confederate: Reunion Will Begin Tuesday at New Orleans," *Courier-Journal* (Louisville, KY), May 17, 1903, A2; "Confederate Veterans," *Hartford Courant*, May 21, 1903, 2.
114. "The South Vindicated—Reunion Oration by Hon. J. H. Rogers," *Confederate Veteran* 11 (June 1903): 255.
115. "The South Vindicated," *Confederate Veteran*, 257.
116. "The Black Specter," *Daily States* (New Orleans, LA), May 19, 1903, 4, in United Confederate Veterans Reunion Scrapbooks, 1903–1914, vol. 1: U.C.V. Reunion: New Orleans, 1903, Louisiana and Lower Mississippi Valley Collections (Baton Rouge: Louisiana State University Libraries).
117. "Confederate: Reunion Will Begin Tuesday at New Orleans," *Courier-Journal* (Louisville, KY), May 17, 1903, A2.
118. "Confederate: Reunion Will Begin Tuesday at New Orleans," A2.
119. "Reunion of the Gray: Confederate Veterans in Session at New Orleans," *Washington Post*, May 22, 1903, 11.
120. "Reunion Retrospect," *Confederate Veteran* 11 (June 1903): 243–44.
121. "Why Confederates Snubbed Wheeler," *New York Times*, May 25, 1903, 5. In the *Confederate Veteran*, Wheeler denied any problems at the reunion. See "Discourtesy to Gen. Wheeler Denied," *Confederate Veteran* 11 (July 1903): 299–300.
122. Many historians have portrayed the Spanish-American War as a turning point in the reconciliation of the nation. By uniting under a single flag to fight a common enemy, the North and South reconciled their differences. Although the Spanish-American War may have eased tensions, some historians argue that passionate sectionalism remained. See Janney, *Remembering the Civil War*; Blight, *Race and Reunion*.
123. "Amusements," *Times-Democrat* (New Orleans, LA), May 19, 1903, 15, in United Confederate Veterans Reunion Scrapbooks, 1903–1914, vol. 1: U.C.V. Reunion: New Orleans, 1903, Louisiana and Lower Mississippi Valley Collections (Baton Rouge: Louisiana State

University Libraries); "West End," *Times-Democrat* (New Orleans, LA), May 19, 1903, 15, in United Confederate Veterans Reunion Scrapbooks, 1903–1914, vol. 1: U.C.V. Reunion: New Orleans, 1903, Louisiana and Lower Mississippi Valley Collections (Baton Rouge: Louisiana State University Libraries).

124. "April Demands of Local Labor," *Daily Picayune* (New Orleans, LA), April 7, 1903.

125. "Concert of Antebellum Songs," *Times-Democrat* (New Orleans, LA), May 19, 1903, 15, in United Confederate Veterans Reunion Scrapbooks, 1903–1914, vol. 1: U.C.V. Reunion: New Orleans, 1903, Louisiana and Lower Mississippi Valley Collections (Baton Rouge: Louisiana State University Libraries); *Three Centuries of American Ballads: In Costume*, Redpath Cautauqua Collection, Traveling Culture: Circuit Chautauqua in the Twentieth Century, Iowa Digital Library, https://digital.lib.uiowa.edu/islandora/object/ui%3Atc_40336.

126. "The Old South and the Young South," *Lafayette Gazette* (Lafayette, LA), May 30, 1903, 2. They reprinted the editorial from the *Daily Picayune*.

127. "Parade Most Notable," *The Caucasian* (Shreveport, LA), May 24, 1903, 1.

128. "Most Successful of All Reunions," *The American* (Nashville, TN), May 23, 1903, 1; Dudley M. Watson, *Confederate Veteran* 11 (July 1903): 299–300.

129. Watson, "The Gray Parade," 299.

130. Bettina Ruth Bush, "Missouri Girl at the Reunion," *Confederate Veteran* 11 (August 1903): 343.

131. "Parade Most Notable," 1; "Veterans in Gray March," *The Sun* (Baltimore, MD), May 23, 1903, 1.

132. "Parade Most Notable," 1; "Veterans in Gray March," 1.

133. "Girl Heralds for Veterans: Novel Features Will Mark Confederate Reunion at New Orleans," *Atlanta Constitution*, April 3, 1903, 5; Lucille Webb Banks, "Enthusiasm, Unity, Pathos, Marked Thirteenth Annual Confederate Reunion," *Atlanta Constitution*, May 24, 1903, E5.

134. "The Old South and the Young South," 2.

135. "Most Successful of All Reunions," 1.

136. "The Confederate Veterans," *The Chronicle* (Colfax, LA), May 30, 1903, 1.

137. "Next U.C.V. Reunion," *Daily Ardmoreite* (Ardmore, OK), May 31, 1903, 6.

138. Bush, "Missouri Girl at the Reunion," 343.

139. Editorial, *The Caucasian* (Shreveport, LA), May 28, 1903, 4.

CHAPTER 3: "FURIOUS MUSIC": AFRICAN AMERICANS, POLITICAL SPECTACLES, AND STREET THEATER IN THE POST-DISFRANCHISEMENT SOUTH, 1909–32

1. Perman, *Struggle for Mastery*, 204–6, 215, 218–23.

2. "Good Day for Republicans," *Tazewell Republican* (Tazewell, VA), August 25, 1904, 1; "Editorial Paragraphs," *Tazewell Republican* (Tazewell, VA), August 26, 1904, 1.

3. "A Field Day in Tazewell," *Times-Dispatch* (Richmond, VA), August 28, 1904, 1.

4. "A Field Day," 1.

5. "Editorial Paragraphs," *Tazewell Republican*, 1.

6. McGerr, *The Decline of Popular Politics*, 6–7. In this section, McGerr identifies disfranchisement as the harbinger of popular politics in the South. He points out the massive decline in voter turnout but does not seem to pursue whether or not popular politics continued.

7. Perman, *Struggle for Mastery*, 9–11.

8. McGerr, *The Decline of Popular Politics*, 43–70, 107–37.

9. McGerr, *The Decline of Popular Politics*, 149.

10. Sotiropoulos, *Staging Race*, 1, 4–6; Davarian L. Baldwin, *Chicago's New Negroes: Modernity, The Great Migration, and Black Urban Life* (Chapel Hill: University of North Carolina Press, 2007), 5–8; Barbara L. Webb, "Authentic Possibilities: Plantation Performance of the 1890s," *Theatre Journal* 56 (March 2004): 63–65; Lawson, *Jim Crow's Counterculture*, 28–32; Hale, *Making Whiteness*; Wood, *Lynching and Spectacle*; Crystal N. Feimster, *Southern Horrors: Women and the Politics of Rape and Lynching* (Cambridge, MA: Harvard University Press, 2009).

11. Schwartz, *Spectacular Realities*, 2–6, 10–12.

12. Thompson, *A Most Stirring and Significant Episode*, 57–65; Michael Lewis, "Access to Saloons, Wet Voter Turnout, and Statewide Prohibition Referenda," *Social Science History* 32:3 (Fall 2008): 379–80; Walton and Taylor, "Blacks and the Southern Prohibition Movement," 247, 249, 251–56.

13. Ferdinand Cowle Iglehart, "The Nation's Anti-Drink Crusade," *Nashville Tennessean*, June 16, 1908, 4.

14. "Mighty Wave of Reform Sweeps the Entire South: Prohibition and Local Option Laws Rapidly Closing the Saloons of the Entire Region south of Mason and Dixon's Line—Negro Problem an Impelling Motive," *New York Times*, June 2, 1907, SM6; Walton and Taylor, "Blacks and the Southern Prohibition Movement," 247, 249, 251–56.

15. Walton and Taylor, "Blacks and the Southern Prohibition Movement," 252–53, 256–57; Perman, *Struggle for Mastery*, 173–94.

16. Perman, *Struggle for Mastery*, 173–94.

17. "How Prohibition Was Turned Down in Alabama," *New York Times*, December 5, 1909, SM6.

18. J. E. Stanley, "Campaign Ends in Calhoun County," *Birmingham Age-Herald*, November 28, 1909, 2.

19. "Great Rally Closes Fight in Montgomery," *Birmingham News*, November 29, 1909, 9.

20. "Must Have Absolute Fairness," *Birmingham Age-Herald*, November 27, 1909, 2.

21. "How Prohibition Was Turned Down in Alabama," *New York Times*, December 5, 1909, SM6.

22. "Great Crowds Read Returns," *Mobile Register*, November 30, 1909, 5;

23. "Wets Win at Sedalia: Drys, After Spectacular Campaign, Are Surprised at Sweeping Defeat," *Mexico Weekly Ledger* (Mexico, MO), June 18, 1908, 1.

24. "'Wets' Paid Cash," *Mexico Missouri Message* (Mexico, MO), June 18, 1908, 1.

25. "No More Saloons, Says Knoxville: By a Majority of Nearly 2,000 Town Climbs on the Water Wagon," *The American* (Nashville, TN), March 12, 1907, 1.

26. Perman, *Struggle for Mastery*, 195–223.

27. Robert A. Hohner, "Prohibition Comes to Virginia: The Referendum of 1914," *Virginia Magazine of History and Biography* 75 (October 1967): 476–77.

28. "All Who Oppose Enabling Act Are Hotly Assailed," *Times-Dispatch* (Richmond, VA), January 23, 1914, 1.

29. Perman, *Struggle for Mastery*, 271–81.

30. "Big Prohibition Meetings Over the County Sunday," *Wichita Daily Times* (Wichita Falls, TX), July 26, 1915, 5.

31. "In Suburbs and County," *The Sun* (Baltimore, MD), October 25, 1916, 5.

32. "Fewer than 20,000 in Anti-Dry Parade; Slogans from Bible," *New York Times*, July 5, 1921, 1.

33. National Urban League, *Negro Membership in American Labor Unions*. Department of Research and Investigations of the National Urban League (New York: Alexander Press, 1930), 101–3, 106–9.

34. Programme for Labor Day," *Atlanta Constitution*, August 9, 1901.

35. "Big Negro Parade: Norfolk Celebrates Labor Day," *The Sun* (Baltimore, MD), August 5, 1905, 2.

36. "Labor's Army Given Ovation by Thousands," *Atlanta Constitution*, September 3, 1907, 1.

37. "Brunswick Has Planned Big Labor Day Fete," *Atlanta Constitution*, September 1, 1918, A1.

38. "Negroes Win First Place," *Los Angeles Times*, August 21, 1911, 13.

39. "The Servant Problem," *The Sun* (Baltimore, MD), February 27, 1900, 10.

40. "The Campaign: At Walterboro," *Kingstree County Record* (Kingstree, SC), July 24, 1902, 2; "The Campaign: At Walterboro," *News and Herald* (Winnsboro, SC), July 23, 1902, 2.

41. J. Chal Vinson, "Hoke Smith and the 'Battle of the Standards' in Georgia, 1895–1896," *Georgia Historical Quarterly* 26 (September 1952): 201–19; Dewey W. Grantham Jr., "Hoke Smith: Progressive Governor of Georgia, 1907–1909," *Journal of Southern History* 15 (November 1949): 423–40.

42. "Great Crowd Hears Howell at Swainsboro," *Atlanta Constitution*, April 17, 1906, 1.

43. "Howell in Emanuel," *Atlanta Constitution*, April 29, 1906, A5; "Great Crowd Hears Howell at Swainsboro," 1–2; "Hon. Clark Howell in Swainsboro," *Forest-Blade* (Swainsboro, GA), April 19, 1906, 1.

44. "Negro Band Plays 'Hail to the Chief' for Clark Howell," *Atlanta Journal*, April 16, 1906, 1.

45. "Another Mare's Nest," *Atlanta Constitution*, April 29, 1906, A5. According to the *Atlanta Constitution*, someone penned this letter to *Americus Times-Recorder*, but I could not find any evidence of the original letter in that newspaper.

46. "A Negro Band in Vardaman Parade," *Times Dispatch* (Richmond, VA), August 2, 1907, 3; "The Williams-Vardaman Contest," *New York Tribune*, August 1, 1907, 1.

47. "The Mississippi Senatorship," *Hartford Courant*, August 5, 1907, 8.

48. "Death Takes Vardaman of Mississippi," *Chicago Defender*, July 5, 1930, 3; "Vardaman in Senate," *Pittsburgh Courier*, August 12, 1911, 4.

49. Eugene E. White, "Mississippi's Great White Chief: The Speaking of James K. Vardaman in the Mississippi Gubernatorial Campaign of 1903," *Quarterly Journal of Speech* 32 (December 1946): 442–47.

50. "Death Takes Vardaman of Mississippi," 3; "Vardaman in Senate," 4.

51. "Both Candidates Claiming Victory in Mississippi," *The Tennessean* (Nashville, TN), August 1, 1907, 1.

52. Handy, *Father of the Blues*, 79–82; Gussow, "'Make My Getaway,'" 5–28; Gussow, "Racial Violence," 56–77.

53. "Played 'Hang Jeff Davis,'" *The Sun* (Baltimore, MD), November 10, 1905, 1.

54. John Stauffer, "The Song That Marches On," *Civil War Times* 54 (February 2015): 58–65.

55. "Played 'Hang Jeff Davis,'" 1.

56. "Shoulder to Shoulder Democratic Hosts March," *Courier-Journal* (Louisville, KY), September 1, 1909, 1.

57. "Negro Band Cuts Ku Klux Picnic," *Helena Independent*, July 26, 1925, 1.

58. "Klan K. of C., Jews and Negroes Parade," *Washington Post*, November 12, 1925, 1.

59. John Corrigan, "With Roosevelt on Georgia Tour: Bull Moose Candidate Greeted by Great Crowds," *Atlanta Constitution*, September 29, 1912, A4.

60. "Unique Meeting at Auditorium: Roosevelt Gathering Tonight Will Have Nature of Crusade," *Atlanta Constitution*, September 28, 1912, 1.

61. Roosevelt refused to recognize the Black delegates from the southern states, which according to *New York Times*, "will not get him any Southern electoral votes, and may lose him some Northern ones, but one thing it has done, it has made it possible for Southerners to leave the Democratic Party." "Wilson At Last Put in the Ananias Club," *New York Times*, September 29, 1912, 3.

62. "Bull Moose on Parade: Stay-At-Homes Welcome Back Contingent from Chicago," *The Sun* (Baltimore, MD), August 10, 1912, 12.

63. Robin D. G. Kelley, *Hammer and Hoe: Alabama Communists During the Great Depression* (Chapel Hill: University of North Carolina Press, 1990), 15–16.

64. "Dixie Socialists Called Similar to Purists," *Atlanta Daily World*, November 17, 1932, 4A.

65. "Wilson Stirs Baltimore," *New York Times*, April 7, 1918, 1.

66. "Drum Major on Way: Ragtime Baton-Twirler of 368th Infantry Awaited at Meade," *The Sun* (Baltimore, MD), February 10, 1919, 12.

67. "Colored People Barred from Patriotic Rally," *Afro-American* (Baltimore, MD), April 19, 1918, 1.

68. "Colored People Barred," 1.

69. "W. S. S. Rally Nets $5,000," *The Sun* (Baltimore, MD), April 29, 1918, 12.

70. "600 Negroes at Camp Get Colors and Big Slice of Watermelon," *Atlanta Constitution*, July 5, 1918, 8.

71. "To Martial Music Atlanta Manhood Registers Today," *Atlanta Constitution*, September 12, 1918, 1.

72. Adriane Lentz-Smith, *Freedom Struggles: African Americans and World War I* (Cambridge, MA: Harvard University Press, 2009); Cornelius L. Bynum, *A. Philip Randolph and the Struggle for Civil Rights* (Urbana: University of Illinois Press, 2010), 87–88.

73. "City's Negro Fighters Parade 5th Av. Today," *New York Times*, February 17, 1919, 1; Lentz-Smith, *Freedom Struggles*, 90; "Harlem Hellfighters," *MAAP: Mapping the African American Past*, accessed October 20, 2015, http://maap.columbia.edu/place/43.

74. "Jim Europe Killed in Boston Quarrel," *New York Times*, May 10, 1919, 1.

75. "Arrangements for Reception Now Completed," *Nashville Tennessean and the Nashville American*, March 26, 1919, 13.

76. "Candidates Ignore Colored Bands," *Chicago Defender*, April 6, 1912, 4.

77. "George Negro Speaks in City for Broening," *The Sun* (Baltimore, MD), May 5, 1923, 12.

78. "Smith Greeted by Cheers at Topeka," *Galveston Daily News* (Galveston, TX), September 20, 1928, 1.

79. "Final G. O. P. Rally Held in Baltimore," *The Sun* (Baltimore, MD), November 5, 1929, 22.
80. "Smith Ends 16 Days of Campaigning," *Bradford Era* (Bradford, PA), October 3, 1928, 1.
81. "Winter Campaign Opens at Home," *Monitor-Index and Democrat* (Moberly, MO), September 16, 1932, 2.
82. "Watson Sits Silent Through Colored Rally," *Chicago Daily Tribune*, October 15, 1928, 9.
83. "Gov. Roosevelt Invades Indiana," *Billings Gazette*, October 21, 1932, 2.
84. "Hold GOP Political Rally in Ark.; Negro Support Urged," *Atlanta Daily World*, July 27, 1932, 1.

CHAPTER 4: "TO DO OUR BIT FOR GOOD GOVERNMENT": W. C. HANDY, E. H. CRUMP, AND THE 1909 MEMPHIS MAYORAL ELECTION

1. Handy, *Father of the Blues*, 98.
2. Kathleen C. Berkeley, *"Like a Plague of Locusts": From an Antebellum Town to a New South City, Memphis, Tennessee, 1850–1880* (New York: Garland, 1991), 4–5, 119–20.
3. Gritter, *River of Hope*, 1–3, 16–17; Stephen V. Ash, *A Massacre in Memphis: The Race Riot That Shook the Nation One Year after the Civil War* (New York: Hill and Wang, 2013).
4. Gritter, *River of Hope*, 1–3, 16–20, 26–29.
5. Berkeley, *"Like a Plague of Locusts,"* 119–25.
6. Berkeley, *"Like a Plague of Locusts,"* 159–71.
7. Gritter, *River of Hope*, 1–3, 17–18.
8. Berkeley, *"Like a Plague of Locusts,"* 180–81, 186–87, 236–41.
9. Berkeley, *"Like a Plague of Locusts,"* 180–81, 186–87, 236–41.
10. Editorial, *Memphis Appeal*, April 3, 1889, 4; Perman, *Struggle for Mastery*, 53–56.
11. Perman, *Struggle for Mastery*, 57–59.
12. "The Unterrified," *Memphis Avalanche*, August 8, 1890, 1; Perman, *Struggle for Mastery*, 58–59.
13. Editorial, *Memphis Appeal*, August 9, 1890, 4; Perman, *Struggle for Mastery*, 58–59.
14. George W. Lee, *Beale Street: Where the Blues Began* (College Park, MD: McGrath, 1969), 240–43.
15. Gritter, *River of Hope*, 21–22, 35; David Robertson, *W. C. Handy: The Life and Times of the Man Who Made the Blues* (New York: Alfred A. Knopf, 2009), 111.
16. Barnett, *Southern Horrors*.
17. Gritter, *River of Hope*, 22–23.
18. G. Wayne Dowdy, *A Brief History of Memphis* (Charleston: History Press, 2011), 76–77.
19. Handy, *Father of the Blues*, 7–10.
20. Lynn Abbott and Doug Seroff, *Out of Sight: The Rise of African American Popular Music, 1889–1895* (Jackson: University Press of Mississippi, 2002), 115–19.
21. Lee, *Beale Street*, 130–32; Robertson, *W. C. Handy*, 52–65.
22. Robertson, *W. C. Handy*, 114–15.
23. G. Wayne Dowdy, *Mayor Crump Don't Like It: Machine Politics in Memphis* (Jackson: University Press of Mississippi, 2006), ix–xii, 3–5; Dowdy, *A Brief History of Memphis*, 74–75.

24. "Registration Opens Today: Strict Check Will Be Kept," *Memphis Commercial-Appeal*, August 9, 1909, 4.

25. "Registration Books Opened: Many Changes Are Made," *Memphis Commercial-Appeal*, August 10 1909, 5.

26. "Registration Books Opened," 5.

27. "Registration Books Opened," 5.

28. Roberson, *W. C. Handy*, 118.

29. Handy, *Father of the Blues*, 98–99.

30. Lee, *Beale Street*, 133–35; Robertson, *W. C. Handy*, 118–19; Margaret McKee and Fred Chisenhall, *Beale Black and Blue: Life and Music on Black America's Main Street* (Baton Rouge: Louisiana State University Press, 1993), 17–18.

31. Robertson, *W. C. Handy*, 118–19.

32. Handy, *Father of the Blues*, 98–99.

33. Lee, *Beale Street*, 97, 127–28; Bob L. Eagle and Eric S. Leblanc, *Blues: A Regional Exploration* (Santa Barbara, CA: ABC-CLIO, 2013), 142.

34. Handy, *Father of the Blues*, 98–99.

35. Robertson, *W. C. Handy*, 115.

36. Rosen, *Terror in the Heart of Freedom*, 272n122.

37. "Registration Books Opened," 5.

38. "Register," *Memphis Commercial-Appeal*, August 11, 1909, 6.

39. "11,000 Voters in the City," *Memphis Commercial-Appeal*, August 20, 1909, 4.

40. "Mayor's Race Open Question," *Memphis Commercial-Appeal*, August 8, 1909, 9.

41. William D. Miller, *Mr. Crump of Memphis* (Baton Rouge: Louisiana State University Press, 1964), 71–74.

42. "Registration Opens Tuesday," *Memphis Commercial-Appeal*, October 10, 1909, 10.

43. "Build Armory for Memphis: Walter W. Talbert's Plan," *Memphis Commercial-Appeal*, August 1, 1909, 8.

44. Dowdy, *A Brief History of Memphis*, 63–73.

45. Dowdy, *A Brief History of Memphis*, 62–63.

46. Dowdy, *Mayor Crump Don't Like It*, 5.

47. "Mayoralty Race Candidates Off: Campaign Will Open Today," *Memphis Commercial-Appeal*, August 30, 1909, 5.

48. Miller, *Mr. Crump of Memphis*, 72–73.

49. "Mayoralty Race Candidates Off: Campaign Will Open Today," 5.

50. E. A. Bushnell, "Intimate Impressions of Mayoralty Candidates: No. 3—E. H. Crump," *News Scimitar* (Memphis, TN), September 27, 1909, 1; Miller, *Mr. Crump of Memphis*, 72–73.

51. Dowdy, *A Brief History of Memphis*, 61–72; Miller, *Mr. Crump of Memphis*, 50–51, 53–54.

52. Walter W. Talbert, "Talbert Asks Some Questions: Takes Up Crump's Record," *Memphis Commercial-Appeal*, September 12, 1909, 4.

53. Walter W. Talbert, "Talbert on Crump's Record," *Memphis Commercial-Appeal*, October 6, 1909, 2.

54. J. J. Williams, "To the Citizens of Memphis," *Memphis Commercial-Appeal*, August 29, 1909, 4.

55. "J. J. Williams Issues Platform," *Memphis Commercial-Appeal*, August 29, 1909, 5.

56. Williams, "To the Citizens of Memphis," 4.
57. "Mayoralty Race Candidates Off: Campaign Will Open Today," 5.
58. "City Campaign Grows Warmer: Candidates for Mayor Busy," *Memphis Commercial-Appeal*, September 19, 1909, 5.
59. "Registration Opens Tuesday," *Memphis Commercial-Appeal*, October 10, 1909, 10.
60. "City Campaign Grows Warmer: Candidates for Mayor Busy," 5.
61. "Fair Election is Demanded," *Memphis Commercial-Appeal*, September 26, 1909, 8.
62. E. H. Crump, "Crump for a Commission," *Memphis Commercial-Appeal*, September 26, 1909, 8.
63. Edwards, *Angels in the Machinery*, 1–9, 70, 72, 145.
64. Advertisement, *News Scimitar* (Memphis, TN), October 21, 1909, 6.
65. Advertisement, *News Scimitar* (Memphis, TN), October 29, 1909, 4.
66. Advertisement, *Memphis Commercial-Appeal*, October 17, 1909.
67. Advertisement, *News Scimitar* (Memphis, TN), October 30, 1909, 8.
68. Advertisement, *Memphis Commercial-Appeal*, October 31, 1909.
69. Advertisement, *Memphis Commercial-Appeal*, 1909.
70. David Evans, "Blues: Chronological Overview," in *African American Music: An Introduction*, ed. Mellonee V. Burnim and Portia K. Maultsby, Chapter 7 (New York: Routledge, 2006), 82.
71. Handy, *Father of the Blues*, 99.
72. Evans, "Blues," 82.
73. Handy, *Father of the Blues*, 99.
74. Handy, *Father of the Blues*, 93.
75. Roberson, *W. C. Handy*, 124–25.
76. Handy, *Father of the Blues*, 100.
77. Handy, *Father of the Blues*, 100–101.
78. "Final Rallies Held Tonight," *Memphis Commercial-Appeal*, November 3, 1909, 4.
79. "Votes Will Decide Today," *Memphis Commercial-Appeal*, November 4, 1909, 4.
80. Patrick Bolton, "'The Oldest High School Band in America': The Christian Brothers Band of Memphis, 1872–1947," master's thesis, University of Memphis, 2011, 115–16.
81. "Votes Will Decide Today," 4.
82. "Final Rallies Held Tonight," 4; "Votes Will Decide Today," 4.
83. "Final Rallies Held Tonight," 4.
84. "Davis Visits Wards: Chief of Police Finds Officers Non-Partisan," *Memphis Commercial-Appeal*, November 5, 1909, 5.
85. "Warns Against Raids on Ballot Boxes; Fight Breaks Out in Fifth," *News Scimitar* (Memphis, TN), November 4, 1909, 1.
86. "Warns Against Raids," 1.
87. "Crump Charged with Assault: Disturbance in Fifth Ward," *Memphis Commercial-Appeal*, November 5, 1909, 5; "Voting Places Selected," *Memphis Commercial-Appeal*, November 3, 1909, 8; Gritter, *River of Hope*, 33–34.
88. Handy, *Father of the Blues*, xiv.
89. "E. H. Crump Chosen Mayor of Memphis," *Memphis Commercial-Appeal*, November 5, 1909, 1; "Surprises in Some Wards," *Memphis Commercial-Appeal*, November 5, 1909, 2; Gritter, River of Hope, 34.

90. "Voting Places Selected," *Memphis Commercial-Appeal*, November 3, 1909, 8; "E. H. Crump Chosen Mayor of Memphis," 1; "Davis Visits Wards," *Memphis Commercial-Appeal*, November 5, 1909.

91. "Must Go to the Polls in a Body," *News Scimitar* (Memphis, TN), November 4, 1909, 1.

92. "Warns Against Raids," 1.

93. "E. H. Crump Chosen Mayor of Memphis," 2.

94. "E. H. Crump Chosen Mayor of Memphis," 2.

95. "The Election," *Memphis Commercial-Appeal*, November 5, 1909, 6.

96. "The Memphis Election," *News Scimitar*, November 5, 1909, 4.

97. Newspaper clipping, E. H. Crump Collection, Box 20, Folder 9L-City Business 1910. To determine a relative date of this clipping, I cross-referenced it against a letter from A. C. Lake dated April 27, 1910. In this letter, Lake opposes the joining of the federal grounds with Confederate Park via a bridge over Court Avenue. She argues that African Americans "will flood over into Confederate Park." A. C. Lake to E. H. Crump, April 27, 1910, Letter. Box 20, Folder 9L-City Business 1910, E. H. Crump Collection, Memphis and Shelby County Room, Memphis Public Library and Information Center, Memphis, TN.

98. Colored Citizens of the City of Memphis, Letter to E. H. Crump, undated. Box 7 Folder 4C-Personal 1912, E. H. Crump Collection, Memphis and Shelby County Room, Memphis Public Library and Information Center, Memphis, TN.

99. J. H. Cannon to E. H. Crump, April 18, 1914, Letter. E. H. Crump Collection Box 6, Folder 2C-City Business 1914; E. H. Crump to J. H. Cannon, April 20, 1914, Letter. Box 6, Folder 2 City Business 1914, E. H. Crump Collection, Memphis and Shelby County Room, Memphis Public Library and Information Center, Memphis, TN.

100. Robert R. Church Jr. to E. H. Crump, November 24, 1914, Letter. Box 7, Folder 6 C-Personal 1914, E. H. Crump Collection, Memphis and Shelby County Room, Memphis Public Library and Information Center, Memphis, TN.

101. Gritter, *River of Hope*, 35–36.

102. Julia A. Hooks to E. H. Crump, July 24, 1910, Letter. Box 15, Folder 1 H-City Business, E. H. Crump Collection, Memphis and Shelby County Room, Memphis Public Library and Information Center, Memphis, TN.

103. E. H. Crump to Julia A. Hooks, July 27, 1910, Letter. Box 15, Folder 1 H-City Business 1910, E. H. Crump Collection, Memphis and Shelby County Room, Memphis Public Library and Information Center, Memphis, TN.

104. L. W. Dutro to E. H. Crump, January 10, 1912, Letter. Box 9, Folder 6 City Departments 1912, E. H. Crump Collection, Memphis and Shelby County Room, Memphis Public Library and Information Center, Memphis, TN; William Duecker to E. H. Crump, January 6, 1912, Letter. Box 9, Folder 6 City Departments 1912, E. H. Crump Collection, Memphis and Shelby County Room, Memphis Public Library and Information Center, Memphis, TN.

105. T. O. Fuller to E. H. Crump, May 1, 1912, Letter. Box 11, Folder 19 F-City Business 1912, E. H. Crump Collection, Memphis and Shelby County Room, Memphis Public Library and Information Center, Memphis, TN.

106. E. H. Crump to the Committee on Location, June 9, 1914, Letter. Box 6 Folder 2 C-City Business 1914, E. H. Crump Collection, Memphis and Shelby County Room, Memphis Public Library and Information Center, Memphis, TN.

107. Gritter, River of Hope, 35–36. She discusses the relationship between Crump and Memphis's Black community and points out the "two-way relationship" existing between them.

108. Miller, *Mr. Crump of Memphis*, 102–3.

109. Dowdy, *Mayor Crump Don't Like It*, 108–11.

110. For an explanation and description of Crump's rise to power and his control of Memphis and Tennessee for fifty years, see Dowdy, *Mayor Crump Don't Like It*.

111. Roberson, *W. C. Handy*, 126.

112. Handy, *Father of the Blues*, 101.

113. Miller, *Mr. Crump of Memphis*, 101–2.

114. Joel Dreyfuss, "The Man Who Made the Blues," *Washington Post*, November 16, 1973, B1; "W. C. Handy, Composer, Is Dead; Author of 'St. Louis Blues'; 84," *New York Times*, March 29, 1958, 17; Handy, *Father of the Blues*.

115. Lewis Nichols, "The End of the Sky Blue Decade: W. C. Handy, Historian of Memphis, Beale Street and St. Louis, Now Tills Greener Fields," *New York Times*, November 11, 1934, X3.

116. "W. C. Handy, Composer, Is Dead; Author of 'St. Louis Blues,' 84," *New York Times*, March 29, 1958, 17.

117. Henry Louis Gates Jr., *The Signifying Monkey: A Theory of Afro-American Literary Criticism* (New York: Oxford University Press, 1989), Introduction.

EPILOGUE: "I DIDN'T REALLY KNOW HOW TO SHOW MY OPPOSITION": STREET THEATER IN THE TWENTY-FIRST CENTURY

1. Paul Bowers, "Sousaphonist Serenades Confederate Flag Supporters in Columbia," *Charleston City Paper*, July 20, 2015, http://www.charlestoncitypaper.com/FeedbackFile/archives/2015/07/20/sousaphonist-serenades-confederate-flag-supporters-in-columbia; Imogen Calderwood, "Hilarious Moment Tuba Player Ridicules KKK Supporters with 'Family Guy-Style' Serenade at a Confederate Rally in South Carolina," *Daily Mail* (UK), July 21, 2015, http://www.dailymail.co.uk/news/article-3169567/Hilarious-moment-tuba-player-ridicules-KKK-supporters-Family-Guy-style-serenade-Confederate-rally-South-Carolina.html.

2. Perman, *Struggle for Mastery*, 58–59, 170–72; Kousser, *The Shaping of Southern Politics*, 194, table 7.5.

3. Edwards, *Angels in the Machinery*.

4. Joel Landau, "South Carolina Man Mocks Ku Klux Klan Rally Supporters with Serenade from Sousaphone," *Daily News* (New York), July 21, 2015, http://www.nydailynews.com/news/national/watch-s-man-mocks-kkk-members-sousaphone-article-1.2299317.

5. Donie O'Sullivan, "Taco Trucks Form a 'Wall' Outside Donald Trump's Vegas Hotel," CNN, October 19, 2016, https://www.cnn.com/2016/10/19/politics/taco-truck-trump-hotel-protest-trnd/index.html; Niraj Chokshi, "'Taco Trucks on Every Corner': Trump Supporter's Anti-Immigration Warning," *New York Times*, September 2, 2016, https://www.nytimes.com/2016/09/03/us/politics/taco-trucks-on-every-corner-trump-supporters-anti-immigration-warning.html.

BIBLIOGRAPHY

MANUSCRIPT COLLECTIONS

David M. Rubenstein Rare Book and Manuscript Library Digital Collections, Duke University, Durham, NC
  William Mahone Papers
Hargrett Research Library, University of Georgia, Athens, GA
  Walter B. Hill Papers
Hill Memorial Library, Louisiana State University, Baton Rouge, LA
  Louisiana and Lower Mississippi Valley Collections
  United Confederate Veterans Association Records
Hogan Jazz Archive, Howard-Tilton Memorial Library, Tulane University, New Orleans, LA
  American Federation of Musicians Local 174–496
Memphis Public Library and Information Center, Memphis, TN
  E. H. Crump Collection
Milton S. Eisenhower Library, Johns Hopkins University, Baltimore, MD
  The Lester S. Levy Sheet Music Collection
Kenan Research Center, Atlanta History Center, Atlanta, GA
  Samuel P. Jones Papers
Manuscript, Archives, and Rare Books Library, Emory University, Atlanta, GA
  Women's Christian Temperance Union Papers

NEWSPAPERS AND PERIODICALS

Alexandria Gazette and Virginia Advertiser (Alexandria, VA)
Afro-American (Baltimore, MD)
The American (Nashville, TN)
Augusta Chronicle (Augusta, GA)
Atlanta Constitution (Atlanta, GA)
Atlanta Daily World (Atlanta, GA)
Billings Gazette (Billings, MT)
Birmingham Age-Herald (Birmingham, AL)
Birmingham News (Birmingham, AL)

Bradford Era (Bradford, PA)
The Caucasian (Shreveport, LA)
Charleston Gazette (Charleston, SC)
Charlotte Democrat (Charlotte, NC)
Chicago Daily Tribune (Chicago, IL)
Chicago Defender
Christian Recorder (Philadelphia, PA)
The Chronicle (Colfax, LA)
Colored American (Washington, DC)
Confederate Veteran
Courier-Journal (Louisville, KY)
The Critic (Washington, DC)
Daily American (Nashville, TN)
Daily Ardmoreite (Ardmore, OK)
Daily Charlotte Observer (Charlotte, NC)
Daily Chronicle (Knoxville, TN)
Daily Citizen (Asheville, NC)
Daily Courant (Hartford, CT)
Daily Dispatch (Richmond, VA)
Daily Globe (St. Paul, MN)
Daily Picayune (New Orleans, LA)
Daily States (New Orleans, LA)
Daily Tobacco Leaf-Chronicle (Clarksville, TN)
Davenport Daily Leader (Davenport, IA)
The Enquirer (Yorkville, SC)
Forest-Blade (Swainsboro, GA)
Frank Leslie's Weekly
The Freeman (Indianapolis, IN)
Galveston Daily News (Galveston, TX)
The Gazette (Fort Worth, TX)
Globe and Mail (Toronto, ON)
Greenville Advocate (Greenville, SC)
Hamilton Times (Hamilton, AL)
Helena Independent (Helena, MT)
Herald Dispatch (Decatur, IL)
The Independent: Devoted to the Consideration of Politics, Social and Economic Tendencies, History, Literature, and the Arts
The Intelligencer (Anderson Court House, SC)
Kingstree County Record (Kingstree, SC)
Lafayette Gazette (Lafayette, LA)
The Landmark (Statesville, NC)
Los Angeles Times (Los Angeles, CA)

Macon News (Macon, GA)
Macon Telegraph (Macon, GA)
Maryville Times (Maryville, TN)
Memphis Appeal-Avalanche (Memphis, TN)
Memphis Avalanche (Memphis, TN)
Memphis Appeal (Memphis, TN)
Memphis Commercial-Appeal (Memphis, TN)
Mexico Missouri Message (Mexico, MO)
Mexico Weekly Ledger (Mexico, MO)
Mobile Register (Mobile, AL)
Monitor-Index and Democrat (Moberly, MO)
Morning Oregonian (Portland, OR)
New Journal and Guide (Norfolk, VA)
New York Times (New York, NY)
New York Tribune (New York, NY)
News and Herald (Winnsboro, SC)
News Scimitar (Memphis, TN)
Petersburg Index Appeal (Petersburg, VA)
Pittsburgh Courier (Pittsburgh, PA)
Progressive Farmer (Winston, NC)
Pulaski Citizen (Pulaski, TN)
Richmond Dispatch (Richmond, VA)
Richmond Planet (Richmond, VA)
Sandusky Star (Sandusky, OH)
Savannah Tribune (Savannah, GA)
Shenandoah Herald (Woodstock, VA)
Staunton Spectator (Staunton, VA)
St. Louis Post-Dispatch (St. Louis, MO)
St. Paul Globe (St. Paul, MN)
The Sun (Baltimore, MD)
Sunday States (New Orleans, LA)
Tazewell Republican (Tazewell, VA)
The Tennessean (Nashville, TN)
Times-Democrat (New Orleans, LA)
Times-Dispatch (Richmond, VA)
Trenton Evening Times (Trenton, NJ)
Union Advocate (New Orleans, LA)
Washington Bee (Washington, DC)
Washington Post (Washington, DC)
Watauga Democrat (Boone, NC)
Wichita Daily Times (Wichita Falls, TX)
Yorkville Enquirer (Yorkville, SC)

PUBLISHED PRIMARY SOURCES

Handy, W. C. *Father of the Blues: An Autobiography.* New York: Da Capo Press, 1941.

Harrison, Harold, Jr. "The True Story of Amos Rucker," Know Southern History, http://www.knowsouthernhistory.net/Articles/Minorities/true_story_of_amos_rucker.html.

Lee, George W. *Beale Street: Where the Blues Began.* College Park, MD: McGrath, 1969.

Meader, J. R. *The Cyclopaedia of Temperance and Prohibition: A Reference Book of Facts, Statistics, and General Information on All Phases of the Drink Question, the Temperance Movement, and the Prohibition Agitation.* New York: Funk & Wagnalls, 1891.

National Urban League. *Negro Membership in American Labor Unions.* Department of Research and Investigations of the National Urban League. New York: Alexander Press, 1930.

"Oration of General Lee." *Southern Historical Society Papers.* Vol. 24. Edited by R. A. Brock. Richmond: Southern Historical Society, 1896.

Washington, Booker T. *Up from Slavery.* 1901; New York: Penguin Classics, 1986.

Wells-Barnett, Ida B. *Southern Horrors: Lynch Law in All Its Phases.* New York: New York Age Print, 1892.

SECONDARY SOURCES

Alford, Violet. "Rough Music or Charivari." *Folklore* 70 (December 1959): 505–18.

Ali, Omar H. *In the Lion's Mouth: Black Populism in the New South, 1886–1900.* Jackson: University Press of Mississippi, 2010.

Ash, Stephen V. *A Massacre in Memphis: The Race Riot That Shook the Nation One Year after the Civil War.* New York: Hill and Wang, 2013.

Ayers, Edward L. *The Promise of the New South: Life after Reconstruction.* New York: Oxford University Press, 2007.

Bailey, Harris M., Jr. "The Only Game in Town: The South Carolina Republican Party in the Post-Reconstruction Era." *Proceedings of the South Carolina Historical Association.* Columbia: University of South Carolina Press, 1992.

Baker, Jean H. *The Stevensons: A Biography of an American Family.* New York: W. W. Norton, 1997.

Baker, Paula. "The Domestication of Politics: Women and American Political Society, 1780–1920." *American Historical Review* 89 (1984): 620–47.

Baldwin, Davarian L. *Chicago's New Negroes: Modernity, the Great Migration, and Black Urban Life.* Chapel Hill: University of North Carolina Press, 2007.

Baraka, Imamu Amiri. *Blues People: Negro Music in White America.* 1963; Westport, CT: Greenwood Press, 1980.

Beckel, Deborah. *Radical Reform: Interracial Politics in Post-Emancipation North Carolina.* Charlottesville: University of Virginia Press, 2011.

Berkeley, Kathleen C. *"Like a Plague of Locusts": From an Antebellum Town to a New South City, Memphis, Tennessee, 1850–1880.* New York: Garland, 1991.

Bever, Megan Leigh. "War Is a Terrible Enemy to Temperance: Drinking, Self-Control, and Meaning of Loyalty in the Civil War Era." Unpublished doctoral dissertation, University of Alabama, Tuscaloosa, 2014.

Blair, William A. *Cities of the Dead: Contesting the Memory of the Civil War in the South, 1865–1914*. Chapel Hill: University of North Carolina Press, 2004.

Blight, David W. *Race and Reunion: The Civil War and American Memory*. Cambridge, MA: Belknap Press of Harvard University Press, 2001.

Bolton, Patrick. "'The Oldest High School Band in America': The Christian Brothers Band of Memphis, 1872–1947." Master's thesis, University of Memphis, 2011.

Brandt, Lydia Mattice. "Re-creating Mount Vernon: The Virginia Building at the 1893 Chicago World's Columbian Exposition." *Wintherthur Portfolio* 43 (Spring 2009): 79–114.

Breen, Patrick H. "A Prophet in His Own Land: Support for Nat Turner and His Rebellion within Southampton's Black Community." In *Nat Turner: A Slavery Rebellion in History and Memory*, edited by Kenneth S. Greenberg, 103–18. New York: Oxford University Press, 2003.

Brown, Leslie. *Upbuilding Black Durham: Gender, Class, and Black Community Development in the Jim Crow South*. Chapel Hill: University of North Carolina Press, 2008.

Browne, C. A. *The Story of Our National Ballads*. New York: Thomas Y. Crowell, 1919.

Brundage, W. Fitzhugh. *Where These Memories Grow: History, Memory, and Southern Identity*. Chapel Hill: University of North Carolina Press, 2000.

Bynum, Cornelius L. *A. Philip Randolph and the Struggle for Civil Rights*. Urbana: University of Illinois Press, 2010.

Calhoun, Charles W. *Conceiving a New Republic: The Republican Party and the Southern Question, 1869–1900*. Lawrence: University Press of Kansas, 2006.

Cantrell, George. "'Dark Tactics': Black Politics in the 1887 Texas Prohibition Campaign." *Journal of American Studies* 25 (April 1991): 85–93.

Carder, P. H. *George F. Root, Civil War Songwriter: A Biography*. Jefferson, NC: McFarland, 2008.

Carney, Court. *Cuttin' Up: How Early Jazz Got America's Ear*. Lawrence: University Press of Kansas, 2009.

Carter, Dan. "Southern Political Style." In *The Age of Segregation: Race Relations in the South, 1890–1945*, edited by Robert Haws, 46–66. Jackson: University Press of Mississippi, 1978.

Casper, Scott E. *Sarah Johnson's Mount Vernon: The Forgotten History of an American Shrine*. New York: Hill and Wang, 2008.

Cobb, James C. *Industrialization and Southern Society, 1877–1984*. Lexington: University Press of Kentucky, 1984.

Dailey, Jane. *Before Jim Crow: The Politics of Race in Postemancipation Virginia*. Chapel Hill: University of North Carolina Press, 2000.

Dailey, Jane, Glenda Elizabeth Gilmore, and Bryant Simon. *Jumpin' Jim Crow: Southern Politics from Civil War to Civil Rights*. Princeton, NJ: Princeton University Press, 2000.

David, James Corbett. "The Politics of Emasculation: The Caning of Charles Sumner and Elite Ideologies of Manhood in the Mid-Nineteenth-Century United States." *Gender and History* 19 (August 2007): 324–45.

Davis, Susan G. *Parades and Power: Street Theatre in Nineteenth-Century Philadelphia*. Philadelphia: Temple University Press, 1986.

DeBord, Guy. *Society of the Spectacle*. Detroit: Black and Red, 1967.

Devore, Donald E. *Defying Jim Crow: African American Community Development and the Struggle for Racial Equality in New Orleans, 1900–1960*. Baton Rouge: Louisiana University Press, 2015.

Dinkin, Robert. *Before Equal Suffrage: Women in Partisan Politics from Colonial Times to 1920*. Westport: Greenwood Press, 1995.

Dorr, Lisa Lindquist. *White Women, Rape, and the Power of Race in Virginia, 1900–1960*. Chapel Hill: University of North Carolina Press, 2004.

Dowdy, G. Wayne. *A Brief History of Memphis*. Charleston: History Press, 2011.

Dowdy, G. Wayne. *Mayor Crump Don't Like It: Machine Politics in Memphis*. Jackson: University Press of Mississippi, 2006.

Eagle, Bob L. and Eric S. Leblanc. *Blues: A Regional Exploration*. Santa Barbara, CA: ABC-CLIO, 2013.

Edmonds, Helen G. *The Negro and Fusion Politics in North Carolina, 1894–1901*. Chapel Hill: University of North Carolina Press, 1951.

Edwards, Rebecca. *Angels in the Machinery: Gender in American Party Politics from the Civil War to the Progressive Era*. New York: Oxford University Press, 1997.

Endersby, James W. "Prohibition and Repeal: Voting on Statewide Liquor Referenda in Texas." *Social Science Journal* 49 (2012): 503–12.

Epstein, Dena J., and Rosita Sands. "Secular Folk Music." In *African American Music: An Introduction*, edited by Mellonee V. Burnim and Portia K. Maultsby. New York: Routledge, 2006.

Evans, David. "Blues: Chronological Overview." In *African American Music: An Introduction*, edited by Mellonee V. Burnim and Portia K. Maultsby. New York: Routledge, 2006.

Feimster, Crystal N. *Southern Horrors: Women and the Politics of Rape and Lynching*. Cambridge, MA: Harvard University Press, 2009.

Filene, Bejamine. *Romancing the Folk: Public Memory and American Roots Music*. Chapel Hill: University of North Carolina Press, 2000.

Fink, Leon. *Workingmen's Democracy: The Knights of Labor and American Politics*. Urbana: University of Illinois Press, 1985.

Finson, Jon W. *The Voices That Are Gone: Themes in Nineteenth-Century American Popular Song*. New York: Oxford University Press, 1994.

Foner, Eric. *Freedom's Lawmakers: A Directory of Black Officeholders during Reconstruction*. Baton Rouge: Louisiana State University Press, 1996.

Foner, Eric. *Reconstruction: America's Unfinished Revolution*. New York: Perennial Classics, 2002.

Foner, Jack D. *Blacks and the Military in American History: A New Perspective*. New York: Praeger, 1974.

Foster, Gaines M. *Moral Reconstruction: Christian Lobbyists and the Federal Legislation of Morality, 1865–1920*. Chapel Hill: University of North Carolina Press, 2002.

Friend, Craig Thompson. *Southern Masculinity: Perspectives on Manhood in the South since Reconstruction*. Athens: University of Georgia Press, 2009.

Gates, Henry Louis, Jr. *The Signifying Monkey: A Theory of Afro-American Literary Criticism.* New York: Oxford University Press, 1989.

Gilmore, Glenda Elizabeth. *Gender and Jim Crow: Women and the Politics of White Supremacy in North Carolina, 1896–1920.* Chapel Hill: University of North Carolina Press, 1996.

Ginzberg, Lori D. *Women and the Work of Benevolence: Morality, Politics, and Class in the Nineteenth-Century United States.* New Haven, CT: Yale University Press, 1990.

Grantham, Dewey W., Jr. "Hoke Smith: Progressive Governor of Georgia, 1907–1909." *Journal of Southern History* 15 (November 1949): 423–40.

Gritter, Elizabeth. *River of Hope: Black Politics and the Memphis Freedom Movement, 1865–1954.* Lexington: University Press of Kentucky, 2014.

Gushee, Lawrence. "Black Professional Musicians in New Orleans c1880." *Inter-American Music Review* 11 (Spring Summer 1991): 53–64.

Gussow, Adam. "'Make My Getaway': The Blues Lives of Black Minstrels in W. C. Handy's *Father of the Blues*," *African-American Review* 35 (Spring 2001): 5–28.

Gussow, Adam. "Racial Violence, 'Primitive' Music, and the Blues Entrepreneur: W. C. Handy's Mississippi Problem." *Southern Cultures* 8 (Fall 2002): 56–77.

Gussow, Adam. *Seems Like Murder Here: Southern Violence and the Blues Tradition.* Chicago: University of Chicago Press, 2002.

Gustafson, Melanie Susan. "Partisan Women in the Progressive Era: The Struggle for Inclusion in American Political Parties." *Journal of Women's History* 9 (Summer 1997): 8–30.

Hahn, Steven. *A Nation under Our Feet: Black Political Struggles in the Rural South from Slavery to the Great Migration.* Cambridge: Belknap Press of Harvard University Press, 2003.

Hale, Grace Elizabeth. *Making Whiteness: The Culture of Segregation in the South, 1890–1940.* New York: Pantheon, 1998.

"Harlem Hellfighters." *MAAP: Mapping the African American Past.* Accessed October 20, 2015. http://maap.columbia.edu/place/43.

Harris, Trudier. "The Trickster in African American Literature." National Humanities Center. http://nationalhumanitiescenter.org/tserve/freedom/1865-1917/essays/trickster.htm.

Higginbotham, Evelyn Brooks. *Righteous Discontent: The Women's Movement in the Black Baptist Church, 1880–1920.* Cambridge, MA: Harvard University Press, 1993.

Higgs, Robert. "Race and Economy in the South, 1890–1950." In *The Age of Segregation: Race Relations in the South, 1890–1945*, edited by Robert Haws, 89–116. Jackson: University Press of Mississippi, 1978.

Hild, Matthew. *Greenbackers, Knights of Labor, and Populists: Farmer-Labor Insurgency in the Late-Nineteenth-Century South.* Athens: University of Georgia Press, 2007.

Hill Errol G., and James V. Hatch. *A History of African American Theatre.* Cambridge: Cambridge University Press, 2003.

Hillyer, Reiko. "Relics of Reconciliation: The Confederate Museum and Civil War Memory in the New South." *Public Historian* 33 (November 2011): 35–62.

Hirshson, Stanley. *Farewell to the Bloody Shirt: Northern Republicans and the Southern Negro, 1877-1893*. Bloomington: Indiana University Press, 1962.

Hohner, Robert A. "Prohibition Comes to Virginia: The Referendum of 1914." *Virginia Magazine of History and Biography* 75 (October 1967): 473-88.

Honey, Michael. "Class, Race, and Power in the New South: Racial Violence and the Delusions of White Supremacy." In *Democracy Betrayed: The Wilmington Race Riot of 1898 and Its Legacy*, edited by David S. Cecelski and Timothy B. Tyson, 163-84. Chapel Hill: University of North Carolina Press, 1998.

Howe, Daniel Walker. *What Hath God Wrought: The Transformation of America, 1815-1848*. New York: Oxford University Press, 2007.

Hunt, James L. *Marion Butler and American Populism*. Chapel Hill: University of North Carolina Press, 2003.

Janney, Caroline E. *Burying the Dead but Not the Past: Ladies' Memorial Associations and the Lost Cause*. Chapel Hill: University of North Carolina Press, 2008.

Janney, Caroline E. *Remembering the Civil War: Reunion and the Limits of Reconciliation*. Chapel Hill: University of North Carolina Press, 2013.

Janney, Caroline E. "Written in Stone: Gender, Race, and the Heyward Shepherd Memorial." *Civil War History* 52 (2006): 117-41.

Jeffrey, Julie Roy. "Women in the Southern Farmers' Alliance: A Reconsideration of the Role and Status of Women in the Late Nineteenth-Century South." *Feminist Studies* 3 (1975): 72-91.

Kazin, Michael, and Steven J. Ross. "America's Labor Day: The Dilemma of Workers' Celebration." *Journal of American History* 78 (March 1992): 1294-1323.

Keith, LeeAnna. *The Colfax Massacre: The Untold Story of Black Power, White Terror, and the Death of Reconstruction*. New York: Oxford University Press, 2009.

Kelley, Robin D. G. *Hammer and Hoe: Alabama Communists during the Great Depression*. Chapel Hill: University of North Carolina Press, 1990.

Kellner, Douglas. "Media Culture and the Triumph of the Spectacle." In *The Spectacle of the Real: From Hollywood to Reality TV and Beyond*, edited by Geoff King. Bristol, UK: Intellect Press, 2005.

Kellner, Douglas. *Media Spectacle*. New York: Routledge, 2003.

Kelly, Brian. "Sentinels for New South Industry: Booker T. Washington, Industrial Accommodation and Black Workers in the Jim Crow South." *Labor History* 44 (2003): 337-57.

Kerber, Linda K. *Women of the Republic: Intellect and Ideology in Revolutionary America*. Chapel Hill: University of North Carolina Press, 1980.

Kousser, J. Morgan. *The Shaping of Southern Politics: Suffrage Restriction and the Establishment of the One-Party South*. New Haven, CT: Yale University Press, 1974.

Krasner, David. "The Real Thing." In *Beyond Blackface: African Americans and the Creation of American Popular Culture, 1890-1930*, edited by W. Fitzhugh Brundage, 99-123. Chapel Hill: University of North Carolina Press, 2011.

Lavergne, Gary M. *Before Brown: Heman Marion Sweatt, Thurgood Marshall, and the Long Road to Justice*. Austin: University of Texas Press, 2011.

Lawson, R. A. *Jim Crow's Counterculture: The Blues and Black Southerners*. Baton Rouge: Louisiana State University Press, 2010.

Lemann, Nicholas. *Redemption: The Last Battle of the Civil War*. New York: Farrar, Straus & Giroux, 2007.

Lender, Mark Edward, and James Kirby Martin. *Drinking in America: A History*. New York: Free Press, 26–30.

Lentz-Smith, Adriane. *Freedom Struggles: African Americans and World War I*. Cambridge, MA: Harvard University Press, 2009.

Levine, Lawrence W. "African American Music as Resistance." In *African American Music: An Introduction*, edited by Mellonee V. Burnim and Portia K. Maultsby. New York: Routledge, 2006.

Levine, Lawrence W. *Black Culture and Black Consciousness: Afro-American Folk Thought from Slavery to Freedom*. New York: Oxford University Press, 2007.

Lewis, Michael. "Access to Saloons, Wet Voter Turnout, and Statewide Prohibition Referenda." *Social Science History* 32 (Fall 2008): 373–404.

Litwack, Leon F. *Trouble in Mind: Black Southerners in the Age of Jim Crow*. New York: Alfred A. Knopf, 1998.

Lott, Eric T. *Love and Theft: Blackface Minstrelsy and the American Working Class*. 20th Anniversary ed. New York: Oxford University Press, 2013.

Manis, Andrew M. *Macon Black and White: An Unutterable Separation in the American Century*. Macon, GA: Mercer University Press, 2004.

Markovitz, Nathan. *Racial Spectacles: Explorations in Media, Race, and Justice*. New York: Routledge, 2011.

Marszalek, John F. *A Black Congressman in the Age of Jim Crow: South Carolina's George Washington Murray*. Gainesville: University Press of Florida, 2006.

Mason, Herman "Skip," Jr. *Politics, Civil Rights, and Law in Black Atlanta, 1870–1970*. Charleston: Arcadia, 2000.

McConville, Brendan. *The King's Three Faces: The Rise and Fall of Royal America, 1688–1776*. Chapel Hill: University of North Carolina Press, 2006.

McElya, Micki. *Clinging to Mammy: The Faithful Slave in Twentieth-Century America*. Cambridge, MA: Harvard University Press, 2007.

McGerr, Michael E. *The Decline of Popular Politics: The American North, 1865–1928*. New York: Oxford University Press, 1986.

McGerr, Michael E. "Political Style and Women's Power, 1830–1930." *Journal of American History* 77 (December 1990): 864–85.

McKee, Margaret, and Fred Chisenhall. *Beale Black and Blue: Life and Music on Black America's Main Street*. Baton Rouge: Louisiana State University Press, 1993.

McKnight, Mark. "Charivaris, Cowbellions, and Sheet Iron Bands: Nineteenth-Century Rough Music in New Orleans." *American Music* 23 (Winter 2005): 407–25.

McLaurin, Melton Alonzo. *The Knights of Labor in the South*. Westport, CT: Greenwood Press, 1978.

Miller, William D. *Mr. Crump of Memphis*. Baton Rouge: Louisiana State University Press, 1964.

Moran, Rachel F. *Interracial Intimacy: The Regulation of Race and Romance*. Chicago: University of Chicago Press, 2001.

Morgan, Jo-Ann. "Mammy the Huckster: Selling the Old South for the New Century." *American Art* 9 (Spring 1995): 86–109.

Moss, Robert F. *Barbecue: The History of an American Institution*. Tuscaloosa: University of Alabama Press, 2010.

Nash, Gary B. *The Urban Crucible: The Northern Seaports and the Origins of the American Revolution*. Cambridge, MA: Harvard University Press, 1986.

Norton, Mary Beth. *Liberty's Daughters: The Revolutionary Experience of American Women, 1750–1800*. Ithaca, NY: Cornell University Press, 1980.

Ortiz, Paul. *Emancipation Betrayed: The Hidden History of Black Organizing and White Violence in Florida from Reconstruction to the Bloody Election of 1920*. Berkeley: University of California Press, 2005.

Pierce, David. "'Carl Laemmle's Outstanding Achievement': Harry Pollard and the Struggle to Film 'Uncle Tom's Cabin.'" *Film History* 10 (1998): 459–76.

Perman, Michael. *Struggle for Mastery: Disfranchisement in the South, 1888–1908*. Chapel Hill: University of North Carolina Press, 2001.

Postel, Charles. *The Populist Vision*. New York: Oxford University Press, 2007.

Prather, H. Leon. *We Have Taken a City: Wilmington Racial Massacre and Coup of 1898*. Rutherford, NJ: Fairleigh Dickinson University Press, 1984.

Riser, R. Volney. *Defying Disfranchisement: Black Voting Rights Activism in the Jim Crow South, 1890–1908*. Baton Rouge: Louisiana State University Press, 2010.

Robertson, David. *W. C. Handy: The Life and Times of the Man Who Made the Blues*. New York: Alfred A. Knopf, 2009.

Rosenberg, Daniel. *New Orleans Dockworkers: Race, Labor, and Unionism, 1892–1923*. Albany: State University of New York Press, 1988.

Roberts, John W. *From Trickster to Badman: The Black Folk Hero in Slavery and Freedom*. Philadelphia: University of Pennsylvania Press, 1989.

Schaffer, Jason. *Performing Patriotism: National Identity in the Colonial and Revolutionary American Theater*. Philadelphia: University of Pennsylvania Press, 2007.

Schwartz, Vanessa R. *Spectacular Realities: Early Mass Culture in Fin-De-Siècle Paris*. Berkeley: University of California Press, 1998.

Scott, James C. *Weapons of the Weak: Everyday Forms of Peasant Resistance*. New Haven: Yale University Press, 1985.

Somerville, Diane Miller. *Rape and Race in the Nineteenth-Century South*. Chapel Hill: University of North Carolina Press, 2004.

Sotiropoulos, Karen. *Staging Race: Black Performers in Turn of the Century America*. Cambridge, MA: Harvard University Press, 2006.

Stauffer, John. "The Song That Marches On." *Civil War Times* 54 (February 2015): 58–65.

Summers, Mark W. "The Press Gang: Corruption and the Independent Press in the Grant Era." *Congress and the Presidency* 17 (Spring 1990): 29–44.

Szymanski, Ann-Marie. "Beyond Parochialism: Southern Progressivism, Prohibition, and State-Building." *Journal of Southern History* 69 (February 2003): 107–36.

Thompson, E. P. "Rough Music Reconsidered." *Folklore* 103 (1992): 3–26.

Thompson, H. Paul, Jr. *A Most Stirring and Significant Episode: Religion and the Rise and Fall of Prohibition in Black Atlanta, 1865–1887*. DeKalb: Northern Illinois University Press, 2013.

Tribble, Edwin. "Marching Through Georgia." *Georgia Review* 21 (Winter 1967): 423–29.

Turpie, David C. "A Voluntary War: The Spanish-American War, White Southern Manhood, and the Struggle to Recruit Volunteers in the South." *Journal of Southern History* 80 (November 2014): 859–92.

Wagner, Michael A. "'As Gold Is Tried in the Fire, So Hearts Must Be Tried by Pain:' The Temperance Movement in Georgia and the Local Option Law of 1885." *Georgia Historical Quarterly* 93 (Spring 2009): 30–54.

Waldstreicher, David. *In the Midst of Perpetual Fetes: The Making of American Nationalism, 1776–1820*. Chapel Hill: University of North Carolina Press, 1997.

Walton Jr., Hanes, and James E. Taylor. "Blacks and the Southern Prohibition Movement." *Phylon* 32:3 (1971): 247–59.

Ward, Brian. *Just My Soul Responding: Rhythm and Blues, Black Consciousness, and Race Relations*. Berkeley: University of California Press, 1998.

Watts, Jill. "Hattie McDaniel." *Interview* 35 (September 2005): 126–30.

Webb, Barbara L. "Authentic Possibilities: Plantation Performance of the 1890s." *Theatre Journal* 56 (March 2004): 63–82.

West, Stephen A. "'A Hot Municipal Contest': Prohibition and Black Politics in Greenville, South Carolina, after Reconstruction." *Journal of the Gilded Age and Progressive Era* 11 (October 2012): 519–51.

White, Eugene E. "Mississippi's Great White Chief: The Speaking of James K. Vardaman in the Mississippi Gubernatorial Campaign of 1903." *Quarterly Journal of Speech* 32 (December 1946): 442–47.

Wilentz, Sean. "Artisan Republican Festivals and the Rise of Class Conflict in New York City, 1788–1837." In *Working-Class America: Essays on Labor, Community, and American Society*, edited by Michael H. Frisch and Daniel J. Walkowitz, 37–77. Urbana: University of Illinois Press, 1983.

Williamson, Joel. *The Crucible of Race: Black-White Relations in the American South since Emancipation*. New York: Oxford University Press, 1984.

Wolfe, Bernard. "Uncle Remus and the Malevolent Rabbit." In *Mother Wit from the Laughing Barrel: Readings in the Interpretation of Afro-American Folklore*, edited by Alan Dundes, 524–40. Englewood Cliffs, NJ: Prentice-Hall, 1973.

Wood, Amy Louise. *Lynching and Spectacle: Witnessing Racial Violence in America, 1890–1940*. Chapel Hill: University of North Carolina Press, 2009.

Wood, Gordon S. *The Radicalism of the American Revolution*. New York: Vintage, 1991.

Woodward, C. Vann. *The Strange Career of Jim Crow: A Commemorative Edition*. New York: Oxford University Press, 2001.

Wynne, Lewis Nicholas. *The Continuity of Cotton: Planter Politics in Georgia, 1865–1892*. Macon, GA: Mercer University Press, 1986.

Vinson, J. Chal. "Hoke Smith and the 'Battle of the Standards' in Georgia, 1895–1896." *Georgia Historical Quarterly* 26 (September 1952): 201–19.

INDEX

The page numbers in *italics* refer to illustrations.

African Methodist Episcopal Church, 56, 62, 188. *See also* churches
American Federation of Labor, 44, 100, 132
American Revolution, 9
American Temperance Union, 56
Atlanta, Georgia: faithful slave myth in, 98; Labor Day in, 138; partisan rallies in, 31, 49–50; prohibition campaigns in, 11, 52–74, 76, 79, 83–85; racial violence in, 86; Roosevelt in, 147; World War I and, 150–51
Atlanta Fire Department Drum Corps, 103
Atlanta Typographical Union, 138
authenticity, 6

badges, 33, 37, 64, 66, 71, 91
barbecues, 9, 29, 32, 35, 64, 70, 97, 133, 138, 145
"Battle Cry of Freedom," 51
"Battle Hymn of the Republic," 144
Beale Street: Black entrepreneurship on, 95, 159; blues music on, 167, *185*, 185–86; churches on, 162; polling sites on, 178–79; voter mobilization on, 13, 158, *163*, 166, 168, 175, 187
"Beale Street Blues," 186
Bibb County Anti-Saloon League (Georgia), 79
Birmingham, Alabama: communists in, 148; Confederate veterans in, 91; Handy and, 164; labor unions in, 44
Black musicians: harassment of, 16, 22, 30, 128, 138; at Lost Cause spectacles, 12,
87–88, 102, 104, 120, *124*, 126; military, 149, 150–51, 168; motives of, 12, 88, 89, 110–11, 143–44, 146, 164, 187; popularity of, 6, 87, 101, 105, 168; professionalism of, 3, 4, 6, 12, 126, 186; stereotypes of, 12, 25, 82, 87–88, 104–5, 126, 137; unions, 12, 100–101, 104, 110–12, 126; white hiring of, 3–4, 12, 17, 87, 102–3, 137, 140–41, *141*, 158, 166, 168, 173, 187; and white supremacists, 3, 4, 12, 87, 88, 102, 104, 126, 141, 143–44, 146; and white women, 38, 51, 52, 82, 85, 124
blackface minstrelsy, 6, 38, 164, 189
blues music, 3, 6, 104, 158, 164, *167*, 167–68, 174–75, 184–87
bondpeople. *See* enslaved people
"Bonnie Blue Flag, The," 119
Bull Moose Party, 147
Butler, Marion, 14–16
Bryan, William Jennings, 48, 50
Bynum, Charlie, 165, 168
Bynum's Superb Orchestra, 168

campaign rallies: Black musicians at, 3–4, 16–18, 21, 25–26, 28, 37, 48, 127–28, 137, 140–43, 145–47, 155, 158, 173, 187; Black speakers at, 48; Democratic Party, 3–4, 18, 25–26, 127, 140–45, 158, 172–73, 177–78; harassment of African Americans at, 128; patriotic, 149; Populist, 16, 33, 47–49; prohibition and anti-prohibition, 33, 35–37, 52, 58, 60, 71, 133–37; Republican Party, 17–18, 21,

25–26, 127, 155–56; spectacular nature of, 4, 12, 16, 28, 33, 59, 137, 148, 189; third party, 33, 41, 147–48
Capital City Guards, 144
Carnival, 87, 112, 115
Central Trades and Labor Council of New Orleans, Louisiana, 103–4, 109–11, 113
Chase, William Calvin, 92
Chester Democratic Club (South Carolina), 26
Chicago, Illinois, 6, 19, 90, 120, 149, 156, 164
Christian Brothers High School Band, 177
Church, Robert R., 95–96, 103, 159, *163*
Church, Robert R., Jr., 182
churches: Black, 5, 25, 56, 62–63, 67, 70, 85, 136, 154, 159, 161–62, 182, 188; and Lost Cause events, 117; prohibition meetings in, 35, 55, 58–59, 63, 67, 70, 74, 85, 133, 136; and prohibition laws in Georgia, 72–73
citizenship, 7, 9, 10, 148, 160, 168
Civil Rights Act of 1875, 160
civil rights movement, 5, 190
Civil War. *See* Lost Cause
Clarksville Military Band (Tennessee), 24
Cleveland, Grover, 14, 19, 22, 27
Colored Citizens Association of Memphis, Tennessee, 164, 181
Colored Men's Civic League of Memphis, Tennessee, 182–83
Colquitt, Alfred, 31, 55, 59
Communist Party, 13, 148. *See also* labor movement
Confederate States of America, 3, 11, 118, 121, 126, 129, 130. *See also* Lost Cause; United Confederate Veterans
Confederate veterans: and 1894 reunion in Birmingham, 91; and 1903 reunion in New Orleans, 87, 113–26; and Black musicians, 87–88, 104–5, 109–13; and faithful slave myth, 94–95, 97; and Jefferson Davis monument, 92; and Robert E. Lee monument, 91–92. *See also* Sons of Confederate Veterans; United Confederate Veterans

Congress of Racial Equality, 5
conventions: business, 169; labor, 42–44, *44*; nominating, 14, 17, 19, 27, 147, 148; prohibition, 34, 56, 72, 74, 85; religious, 183; state constitutional, 61, 99, 104, 107, 130, 133, 136; UCV, 114, 117–19
Cotton States and International Exposition of 1895, 107
crowd: as claim to citizenship, 7; as political statement, 7, 9; as protection, 9
Crump, Edward Hull: early life, 165; and Handy, 13, 158, 167–68, 174–76, 179, 185–87; as machine boss, 183–84; as mayoral candidate, 4, 158, 166–81; relationship with Black Memphians, 164, 178–83. *See also* "Mr. Crump"
Culinary Workers Union of Nevada, 189

Davis, Jefferson: effigy, 144; and faithful slave myth, 94; memorial service for, 117, 119; monument to, 92–93; and prohibition, 36, 71. *See also* "Hang Jeff Davis"
Davis, Varina, 92, 98
De Droit, George, 103, 106, 111
"Dead March, The," 24
Democratic Colored Band, 26
Democratic National Convention, 27
Dinkins, James, 102–3
discrimination, 112, 151. *See also* Jim Crow; segregation
disfranchisement, 5, 10–13, 32, 130, 134, 137, 151, 157, 188–89; in Georgia, 76–78, 133, 140–41; Lost Cause justification for, 90; in Louisiana, 99, 104; opposition to, 47, 126, 139; and Populism, 76; and prohibition, 131–32; and Solid South, 147; in Tennessee, 181; in Virginia, 128. *See also* Jim Crow
"Dixie," 3, 28, 45, 91, 94, 104, 119, 136, 145
Dixie Colored Band of Atlanta (Georgia), 138
Douglass, Frederick, 22, 91, 145
Du Bois, W. E. B., 159

Early, Jubal, 91–92
Eckford, R. K., 165, 168
Eckford and Higgins Imperial Orchestra, 168
effigies, 7, 14, *15*, 16, 23, 25
Eighteenth Amendment, 137. *See also* prohibition
elections: of 1876, 17; of 1878 midterms, 25, 26; and 1885 Atlanta prohibition, 51–54, 57, 62–71; and 1887 Atlanta prohibition, 71; of 1888, 19, 27, 130; of 1890 midterms, 161–62; of 1892, 14, 24; of 1896, 50; and 1898 Macon prohibition, 72–74, 76–80, 82–85; and 1905 Georgia gubernatorial, 133; and 1907 Mississippi senatorial, 142; and 1909 Memphis mayoral, 158, 165–73, 177–81, *184*, 187; of 1928, 155; of 1932, 4, 189; of Black officeholders, 5, 39; charges of fraud, 83, 134, 161; fraud and violence, 129, 166; municipal, 28, 61, 131, 161; popular approval of, 8–9, 19; and Populism, 47, 50; and prohibition, 34, 36, 38, 133–35; and Readjuster Party, 39–41; as spectacle, 11, 40, 57, 133
emancipation: and Black migration, 55, 159; and Black political power, 61, 129, 160; and Lost Cause, 90, 118; and music, 52; and racial progress, 163; and reform movements, 74, 131; and Republican Party, 17, 19, 31, 53, 139, 160; and segregation, 100. *See also* faithful slave myth
Emancipation Proclamation, 17, 53
Emanuel African Methodist Episcopal Church of Charleston, South Carolina, 188
enslaved people, 6, 9, 22, 126, 145; and prohibition, 54–56, 62. *See also* emancipation; faithful slave myth; slavery
Europe, James Reese, 152–53

faithful slave myth, 3, 90, 92, 94–98, 104, 106–7, 116, 126. *See also* Lost Cause; slavery
Farmer's Alliance, 14, 16, 24. *See also* People's Party; Populism

Febiger, J. C., Jr., 99, 112
Federal Council of Negro Affairs, 5
Felton, Rebecca Latimore, 78–79, *79*
Ferrell, Frank J., 43–44, *44*
Fifteenth Amendment, 5, 9
15th New York National Guard. *See* Europe; Harlem's Hellfighters; Reese, James
517th Engineer Reserve Corps, 150
folk music, 6
Foster, Stephen, 65, 145
Fourteenth Amendment, 5
Freedmen's Bureau, 159

Gaines, J. W., 99, 102
Garfield, James, 17, 19
Georgia Prohibition Association, 56
Gordon, John B., 91–92, 98–99, *99*, 117, 119. *See also* United Confederate Veterans
Gordon, William A., 95
Grady, Henry, 31, 53–55, 140. *See also* New South
Great Migration, 6, 154
gun clubs, 129

"Hail to the Chief," 17, 28
Hampton, Wade, III, 26, 129
Handy, W. C. (William Christopher), *163*, 163–64, *174*, 184–85; and 1909 Memphis mayoral campaign, 13, 158, 165, 167, 174–78, 186–87; at political rallies, 3, 4, *143*, 143–44, 158
"Hang Jeff Davis," 144
Harlem's Hellfighter's, 152–53
Harris, Hattie Gibson Jobe, 80
Harrison, Benjamin, 19, 27, 130
Haygood, Atticus, 55, 56
Higgins, George, 168, 176
Hill, David B., 27–28
Hill, Sallie B., 80
Hill, Walter B., 73, 83
Hill Club of Savannah, 27–28
Hollingsworth-Watkins, Ada, 120
Hoover, Herbert, 156
Houston Riot of 1917, 149
Howell, Clark, 140–42, *142*

humiliation: of community violators, 8, 23; of Democrats, 13, 24–25, 143–44, 156, 170; of Populists, 15; of public officials, 7, 20; of white supremacists, 139, 143–44, 146, 188–90. *See also* rough music

immigration, 6, 129, 189
inauguration, 30, 156
Independent Order of Immaculates, 45

Jackson, Thomas "Stonewall," 120, 122
jazz, 6, 152
Jim Crow, 8, 13, 187; legal challenges to, 5. *See also* discrimination; disfranchisement; lynching; segregation
"John Brown's Body," 144
Johnston, Joseph E., 91
Jones, Sam, 55, 57, 59, 73

Kit, Yellowstone, 71
Knights of Labor, 42–44, 100
Knoxville, Tennessee, 17, 20, 135, 149, 161
Kruttschnitt, E. B., 99, 117
Ku Klux Klan, 26, 86, 145–46, 156, 161, 188

Labor Day, 24, 42–46, 138–39
labor movement, 11, 13, 42, 43, 45, 46, 137; biracialism and, 107, 108, 110, 138; and Lost Cause, 88, 100, 104, 106, 126. *See also* Labor Day
Lee, Fitzhugh, 43
Lee, George W., 162–63, *163*, 167, *185*, *186*
Lee, Robert E. (Central Trades and Labor Council president), 103
Lee, Robert E. (General): and Lost Cause rhetoric, 120; monument in New Orleans, 121; monument in Richmond, 91–93
Lee, Stephen D., 93, 118
Liberal Anti-Prohibition Party, 34
Lincoln, Abraham, 139
literacy test, 5, 127, 129–30, 162. *See also* disfranchisement
Lodge, Henry Cabot, 24, 29

Lodge Bill, 24, 29. *See also* disfranchisement
Lost Cause, 13, 89, 118; and faithful slave myth, 94–95, 97, 126; and labor movement, 88, 108; spectacles, 91–93, 97–98, 119, 126, 146; and white supremacy, 3–4, 12–13, 88, 90, 105, 145–46. *See also* faithful slave myth; United Confederate Veterans; United Daughters of the Confederacy
lynching, 5, 7, 10–11, 13, 49, 60, 78, 90, 143, 151, 162–63, 188–90; and spectacle, 5, 131; as subject in Black music, 7; white women and, 38, 52, 79

machine politics, 78, 106, 129, 132; in Memphis, 162, 164, 167–68, 172, 183–84
Macon, Georgia: and Atlanta prohibition campaigns of 1885 and 1887, 65, 70, 72; liquor interest in, 72–73; prohibition campaign in, 11, 51, 72–86, 181
Mahara's Colored Minstrels, 164, 168. *See also* Handy, W. C. (William Christopher)
Mahone, William, 39, 40, 42. *See also* Readjuster Party
Manly, Alexander, 78, *79*
marching clubs, 9, 62, 64–65, 145, 179
"Marching Through Georgia," 21
Mardi Gras, 101, 111, 116
McDonald, Frank, 168
Memphis, Tennessee, 19; and 1866 riot, 95, 159; and 1901 UCV reunion, 95–96, 103, 114; and 1909 mayoral campaign, 4, 13, 158, 165–81; and Black entrepreneurship, 159; and Black political mobilization, 159–64, 175, 181–83; and Black schools, 160; and blues music, 167, 175, 184–87; Crump arrives in, 165; Crump machine in, 183–84; disfranchisement in, 161–62, 165–66; Handy arrives in, 164; musicians in, 165–66, 168, 173; and Wells, 163
"Memphis Blues," *174*, 185
Memphis Business Men's Club, 165

Memphis Drum and Bugle Corps, 103, 119, 121
Memphis Philharmonic Orchestra Association, 177
Memphis Riot of 1866, 95, 159, 168
Mickle, William E., 98, 117
Middleton's Cornet Band, 140
Mississippi Republican State Executive Committee, 156
Missouri Anti-Saloon League, 135
"Mocking Bird," 104
Mount Vernon Ladies Association, 91
"Mr. Crump," 174–76, 179, 184. *See also* "Memphis Blues"
Mulcahy, Jim, 167
municipal elections, 131; in 1875 Memphis, 161; in 1883 Greenville, 34; in 1895 Fort Worth, 28; in 1909 Memphis, 4, 13, 158, 165–81
Municipal Park Band, 177
Musicians' Union: and biracialism in New Orleans, 87, 100; conflict with UCV, 89, 101–13; Local 174 (white) of A.F.M., 101–3, 110–13, 120; Local 242 (Black) of A.F.M., 101
"My Old Kentucky Home," 145

Nashville, Tennessee: disfranchisement in, 161; Labor Day in, 45; prohibition in, 36, 37; World War I and, 154
National Association for the Advancement of Colored People, 5
National Prohibition Party, 34
"New Coon in Town, A," 22
New Orleans, Louisiana: and 1903 UCV Reunion, 12, 87, 89, 94, 98–100, 106, 108, 110–11, 113–26; biracial labor movement in, 44, 100–101, 106–13; and reputation for music, 116
New South: and Grady, 54; and labor movement, 106–9; and lack of racial progress, 163; and Lost Cause, 124–25; and prohibition, 53–55. *See also* Grady, Henry

"Old Frank Johnson," 104
"Old Gray Mare," 146
Old South: Black musicians in, 12, 28, 87–88, 105, 126, 144; celebration of, 119, 126; and Lost Cause, 89, 96; nostalgia for, 3, 12, 32, 91, 94, 100, 103–4, 118; recreating racial hierarchy of, 90, 106, 117, 124. *See also* faithful slave myth; Lost Cause; United Confederate Veterans
"Our Days Are Numbered," 24
Owen, Chandler, 151

partisanship, 9, 10, 28, 130
patriotism, 9, 13, 131, 145, 149, 151
People's Party, 11–12, 14, 16, 39, 46–48, 50, 76, 146–47. *See also* Populism
performance: blackface, 6; Lost Cause, 91; and partisan politics, 32, 45, 144–45, 148, 188–89; as resistance, 13; theory of, 8; and World War I, 149–50, 152–53, *153*
plantation songs, 28–29, 91, 98, 104
Pledger, W. A., 60–61, *61*
pole raising, 9, 27
political clubs, 33, 37, 129, 160, 172–73. *See also* marching clubs
poll tax, 5, 78, 129, 130; in Georgia, 61, 76; in Tennessee, 24, 161–62, 167, 181; in Texas, 136; in Virginia, 127. *See also* disfranchisement; Jim Crow
"Pompey Long," 104
Populism, 14–16, 24–25, 32–33, 46–50, 140; disfranchisement and, 76–78, 86, 130. *See also* People's Party
Powderly, Terrence V., 43–44, *44*
professionalism, 6–7, 12, 88–89, 108, 110–11, 126, 164
Progressive Party. *See* Bull Moose Party
prohibition, 13, 33, 53; in 1885 Atlanta, 54–71; in 1887 Atlanta, 71–72; in 1898 Macon, 51, 72–86; African Americans and, 34, 38–39, 46, 56, 59–71; conventions, 34, 56, 72, 74, 85; divisions within, 33; in Georgia, 11–12, 31, 49, 53; in South Carolina, 34; in Tennessee, 34, 36–37; in Texas, 34–35

ragtime, 6, 22, 51, 81, 134, 150
Randolph, A. Phillip, 151
rape, 38, 159
Readjuster Party, 11, 23, 39, 40–42. *See also* Mahone, William
Reconstruction: amendments, 5, 9; Black political power during, 4–5, 90, 118, 134, 139, 156, 160, 187; end of, 39, 53, 129, 139, 189; portrayed as unjust, 47, 86, 90–91, 118, 129, 134, 173, 189
Red Shirts, 26, 129. *See also* Hampton, Wade, III
reform movements, 11, 13, 188; and African Americans, 54–56; and reliance on Black support, 33; and reliance on spectacle, 33, 129–30, 136; and women, 173
Republican National Convention, 19
respectability, 5, 34, 53, 56, 111
Rice, Frank D., 165, 170, 183
Richmond, Virginia, 21; election day spectacle in, 41; Jefferson Davis monument, 92–94; Knights of Labor in, 42–44; Readjusters in, 23; Republicans in, 21; Robert E. Lee monument, 91–92; socialists in, 148; state constitutional convention in, 136
Rodgers, Clinton, 94–95, 98. *See also* faithful slave myth
Roosevelt, Franklin Delano, 4–5, 11, 154, 156, 189
Roosevelt, Theodore, 143, 147
Root, George F., 51
rough music: examples of, 23–25, 32, 52, 82, 128, 157; theory of, 8. *See also* humiliation

saloons, 60, 70, 132, 135–36, 159, 167, 170, 178
Sandy River Band, 26
Saxby, Wallace, Jr., 177
schools, 30, 49, 60, 64, 72–74, 100, *121*, 134, 162, 177; Black, 3, 5, 34, 39, 56, 85, 95, 146, 159–61, 183
"See, the Conquering Hero Comes," 17
segregation, 5, 12, 100, 141, 188; limits of, 10; and Lost Cause, 90; and migration, 163; music and, 6; opposition to, 6; Supreme Court and, 5; and white women, 38; and World War I, 149–51. *See also* Jim Crow
sensationalism, 8, 57, 130, *152*, 178
"She Is Sleeping in the Valley," 24
"Sidewalks of New York, The," 155
slavery, 3, 74; Lost Cause portrayal of, 88–96, 104, 107, 117–18, 129. *See also* enslaved people; faithful slave myth
Small, Samuel, 31, 62
Smith, Al, 155
Smith, Michael Hoke, 133, 140–42, *142*
Spanish-American War, 12, 52, 74–75, 81, 120
spectacle: commentary on, 27, 79–80; and community formation, 23, 68, 81, 125–26, 156, 179; election day as, 36, 71, 83, 178; end of, 155, 161; historical use of, 9, 10; Labor Day as, 44–45, 138; lynching as, 5, 10, 131; militaristic character of, 25, 37, 70, 154; newspapers and, 57, 64, 69, 121, 130, 145, 179; opposition to, 9–11, 40, 129, 134, 136, 155, 161; theory of, 7, 8, 38, 131, 151; types of, 4, 7, 15, 17, 23, 33, 58, 90, 135, 188
spectators, 12; as active participants, 4, 7, 8; and citizenship, 7
Sporer, Frank, 110, 112
St. Louis, Missouri, 28, 45, 82, 149
"St. Louis Blues," 186
stereotypes: of African Americans, 67, 150, 151; of Black intemperance, 56, 74–78, 82–83, 85; of Black performers, 25, 88, 105, 126; manipulation of, 6, 12, 32, 149. *See also* faithful slave myth
street theater, 4, 7, 8, 9, 11–12, 23, 32, 139. *See also* rough music; spectacle
Supreme Court of the United States, 5, 118, 130
"Suwanee River," 104

Talbert, Walter W.: hiring of Black musicians, 158, 168; as Memphis mayoral candidate, 158, 166, 169–73, 177–78
temperance. *See* prohibition

"There Will Be a Hot Time in the Old Town Tonight," 81
third parties, 11, 13, 14, 33, 39, 42, 46, 48, 50, 77, 126, 146
Third US Colored Heavy Artillery Band, 168
Third Ward Colored Club of Atlanta, Georgia, 65
Thirteenth Amendment, 53
Towson Colored Band (Maryland), 137
Truman, Harry, 154
Turner, Jim, 168
251st Field Artillery Band, 150

uniforms: band, 4, 17; military, 119–20, 123, 149, 151; military-style, 7, 9, 40; political, 33, 35, 45, 138; white aggression toward African Americans in, 9
United Confederate Veterans: and 1903 reunion, 12, 87, 98, 113–26; conflict with musicians, 87, 98–113; faithful slave myth and, 95; formation of, 89–90; leadership of, 92. See also Confederate States of America; Lost Cause
United Daughters of the Confederacy, 89, 97

Vardaman, James K., 3–4, 141–44
Veazey, Armand, 120
violence: domestic, 8; and labor movement, 106; and lynching, 10; opposition to, 6; racial, 75, 77, 149, 159; rhetorical, 59; threat of, 26, 57, 164; and voter intimidation, 5, 49. See also lynching
Volstead Act, 137. See also prohibition
"Vote as You Pray," 81

Washington, Booker T., 107, 143, 147
Washington, DC, 17, 22, 28, 95, 97, 141

Washington, George, 90–91
Watson, Tom, 47–50
"We Are Few and Far Between," 24
"We Won't Get Drunk Any More," 65
"We Won't Go Home 'til Morning," 65
Wells, Ida B., 91, 162–63
"We're Out for Prohibition," 136
Wheeler, Joseph, 119–20, 122
white supremacy: and Democratic Party, 143, 146; and Lost Cause, 3–4, 12–13, 88, 90, 96, 106, 117, 188; and Populism, 15, 16; and prohibition, 76; and reaction to Black political power, 77; resistance to, 4–5, 10, 13, 38, 139, 190. See also lynching
Whitecaps, 3
Willard, Frances, 55. See also Women's Christian Temperance Union
Williams, John J.: as 1909 Memphis mayoral candidate, 158, 166, 169–73, 177–79, 183; hiring of Black musicians, 158, 168
Williams, John Sharpe, 4, 141
Wilmington Insurrection of 1898, 12, 52, 77–79, 81, 83–85
Women's Christian Temperance Union, 35, 55–57, 74, 85, 136
Work, Henry Clay, 21
World Columbian Exposition of 1893, 90, 91
World War I, 13, 131, 148, 149–55
World War II, 5
Wright, Seaborn, 49, 50

"Yellow Dog Blues," 186
Young Men's Democratic Club of Brookhaven, Mississippi, 32
Young Men's Garfield and Arthur Club of Knoxville, Tennessee, 17
Young Men's Prohibition Club of Atlanta, Georgia, 59, 63–64

ABOUT THE AUTHOR

Mark A. Johnson, from Milwaukee, graduated in 2016 with a PhD in history from the University of Alabama. Previously, he earned an MA from the University of Maryland and a BA from Purdue University. As a professional historian, he specializes in the history of the United States and the U.S. South, and currently teaches at the University of Tennessee at Chattanooga. He is also the author of *An Irresistible History of Alabama Barbecue: From Wood Pit to White Sauce.*

www.ingramcontent.com/pod-product-compliance
Lightning Source LLC
Chambersburg PA
CBHW022006220426
43663CB00007B/983